A Woman's Place

Rosemary O. Joyce

A WOMAN'S PLACE

The Life History of a Rural Ohio Grandmother

OHIO STATE UNIVERSITY PRESS : COLUMBUS

Portions of the text have appeared in A WORLD OF WOMEN, ed. Erika Bourguignon, and are reprinted with permission of J. F. Bergin Publishers.

Portions of the text are excerpted from the book WOMEN OF CRISIS II: Lives of Work and Dreams, by Robert Coles and Jane Hallowell Coles. Copyright © 1980 by Robert Coles and Jane Hallowell Coles. Reprinted by permission of DELACORTE PRESS/SEYMOUR LAWRENCE. A Merloyd Lawrence Book.

The frontispiece photograph, taken in southeastern Ohio by Michael Houghton, is used with permission.

Copyright © 1983 by the Ohio State University Press

All right reserved.

Library of Congress Cataloging in Publication Data

Joyce, Rosemary O., 1927–
  A woman's place

  Bibliography: p.
  Includes index.
  1. Penfield, Sarah Flynn. 2. Rural women—Ohio—Biography. 3. Grandmothers—Ohio—Biography. 4. Rural Women—Ohio—Attitudes. I. Title.
HQ1438.03J465   1983   305.4′2′0924   83-13188
ISBN 0-8142-0344-2

To Sarah Flynn Penfield
with affection, with admiration
and with fond memories
and to her daughters and my daughters
with love and with hope for what a
woman's place can and will become

Contents

Acknowledgments	xi
1. Doing a Life History: Historical Tradition, Personal Experience	3
2. Sarah Flynn Penfield in Geographic and Personal Space	41
3. Sarah's Grandparents: The First Generation in Ohio, 1853–1880	51
4. Sarah's Parents: The Second Generation of Flynns in Ohio, 1880–1951	71
5. Sarah and Robert: The Third Generation of Penfields in Ohio, 1927–1946	119
6. The Years of Change: 1947–1983	157
7. Sarah Today	173
8. Sarah, the Capable Wife, and Other Women	211
Appendixes	
A. Chart of Numbered Interviews	241
B. Transcription of "Autobiography" Recording	244

C.	Genealogy of Sarah Flynn Penfield	246
D.	Other Versions of Personal Experience Story	248
E.	Sarah's Verbal Genres	250
List of Works Consulted	263
Index	289

Illustrations

1. Ground floor plan of Penfield House, 1900–1983   44
2. Residence proximities of the Flynn and
   Penfield families   56
3. Layout of Flynn farmstead, 1896–1936   76
4. Flynn house ground floor plan, ca. 1909   94
5. Layout of Penfield farm, ca. 1900–1983   122

The photographs used on chapter opening pages are from the personal records of either the author or Sarah's daughters and neighbors.

Acknowledgments

It is a delight to have an opportunity to publicly thank the many people who enabled me, directly or indirectly, to write this book. It is also an impossible task to convey my appreciation adequately in these few words.

A great debt is clearly owed—and happily acknowledged—to "Sarah Flynn Penfield," for her generosity in sharing her time and her life story, for her patience in answering my surely repetitive and seemingly naïve questions. Her daughter, "Anne Penfield Hoffman," was also my consultant as well as my adviser on all Penfield family matters, and her steady interest and advice, along with her friendship, continue to be invaluable. Two other daughters of Sarah's, and two neighbors, graciously offered their treasured family photographs for reproducing here.

A number of faculty and staff members at the Ohio State University were particularly helpful, both with my doctoral program there and with the original manuscript of *A Woman's Place*. Professor Daniel Barnes has been unfailing in his strong support and learned guidance, since I first interviewed Sarah Penfield those many years ago. Professor Erika Bourguignon was particularly helpful; her invitation to me to contribute to

Acknowledgments

her anthology *A World of Women* was only one example of her dedication to, and encouragement of, her students and colleagues. Professor Robert Bremner has remained a model for efficiency, kindness, and scholarly work. Professor John Messenger's advice on research techniques was beneficial, and Professor Patrick Mullen, my original advocate for a graduate degree program, continues to advise and assist me on a broad range of folklore topics. Elmer Baumer, as associate dean of the Graduate School, has been an invaluable supporter, along with William Poland.

Dr. Gay Hadley has given me singular support and reinforcement through all the highs and lows, ups and downs, goods and bads that are endemic both to finishing a graduate degree and to finishing a book. Mim Chenfeld has remained an extraordinary advocate through the years. Few are privileged to have such friends. Dr. Judith Cook gave invaluable bibliographic help, especially on women's research literature and conflict management theories.

Professors Patricia Williams Sabine, Mary Irene Moffitt, Martha Lawry, and Amy Shuman gave excellent suggestions for improving drafts of the manuscript, as did Ann Joyce, James Barry, director of the Martha Kinney Cooper Ohioana Library, Anne Barry, Sally Soliday, and Tad Jeffrey. Virginia Reynolds was always exceptionally generous with her advice and her encyclopedic understanding of the Women's Studies Library holdings, where Abby Kratz and Adrienne Zahniser helped as well. Professors Laurel Richardson and Barbara Rigney were astute and cooperative, and special points were made by Professors Bill Ellis, Jean MacLaughlin, Harold Pepinsky, Leila Rupp, Theodore Napier, Nancy Clatworthy, and Brewton Berry. Perspectives from different academic areas came from Nancy Kelsik, Dr. Patricia Pohlman, Dixie Miller, Dr. Beth Hunker, and Annette Fromm.

Scholars from other institutions also contributed: Professor Claire Farrer, of the University of Illinois, has been a faithful teacher/friend, as have Professor Archie Green, of the University of Texas, and Professor Ellen Stekert, of the University of Minnesota. Instructive correspondence came from Linda

Acknowledgments

Dégh, of Indiana University; Charles Camp, of the Maryland Arts Council; Sidney Farr, of the Hutchins Library, Berea College, Kentucky; and Rosan Jordan, of Louisana State University.

David Blyth, Barbara Hyer, Mary Rhodes, and Marcia Epstein gave practical aid, and Norma Lind's fine typing and tape transcriptions were invaluable; she maintained professional calm and expertise through all the deadline crises I subjected her to. Special appreciation goes to Martha Morss for her splendid help with the manuscript, and to Robert Demorest, my expert and efficient editor.

My sister, Suzanne White, has provided physical backing and moral support through these years. My children—Jay, Ann, Lucy, and Mary—have been cheerfully understanding of my "benign neglect," and their active encouragement has been delightful. My final acknowledgment is to my husband, John, whose suggestions and interest have not only added materially to the book, but have also sustained me innumerable times. It is a privilege now to say "Thank you"!

A Woman's Place

1. Doing a Life History: Historical Tradition, Personal Experience

"What do you think woman's role is?" It was a simple question to the energetic farm woman, my hostess and consultant.[1] As we talked, she continued to thrust her needle through the several layers of a bright Double Wedding Ring quilt. I was startled, then, when she jumped up, flipped through the pages of her dark green Bible, and ordered me to "read that!" Feeling a bit foolish in this unexpected Thespian pose in front of her and her sister, I obediently recited the long chapter she pointed to:

> A capable wife who can find? Her value is far more than that of corals.
> In her the heart of her owner has put trust. And there is no gain lacking.
> She has rewarded him with good and not bad all the days of her life.
> She has sought wool and linen and she works with whatever is in the delight of her hands.
> She has proved to be like the ships of a merchant: from faraway she brings in her food.
> She also gets up while it is still night and gives food to her household and the prescribed portion of her young women.
> She has considered a field and proceeded to obtain it. From the fruitage of her hands she has planted a vineyard.
> She has girded her hips with strength and she invigorates her arms. She has sensed that her trading is good.
> Her lamp does not go out at night.
> Her hands she has thrust out with a distaff, and her own hands take hold of the spindle.

> Her palms she has stretched out to the afflicted one and her hands she has thrust out to the poor ones.
> She does not fear for her household because of the snow for all her household are clothed with double garments.
> Coverlets she has made for herself. Her clothing is of linen and wool dyed reddish purple.
> Her owner is someone known in the gates, when he sits down with the older men of the land.
> She has made even undergarments and proceeded to sell them, and belts she has given to the tradesmen.
> Strength and splendor are her clothing, and she laughs at a future day.
> Her mouth she has opened in wisdom, and the law of loving kindness is on her tongue.
> She is watching over the goings on of her household and the bread of laziness she does not eat.
> Her sons have risen up and proceeded to pronounce her happy; her owner (rises up), and he praises her.
> There are many daughters that have shown capableness, but you, you have ascended above them all.
> Favour may be false, and prettiness may be vain, but the woman that fears Jehovah is the one that procures praise for herself.
> Give her the fruitage of her hands, and let her works praise her, even in the gates.[2]

"That's what God really thought, you know!" the grandmother stated flatly. She then shut the pages of her worn Bible, apparently closing, too, the subject of woman's role.

Relinquishing the stage, I sipped my cup of peppermint tea and munched fresh apple pie (a typical bonus at nearly all our interviewing sessions), as I reflected on our numerous conversations and several interviews over the past three years. (Originally my interviews with her had concentrated on my family's interest in county history; later, as I entered graduate school in folklore studies, the interviewing evolved toward local folk life traditions in this southeastern Ohio region. On the day of the Bible passage reading, the interviews were pointed to discovering more about women and women's role there, with an anthropological focus.)

Suddenly a jarring series of conflicts crystallized for me, conflicts before and now between her spoken statement and her body language, between vehement pronouncement and actual performance, between real and ideal concepts—not only of her own life, but of other women's lives. The "tea party" abruptly acquired new dimension for me, and I was jolted into posing new kinds of questions. Did this dynamic woman actually view herself as "owned," as a "chattel" of her husband's? Had her mother? Do her daughters? Will her granddaughters? If so, why? What family history and personal history was the background? What implication would such a viewpoint have for her family, males and females both? And would such implication reach even beyond that rural community?

Subsequently the questions multiplied as I reflected on my visit. How much did family traditions influence her beliefs and attitudes? Was she typical of women in that rural midwest community? Could a study of her life uncover some of the complexities of her value system? And could it also bring new insights to understanding other women with traditional backgrounds? It was apparent that my research would need to be broadened considerably to include this wider scope. But on that blustery October day in 1975 in a white farmhouse in southeastern Ohio, I had begun to record the life history of Sarah Flynn Penfield.[3]

DOING A LIFE HISTORY

Assuming the major responsibility of recording a person's life was just short of overwhelming. I needed methodological, theoretical, and analytical help. This involved, first, a literature search. Subsequently, study of the historical traditions and discrete methodologies of biographical writings influenced the content of this introductory chapter.

Uses of Biography

Biography is used universally, though with different methods and goals, in the humanities and the psychological, social, and medical sciences. *Life history* is the specialized term used in anthropology and generally in sociology to incorporate both biographical and autobiographical features (the difference is sometimes difficult to distinguish because of differing amounts of available information on fieldwork conditions and on practices of editing field notes or tape transcriptions). *Life history* in psychology and psychiatry refers to the method used as an extension of the "case history," especially in psychoanalysis, to investigate the historical and cultural context of the individual's life. *Oral history* is the historian's term for interview-solicited material. Biography and autobiography are, of course, important literary genres as well. Psychohistory and psychobiography have been developed in psychology and in political science.[4]

The amount of use has differed historically within these disciplines: interest in the life history in both anthropology and sociology surged and then peaked between 1925 and 1945, when less difficult, time-consuming methods—along with statistical analysis in sociology—moved to the forefront. Conversely, interest in oral history mounted steadily with historians after World War II and intensified in the 1970s. Possibly because the life history interviewing process in psychology tends to rely on less time involvement, interest has remained more steady in its use, especially for psychoanalysis. Attention to life history, or "true experience" stories, has only recently evolved in folkloristics (a term now used to denote the *study* of folklore, so that "folklore" can refer only to the *materials* for study).[5]

Literature Search

My specialty is folkloristics. Because of its interdisciplinary approach, I examined the literature of several disciplines—anthropology, history, folkloristics, and also sociology and psychology—for their uses of the life history. When I began this search, instructive comparisons were few. There was nothing in the scholarly literature on women in southeastern Ohio or Ohio, and little on either southeastern Ohio or Ohio with any relation to my subject.[6] Few academic studies had addressed the topic of rural women;[7] in fact, most of the literature of these disciplines focused on other topics: in anthropology, on primitive, nonliterate peoples, the life histories confined generally to American Indians, with only a few of these women; in history, on significant events and famous persons; in folkloristics, on texts or artifacts, that is, the product rather than the producer; in sociology, on urban populations, with the life histories used in criminology.[8] Consequently, my decision to pursue an in-depth life history hinged on several aspects: my personal concern with woman's role, the interesting relevant scholarly literature—on rural society, on the role of women in that society—and on the use of the life history, especially with regard to women.

As I continued my research over the next few years, however, there was great expansion of similar interest in topics concerning women. Suddenly most disciplines offered a steadily lengthening list of woman-focused literature and of bibliographies alerting the reader to these and to earlier—but little known—works.[9] In addition, scholars in several disciplines exhibited new interest in life history research, some with female subjects.[10]

Significant gaps remained nonetheless, concerning Ohio and the Midwest, rural society, women in those geographic areas, the "common person" in America, and scholarly development of the life history—especially as research with explication and analysis of women's lives. I therefore pursued my study of Sarah Flynn Penfield. And out of that pursuit has come my contention, as I propose to show, that the life history is a viable form of research; that a well-founded life history can effect a cross-disciplinary contribution to the scholarly literature; and that it can bring new insights to our understanding of the human condition.

Influences on This Introductory Chapter

My nonacademic friends have groaned at the prospect of my "obscuring this good story with a long, boring introduction: Who cares about all your interviewing techniques?" They railed at an "unnecessary" conclusion: "What's Sarah got to do with other women, anyhow?" My preference was, of course, to have the best of both worlds, the academic *and* the popular, since a larger audience would mean more persons' knowing about Sarah and, possibly, more about women's lives generally. But I soon recognized that it was not possible to have, in today's parlance, a "package deal"—a popular, easy-to-read biography in the same clever bundle with a professional, academically viable life history. Because of my study of existing oral and life histories, I realized that there were at least three stumbling blocks to such a happy combination: the need for (1) an introduction that included details of interviewing techniques and editing procedures; (2) a conclusion that incorporated both summary and analysis; and (3) quotations of Sarah's spoken words in blocks instead of in more flowing quotation-marked passages.

These derive from the lists of shortcomings that scholarly critics have consistently enumerated since 1935: the scarcity of adequate methodological information; the insufficiency of reliability and validity checks; the inclusion of only sketchy biographical material; a lack of annotation; and the inferior quality—or complete absence—of interpretation and analysis.[11] My own research efforts had been handicapped by these kinds of omissions. Therefore, tedious though they may be for some readers, I could not exclude the same details from my own study.

Recently critics have underscored and added to those caveats of nearly fifty years' standing with even stronger appeals: for editing policy information; for contextual data surrounding the consultant's social, cultural, historical, and geographic world; and also for the role and the reactions of the researcher, the "other" person in the life history. Unfortunately, use of the pronoun "I" has had such supranegative connotations of subjectivity in academe that crucial interpersonal data have been eliminated by so-called objective description, thereby obscuring the scholar as a human being. One of the most vocal in calling for this stronger reference to the researcher, Frank asked for a "critical approach to self-description," especially in life histories, since they are—metaphorically speaking—double autobiographies.[12] Since I agree with these viewpoints, I have included my own personal experiences, reactions, and autobiographic references at whatever points seemed logical for understanding my choices or analyses (for example, the next paragraph), especially in this chapter.

My second obstacle to easy readability was the analysis and interpretation in the concluding chapter, in response, as I have noted above, to earlier criticism of the majority of life histories. Analysis offers a way of imposing form on that which "takes on form only in the process of its construction."[13] Further, it is a way to explain that form from the vantage point of the one with (presumably) as complete *and* objective a view as it is possible to have of one life. Without that kind of explication, there is a significant gap in the recording and much of the value of the document is lost. Ultimately I "imposed form" through an analysis based on the pertinence of Sarah's testimonies to my original interest in woman's role. In convergence with Sarah's life, my upbringing was also traditional, and it implanted firm conceptions in my mind of woman's role as wife and mother *in the home*. The divergence in our lives came with our contrasting adaptations to the "empty nest syndrome." Sarah chose to continue—and even to extend—her role as matriarch in the appropriate physical, symbolic locale of the home. Partly because of our differing geographic and cultural environments, partly because of the painful void my young son's death made in my personal environment, I chose the physical and symbolic space of academe rather than home. Gradually I became aware of the whole spectrum of issues, statistics, histories, facts, and fictions that complicate the subject of "woman" and "woman's role." These became a focus of my work with Sarah Penfield not only because of her emphasis on certain values and beliefs but also because of my own confrontations with the attendant issues. The position I ultimately evolved can be stated simply: I believe women are equal to men, and they should have individual choice for the direction of their lives. A simple statement, yes; but strong for such a tradition-bred person, and born of long, difficult experience and introspection. And yet with all my newfound strengths and "strong" opinions about the inherent equality of woman and the basic fairness of role choice for her, the tyrant that is tradition grips me often with unrelenting tentacles of doubt. The strength of this pull of tradition both on Sarah and on me affected the whole direction of my analysis.

The third stumbling block, how to treat Sarah's spoken words, was the most difficult decision for me aesthetically. The standard method of using block quotations does violence to my sense of the poetry of Sarah's speech—of any speech. I aspired to presenting her as sympathetically as the Coleses did their friends in *Women of Crisis* I and II, or Oscar Lewis, in his several life histories: their effective results were due in no small part to the novel-type format of their works. Ultimately my desire to maintain this as a document, *not* a novel, led me to retain the block quotations, rather than (as the Coleses explained their methods) to "shape what we have seen and heard into a kind of story.... We have, so doing, compressed drastically remarks made in leisure. We have moved comments around a bit, placing statements made one time with those of another.... The writers become mediators."[14] I chose a less artistic form of mediation with real regret. Nonetheless, the long block quotations enabled me to present Sarah with far less intrusion of me as editor. The reader knows that this is what *Sarah* said, who was there when she said it, and, when pertinent, what question preceded her commentary.

METHODOLOGY

There are few "how-to" manuals for life history research. After combing the classic ones,[15] I devised a methodological framework, parts of which are presented here: selecting a consultant, the interviewing process, and editing.

Selecting a Consultant

Just as the life history was not begun by careful predetermination, my selection of a consultant was not part of a "grand design."

My husband and I, with our five children, had visited the county where Sarah resides for many years, drawn to its natural beauty for hiking, camping, and, finally, our first timorous purchase of land. Thus we knew the community and many of its inhabitants when we bought more land and a house and began to spend weekends and summers there, away from the "madding crowd." About sixty miles from Columbus, the rural southeastern Ohio region is in a social, economic, and geographic zone different from the urban Ohio capital. With Anne Hoffman, one of our most special friends there, we traveled often to the southeastern section of the county to visit her mother, Sarah Penfield. We first knew Sarah then as a dispenser of interesting, necessary, useful information, and as a contributor of copious garden treasures and luscious fruit pies; she soon became surrogate grandmother to our children as well, complete with the appellation "grandma."[16]

Our family spent increasing periods of time in this second home, and we continued to broaden our community contacts and area friendships. Because of our interest in county history, I conducted my first formal interview with Sarah and her daughter in 1972. She seemed an obvious "prime consultant" (though I did not then know the academic terminology) because of her narrative skill, her knowledge of the community, her family's longevity there (five generations), and our mutual rapport.

At that point the loss of our youngest child had altered our lives dramatically. Despite my traditional upbringing, I subsequently chose to combat the major change in my role in the home by entering graduate school. I became—in today's euphemism for an older woman at college—a "mature student." The thrust of my interviewing therefore evolved toward the academic traditions of folklore and folklife. In 1975 that original question to Sarah on woman's role opened, as I described, new lines of inquiry, and in ensuing interviews I began to focus on a broadened life history approach with Sarah.

"Motivating the consultant" is a major thrust in social science fieldwork. It is difficult to find "average" individuals who will take the time to tell their story, however; deviants—those badly adjusted in their own culture or resentful of their own and the fieldworker's culture—tend to volunteer. Certainly Sarah is in no way a deviant, maladjusted personality. From our personal observation of her and the community, and from testimony of family, friends, and area residents, Sarah is as close to "average" as it is possible to be.[17] Through all the interviews, Sarah was a willing narrator, primarily because of her innate sense of generosity and helpfulness to friends. Even though we are separated by a generation, friendship—and rapport—stemmed from our mutual interests in our families, homes, domestic skills, and concerns as mothers and as women. She is a strong advocate of education, and wished to assist me in furthering mine. Second, she enjoyed the company, the attention, and a chance to tell about her family, best of all the happily recalled days of her youth.[18] For she is proud of the history of her ancestors, her family, and their rural life-style.

There was never any question of pay: it would have been, in my judgment, highly inappropriate. Although Kelley paid her consultants, she affirmed that "direct payment can be construed as inappropriate in relationships characterized as pseudo-kinship or friendship." There are at least two schools of thought among social scientists on this sensitive issue: one is that payment for services rendered by consultants is only fair, and the other is that payment contaminates the relationship, resulting in information skewed by monetary motivations. In agreement with the latter, I still felt a strong obligation to compensate Sarah in some way.[19] Ultimately, in almost humorous circular fashion, I labored to keep abreast of the gifts Sarah gave *me* in return for those I was giving *her* in return for the interviewing time she was giving *me*! We exchanged recipes, herbs, plants, garden produce, baked goods, canned goods, and luncheons. My limits on trading were reached when she papered my kitchen ceiling and "helped" me freeze corn and peaches. The same problem held true in my attempted repayment of her daughter Anne, who had given me uncounted hours of interviewing and consulting time. Finally, I was able to give them each two gifts more unique to my own specialties: copies of my photographs of their houses, yards, flowers, families, and gardens; and copies of the Flynn genealogy I produced for Sarah and each of her children. This in turn gave them all a new awareness of, and interest in, their own family and community history, aided then by my suggestions of methods and sources for research. I finally realized that gifts need not—perhaps should not—be physically or monetarily comparable to be meaningful.

The Interviewing Process

Interviewing is a many-faceted procedure; it is supremely important when—as in the case of life histories—success of the research hinges on the interviewing proficiency of the researcher. Factors of appropriate place, time, audience, types of interview, and types of recording are critical.[20]

My interviews were of two types: (1) formal ones, tape-recorded and transcribed, and (2) informal ones, with typed notes recorded later from field notes or from memory. In addition, a variety of visits, meals, phone conversations, and trips with Sarah and members of her family, as well as with area residents, afforded further perceptions for interpretation and analysis. (For those desiring contextual clarification of the interviewing situation, Appendix A lists the interviews in chronological order, with date, location of interview, persons present, and number of transcription pages. It lists formal and informal interviews with Sarah, her daughter Anne, her son James, and her granddaughter Debbie.)

The formal interviews covered a period of more than six years, the informal ones more than nine years. The formal type varied in length from twenty minutes to nearly four hours; in number of tape transcription pages from 2 to 102; in postinterview typescript pages, 1 to 8. (The time-length figure is misleading, however, since it is calculated only from actual taping time, and the visits themselves often ran far longer, usually including a meal and casual talk as well.) Most of the interviews took place in Sarah's home because she seemed most at ease there.[21] Not only was she more comfortable in her own surroundings but she was also able to continue at least some of her daily activities; she would have quickly become restive were she "just" sitting and visiting. Since one of them was unsuccessful, I conducted only two interviews with Sarah at my own house. That location, however, seemed fully satisfactory for interviews with her daughter Anne.

Another person was present for all but two of my formal interviews with Sarah (with Anne, there was another present for only two). Most often at Sarah's it was her sister Martha. At first I was concerned that Martha's presence would inhibit Sarah's testimony in some way. Instead, the opposite was true: Martha was a catalyst for eliciting memories, attitudes, and beliefs.[22] In addition to contributing information herself, Martha was an invaluable reliability check on Sarah's testimony and a brake on Sarah's tendency to romanticize their childhood years. Interviewing one's consultant alone is often considered advantageous. Yet neither my formal interviews nor my dozens of informal visits alone with Sarah indicated such advantage with her: they elicited no frank or intimate revelations, no filling in the gaps for the period of her married years.

Formal interviews can be either directed, with a question-and-answer format, or nondirected, with the researcher adopting a "blank screen" posture. The directed type may be necessary to draw out less than voluble narrators, or to fill out a shopping list of specific informational items. It is used almost exclusively by historians and by anthropologists with an emphasis on culture. The nondirected type is more nearly autobiographical, since it develops what the consultant—not the researcher—thinks important; it is thus suited to an emphasis on personality.[23] I used a combination of the two, with emphasis on the nondirected; Sarah is such an eager narrator that efforts to maintain a directed interview, and to confine her to short or to specific responses, were usually fruitless. The nondirected method yielded substantially more information, of course, but it did so at the expense of huge amounts of time in both interviewing and—far worse—transcribing.

There was one notable exception to recording a loquacious narrator. In my literature search, I had eagerly read Lurie's accounts of her work with a Winnebago Indian grandmother. After establishing suitable rapport, Lurie hired her to stay at Lurie's home to recount her life story into a tape recorder.

Doing a Life History

Mountain Wolf Woman would "settle herself comfortably in a large chair, fold her hands in her lap, close her eyes and begin to relive events as she recalled them."[24] A beautiful eighty-three-page autobiography rolled forth, in perfect chronology, full of rich cultural detail, with only a few minor additions inserted later!

I was fascinated by (albeit wary of) Lurie's apparent breakthrough in method. Not only could I stop investing such enormous amounts of time in interviewing and transcribing, but I could eliminate my personal intrusion into the data. Because of my school schedule, Sarah and I had had no formal interview for a full year at that point, a logical time to experiment. Carefully the stage was set: a quiet afternoon at my house; no one else there to interrupt; careful suggestions and instructions to Sarah that she simply tell her life story, starting with life as a toddler, remembering even seemingly unimportant details. Emulating Lurie further, I left Sarah with the recorder, but worked quietly in the adjoining kitchen for standby support. It was as if, in some secret conspiracy, an imposter slipped into Sarah's chair. She is noted for her volubility, for both speed and length of deliverance, for firm and forthright declaration, for strong vocal tones. This consultant spoke slowly (even haltingly), timidly, softly, in stilted statement of only the middle childhood stage, no preschool material at all. The dialogue and the content were both inordinately dull. Silence followed. I interjected pump-priming questions and suggestions, but the voice would soon dwindle again. Finally Sarah tiptoed over to me and whispered, in order not to disturb the recorder, that she would "quit for today and mebbe take some notes." Appendix B, a transcription of the tape, demonstrates the amazing comparison between that deliberate, colorless recording and the polychromatic, flowing dialogue that follows in chapters 3 through 7. Sarah needed an audience, in combination with a slight—only slight—interested prompting for that detailed social commentary and often copious discourse. Had this been my first interview, it would have been my last, and Sarah would have been pigeonholed as a nonconsul-

15

tant. She never brought up the subject again; most assuredly I did not, for fear of somehow drying up my source. We visited regularly, and then I resumed my predominantly open-ended, nondirective interviewing three months later, ruefully jealous of Dr. Lurie.

Methods for recording interviews have a wide range: from not making any kind of record (supplanting the visit by typed recall as soon as possible); to personal efforts (jotting key words on small note pads, or attempting full transcription by longhand and shorthand); to, finally, using electronic devices (tape recorders, still cameras, video cameras). Though video cameras remain prohibitively costly and specialized, the advent of less-expensive tape recorders and still cameras has placed a whole new technology at the service of social scientists.[25] Yet use of the tape recorder summons totally opposite kinds of response: for example, one person likens it to a "monster with the appetite of a tapeworm . . . [its] creature, oral history, an artificial survival of trivia of appalling proportions." Still others assert that the resultant product is a new kind of historical document; or that, by providing firsthand data for others' analysis, the recorder somewhat controls the personal bias of the researcher; that it allows the researcher more freedom for observation, and acts as a mnemonic device for recall.[26] It is—and does—all of these and more.

I experimented with all but the video camera, by: using no notes except key-word jottings; attempting longhand transcriptions; and using both a 35 mm camera and a cassette tape recorder, with built-in microphone. The taped transcriptions are far and away the most valuable record for me because I *know*, not *think* I know, what occurred verbally. Furthermore, I can pass on this knowledge to the reader without intruding myself as chronicler. My untaped visits were valuable in some respects, chiefly for maintaining rapport, gaining an intuitive grasp of the subject, and remembering a few facts; but on balance they offered a paucity of translatable material. I simply could not have gained the insights I did without the ability to read and reread my extensive transcriptions. In fact, I would agree with Lurie, who, in working with the Winnebago grandmother, "regretted that it was not possible to have a microphone constantly recording our conversation."[27]

No system is perfect. There are at least three potential hazards in using a recorder: silencing the consultant, "losing" the interview, and acquiring an "embarrassment of riches." Many consultants freeze, their lips glued shut, when that little black box appears. Of course, this varies with the individual and the situation. Fortunately Sarah had no objection to the recorder and no sense of being intimidated by its presence (except for that one disastrous time when I tried to emulate Lurie). Next, the efficiency of the equipment can match only the proficiency of its technician: several interviews, in whole or in part, were forever lost due to malfunction of the recorder—or of my head. Now I take key-word notes while tape recording and check tape results just after the interview (postinterview scripts, if needed to supplement faulty tapes, must be typed immediately for maximum recall). My notes included contextual information as well; for example, body language, special reactions to a subject, voice inflections, interruptions, anything to make the context more clear to me. The third problem pertains to the aptness of that quoted definition—a "monster with the appetite of a tapeworm." The recorder is blessing and curse: for all its remarkable abilities to record full and accurate data, those very profusions of material can create powerful psychological blocks for the researcher. With the incredibly time-consuming job of tape transcription in progress, researchers can suddenly view the recorder as far worse than a voracious monster. At one point I could scarcely force myself to visit Sarah and record her again because of the mathematical progression of transcription that I set in motion: Sarah's speech patterns (characterized by rapid-fire utterances) resulted in almost double the number of words per minute compared with any other consultants on my tapes; one hour of taping her usually translated to at *least* eight hours of transcribing! Ultimately I had to resort to the costly alternative of hiring a transcriber for part of the tapes, and, after considerable trial and error, finally located an excellent technician. (The tapes remain catalogued in my possession.)

Editing

The subject of editing draws more fire than any other in the battle over proper life history methodology. Past researchers have failed to describe not only the conditions and the techniques used to obtain data but also the manner in which they were ultimately reported. For example, when a document is written in the first person, is it actually printed word for word as the consultant said it, or does it have the fine—and invisible—hand of the researcher/author to make it more clear, more convincing, more poetic? When it is written chronologically, did it in fact flow thus from the speaker's lips, or was there extensive manipulation of the texts and the interview situation? More importantly, if this happened are we told so? Is there indication of how the researcher's own comments and questions might have influenced the choice of subject or the quality of answers, or is there even reference to the presence of this third person? Was there need for a third-person translator? Any of these omissions or stylistic devices necessarily removes us another step from what was actually said.[28]

The problems of editing are multiplied in almost direct proportion to the length of transcribed materials. Presumably the ideal would be to present *all* the interviews recorded by whatever method, in unexpurgated form. Kluckhohn, advocating a complex three-volume approach, considered this optimal. In 1945 he admitted it sounded expensive. In 1983 it is utopian.[29]

A reviewer of Dégh's four mini-life histories made the suggestion that a folklorist can, without making thorough checks on contextual data, create a life history simply by turning on the tape recorder. I agree with his call for "thorough checks on contextual data" but would add that this does not resolve questions of editing procedure.[30] Acquiring adequate biographic, interpretive, and contextual data resulted as well in my acquiring more than seven hundred pages of transcription—impossible to publish verbatim. Therefore I edited the material to make it comprehensible to the reader, without, I devoutly hoped, violating the context, meaning, or substance of Sarah's words. I included all the topics of our conversations except those few of obviously too personal a nature; I placed them in chronological sequence to help the reader assimilate this volume of raw data. In the biographical presentations, I have used seven stylistic devices both to expose the reluctant hand of the editor and to enhance contextual perceptions:

(1) Bracketing a transcription number (e.g., [4]) after each conversation quoted. Those interested may then check Appendix A for contextual data relating to date, place, audience present, and length of the full transcription from which the quote is taken. Numbers indicate formal, taped interviews, small letters indicate informal ones. The numeral II before a number or letter indicates interviews with Anne, Sarah's daughter; the numeral III, an interview with James, Sarah's son.

(2) Quoting lengthy excerpts of Sarah's dialogue, in order to present as full a treatment of a subject as possible and to avoid implying meanings out of context. (These excerpts often become overly repetitious, however—as does everyone's daily conversation—and I have used ellipsis points to indicate removal of, for example, excessive repetition, two-word questions, or brief subject change.) They are intended to indicate what holds importance for Sarah and what shapes her world view, to avert at least partially the reader's wondering what *else* she said. They also point up the flavor of her narrative, which in itself uses repetition stylistically.

(3) Including my questions or comments with the letter R to indicate length, placement, and type of question. Though less readable, this also acts as a guide to the directed or nondirected character of the interview itself. It serves, not incidentally, to show that the written word does violence to the spoken: researchers' transcribed speeches sound as ungrammatical and stilted as do consultants'.

(4) Identifying other speakers (primarily Sarah's sister, Martha, and daughter, Anne) to further amplify the context and to increase information.

(5) Using nonstandard punctuation, with few commas, semi-

A Woman's Place

colons, and even periods, to convey the flavor of Sarah's expressivity—her rapid discourse and run-together phrases and sentences. Interruptions (and there are usually many) are designated by a dash at the end of the first speaker's sentence and at the beginning of the interrupter's speech.

(6) Enclosing my explanations in brackets.

(7) Using the vernacular, yet another subject of academic controversy, in the quotations. Some scholars brand the practice—for example, printing the "ain'ts" and the "he don'ts" and dropping the "g" on "ing" endings—a form of academic snobbery, elitism. Since bank presidents, no matter what their form of provincial accent, are quoted in only Etonian English, it is only fair to do the same embellishing for all consultants, they believe. Nonetheless, many accounts use phonetic dialect to faithfully preserve linguistic features of the culture involved. Because faithful reproduction takes us one step closer to the actual data, any deviation becomes an error. Kluckhohn pointed to a recurring fact in the history of science, that is, that another generation of scholars may have a totally different emphasis; thus exact reproduction may be of crucial importance for linguistic study later. It seemed to me a heightened form of snobbery *not* to use the vernacular, a subtle way of saying, "Your speech is strange, and, rather than embarrass either of us, I shall make it proper—like mine." Pure ethnocentrism! Better by far that we quote the bank president, and all of us, with accent intact.[31]

PROBLEM AREAS ENCOUNTERED IN THE RESEARCH

Whether they are delineated or not, problems are an omnipresent aspect of research. The most vexing ones for me were ethical ones. Other disturbing issues were the paradoxes in using fictitious names; the inadequacy of material on Sarah's married life; the enigmatic portions in parts of Sarah's narrative; the limited number of checks that were possible on reliability and validity; and the ambiguity of my position as an outsider in Sarah's culture.

Ethical Considerations

The ethics of presentation, of inclusion, and of conclusion in dealing with the "true story" genre of a real individual constitutes one of its largest problems for the researcher, both personally and professionally.

In the abstractions of a community ethnography, the combined facts and statistics and summaries of a larger population can easily obscure omissions of data, but these become more obvious when there is focus on only one individual. And there *are* omissions in the life history of Sarah Penfield: omissions stemming, first, from the strictures of time (conceivably one could derive new material and new insights as long as interviews were continued); from the consultant's inability to recall portions of her life; from her conscious desire to withhold material for privacy's sake; and from my conscious decisions to withhold material that would, I believed, be considered by Sarah or her family inappropriate for publication.[32]

My decisions to withhold and not to withhold information came only after lengthy, painful introspection. I firmly believed in the validity and importance of these data for scholars in diverse areas, yet my position became increasingly ambiguous: how could I as a private individual be true to my friend and, simultaneously, true to myself as an academic? Most—probably all—researchers wish to portray individuals with respect, shielding them from a public display of their private concerns. The rub is: Can they concurrently submit truly scholarly data, applicable to historical and social comparisons, without either tearing the fabric of authentic relationships or lapsing into mere nostalgic reminiscence?

For a considerable period of time, then, I could see no way to reconcile the seemingly opposing factors of personal honesty and academic truth. As Sarah and I shared cake recipes and peppermint tea and trips to the "herb lady's" garden, I brooded introspectively: Was I using my friendships for selfish (i.e., academic) gain? At first I played a sort of half-conscious game with myself: I never made field notes or data recordings for informal get-togethers, and I logged information only for those times when taping an interview was my stated purpose. Very quickly I realized that I was throwing the baby out with the bath, in a useless kind of charade; since I could not stop internalizing my perceptions of Penfield attitudes and values and even ethnographic information, I was helping no one and fooling only myself. I gave up my research.

Finally, encouragement from friends and mentors pushed me to resume my efforts. Yet the underlying problem remained unsolved. At that time few authors had shared anxieties similar to mine. Instead, Gallagher underscored my fears when she reported that, after publication of her oral history of six generations of women, one of the daughters believed the author was "airing dirty linen."[33] Consequently, a professor friend—upon reading my first short draft of Sarah's life—commented, "She is just too good to be true." And of course she was. In my zeal to portray my friend in a good light, to avoid parading any inconsistencies or shortcomings or problems, I had focused (as Sarah tends to do herself) on the ideal and not the real. Obviously no one—man, woman, or child—lacks inconsistencies or shortcomings or problems. It was not, then, either contribution to scholarship or justice to a friend to present her as a sort of paper doll instead of as the human being she is: a true country woman, wife and mother, with all the heartache and body ache necessarily entailed in that role.

Ultimately, with enormous help, I achieved a middle ground; many competent academic friends guided the scholarly aspects of my report. And Anne Hoffman, my friend and Sarah's daughter, acted as my official Penfield family adviser, reading and approving every page of the final draft, as well as providing additional ethnographic material throughout.

Although these were personal considerations for me, they have become professional concerns for all the social sciences. For example, many Indian tribes are now closed to anthropological research because of real or imagined indiscretions on the part of some scholars and the seeking of sensationalism or profit. The legal ramifications involved are also becoming more central to professional discussions.[34]

Obviously, this aspect of the research had acquired elephantine proportions for me. I knew that field-workers had always been warned to maintain the sense of detachment from their consultants considered absolutely necessary for scientific objectivity, and my detachment and objectivity were worse than suspect. Now scholars have reevaluated both the necessity for, and the practicality of, such a posture.[35] Unfortunately for my peace of mind, the thorough exposition by Langness and Frank on life histories in general, and the whole ethics dilemma in particular, was not available then. Presumably even more will be published concerning these puzzling areas. Consider how grateful I was for the one work that provided glimpses of other researchers as "fully social and occasionally fallible" beings. After all, if even the gods had had at least *toes* of clay (if, for example, Boas—the "father of American anthropology"—was nicknamed the Kwakiutl appellate for "fart," and if Malinowski, famed for his extraordinary empathy, wrote that he was "furious with all those pigs"!), there was, I reasoned, still hope for me with my lapses of detachment and objectivity.[36]

Using Fictitious Names

Electing to use fictitious personal and place- names eased my ethical quandary in large measure (though actually no infallible "cover" can ever be devised). It also illuminated one of the potential problems in an interdisciplinary study: discovering and then mediating opposing stances, in this case methodological. Anthropologists regularly use fictive names; folklorists and literary scholars tend to be divided more along lines of personal opinion and legal liability; sociologists *never* use actual names; yet historians decry the use of pseudonyms, since a whole trainload of fictitious names must necessarily follow— relatives, streets, towns, townships, cities, counties—deleting historical records (and also etiological study of place-names, a valuable source for folklore study). Statistics—for a particular county, for example—cannot be used meaningfully. Providing source references is a further dilemma, since most titles include proper names; and page numbers in larger, more generalized volumes lend even further clues to locale identification. My solution was to use aggregate figures for three southeastern counties to furnish a broad but still accurate picture of the region without specifying an exact location.

I could not use all the interesting variety of photographs I desired. And there was no real solution to the fact that I could not give public recognition to "Sarah" herself and to "Anne," her daughter, without whose help and encouragement and advice I could never have completed the research or the subsequent book. They are such outstanding women and such lovely friends: I would have been joyful to have them receive the public honor and appreciation due them.

Inadequacy of Material on Sarah's Married Life

Large blocks of specific time periods in Sarah's life—most of her married life—remained vague and even obscure after many interviews. This could have been caused by the aging factor,[37] by an unconscious sublimation of a difficult life stage, by a conscious direction toward happier, less traumatic times, or, more probably, by a combination of the three. Sarah and I discussed breaking the interview materials down into four periods for clarification—(1) her childhood and young adulthood, 1903 to 1927; (2) the early married years, 1927 to 1946; (3) the changing married years, 1946 to 1981, when the children began to leave home, she was widowed, and finally alone; and (4) the present—since both ethnographic fact and personal attitude could be different in those disparate periods. For example, when I asked a question about dairying, one of us would specify whether the answer referred to her parents' practices, hers during her early marriage, or hers during later married years.

I combed field research guidebooks and life histories themselves for methods or ideas on eliciting additional information for these inaccessible time periods. One such method I tried was producing a five-generation patrilineal genealogy chart for Sarah, which was somewhat helpful in deriving new information. So were the series of map overlays I constructed of the township: one to represent Sarah's and Robert's grandparents' residences; one, their parents'; and one, hers and her childrens' today. I took numerous photographs over the years: of Sarah, her family, her house, her flowers, her vegetable garden, the neighboring areas, and regional architecture examples. I used them as gifts for her, as clues to social interaction, and also as practice in learning to observe culture in complex detail. Yet my hopes were dashed for discovering new material from her enthusiasms for, or comments on, my pictures.[38] Nor did I have access to old family picture albums to jog her memory; all the mementos and pictures belonging to Sarah's mother had burned in a house fire, and all of Sarah's were in safekeeping with her eldest daughter in Columbus, "because of their safe concrete block home." When we finally did see them, they drew no new material or interesting comment.

I made lists of questions to ask at subsequent interviews, after I had checked my data for gaps in the record. But to say that following such a set "schedule" of questioning was difficult would be gross and ridiculous understatement. Sarah has great penchant for swiftly and frequently changing the subject.[39]

Thus, in spite of my persistence in devising various strategies, the lacunae of Sarah's recollections of her married years were never really filled in satisfactorily. Fortunately, her daughter Anne's contributions fleshed out the period of the later 1930s and 1940s somewhat, both when the children were growing up and then when they were beginning to leave home. There was some help, too, from written sources. I visited cemeteries for dates, and the county courthouse for land acquisition names, locations, and dates; and I consulted local journals and all the available historical literature for southeastern Ohio.[40]

Enigmatic Portions of Sarah's Narrative

There was still another block to expanding my record of the Penfield family: Sarah, too, had techniques—and for purposes diametrically opposed to mine. I sought to uncover information, she to withhold it. There were undoubtedly many aspects of her life she considered "none of Mrs. Joyce's business." So if the conversation ever veered toward what is often termed "ethnographic dynamite"—private matters—she achieved new records in rapid subject change.[41] If there were any skeletons in the family closet, Sarah never rattled them for me.

In addition, she constantly held up an ideal to mirror her reflections on family and on culture. This idealization involved two levels: one, convincing *me* of the superiority of her family, her life-style, her geographic location; the other—far more subtle—convincing *herself* of such superiority, on that unconscious level by which humans internally structure their external environments. Sarah revealed these same kinds of real/ideal dichotomous attitudes toward woman's role and woman's "place" as well (to be discussed in more detail in chapter 7). Such real and ideal conflict is apparently a worldwide phenomenon, one that challenges each discipline in its search for "truth." Langness and Frank, as an example, referred to the "perennial anthropological problem of relating ideals of behavior with the actual behavior itself." Unfortunately no yardstick has been invented to measure the extent of the omissions and the commissions in first-person accounts, yet another hazard of field research. (Fortunately for me, Sarah did not, to my knowledge, ever lie—actually a definite problem with some researchers' consultants.)[42]

Limited Number of Checks on Reliability and Validity

Because of Sarah's constant idealizing of her family, my interviews with her uncovered little of the unpleasant aspects of daily life—the arguments, controversies, religious differences—even in our many visits alone, with no potential censors (after all, I loomed large in that capacity). Nonetheless, a large portion of covert material was still available to me through various devices for checking reliability and validity. One of these was participant observation during my residence there, which included my meeting a broad spectrum of local residents, interviewing many of them, and attending community functions.

The interviews themselves, held as they were at widely spaced intervals and often on the same subjects, were built-in validity checks.[43] So were my discussions of interview results and interpretations with other family members, both Sarah's and my own. Having others present at most of the interviews acted often as a conversation stimulator, but also as a validity check.

Doing a Life History

The open-ended quality of the interviews, which elicited long discourse, was a similar kind of check.

Though my choice of consultant was obviously not based on that favored reliability check, scientific sampling, the sampling ranges in that small community would not have been statistically reliable in any case. And if one is attempting a life history on a particular individual, sampling is irrelevant anyhow. (Mead has argued that *any* individual can be taken as a representative of a culture in a certain sense.)[44] In addition, the choice of a female consultant did help modify the predominance of male consultants in the literature, a predominance improved upon but certainly not eliminated.

Ambiguity as an Outsider in the Culture

As an ethnographer working in my own country, I did not face onerous linguistic and cultural barriers. Sarah and I spoke the same language, so there was no third-person interpreter presenting yet another set of variables. Nonetheless our shared language and nationality often blinded me to the fact that we came from different *sub*cultures. Those differences were subtle. In fact, it is almost axiomatic that one cannot observe the exotic, the unfamiliar within the everyday, the familiar. It was difficult for me, then, to identify ethnographic elements in the seemingly familiar physical environment of southeastern Ohio. At the same time, I did not have the native's built-in understanding of that social environment. One microcosmic example: in an early interview with Sarah, the subtleties of connotative differences in culture—and, correspondingly, in speech—were illustrated when I expressed interest in learning more about "the lives of women in our society." Sarah laughed and warned that she and her sister could not help me then, for they "weren't social people and never went to parties!" (Of course she was too polite to point out similar differences in *my* speech.)

In addition to such linguistic dissimilarities, a number of our values and attitudes are culturally different. One example is the contrast in attitudes toward the physical environment. Most urbanites who seek rural, open spaces—my own family included—are caught up in ecological problems, concerned with preserving the total environment (though sometimes, it should be noted, only for themselves). In general, rural residents have a different outlook, a different world view. Some of it is based in part on the economics of the situation, some on lack of exposure to similar aesthetic or scientific concerns. For the most part, it reflects our country's history of struggle to subjugate the land, that same battle that began when the first white settlers in America set out to "conquer the wilderness." Nature was the enemy, whose tenacity must be fought with tenacity. Wild animals were a source of food or danger, to kill or be killed by; forests and lands, a resource to use and use up.[45] This pragmatic philosophy has been maintained up to the present with rural residents, who still "do battle" with the land. Anne can remember that her mother cleared a whole field herself by "grubbing out tree stumps with an ax, just *hideous* work!" Not surprisingly then, Sarah is not "into ecology," as urbanites see it. For example, she had none of my horror (sublimated when I was with her, admittedly) at the denuding—for no apparent reason—of a forested hillside at the edge of town behind a new shopping mall; she was both satisfied and confident that they would "plant it in grass before spring so it won't wash," apparently minding not at all the ecological and aesthetic loss of a lovely woods. She vehemently pronounces disgust with residents who will not allow the county to spray poison weed killer along their roadsides. Housekeeper always, she decries the resultant "dirty, unsightly views!" Many natives do seem oblivious to the natural features of the land. (This may be the norm for residents of any rural area; after all, urban dwellers have seldom toured the "points of interest" listed in travelogue brochures for their own cities. My exclamations over the natural beauty of the mountain vistas from her porch led a Carolina woman to comment in proverbial style: "I never noticed it much. But then one man's vacation is another man's every day.")[46] Often, however, this holds more true for women, as sex roles are firmly delineated: girls and women belong in the confines of the domestic circle, that is, house, yard, garden—and field only if for the care of domestic animals (as will be seen in chaps. 4 and 5, below). Sarah, too, conforms carefully to societal roles. The head of a magnificent hollow, an incomparable setting of sandstone cliffs and lacy hemlocks, protrudes into Sarah's land within sight of her kitchen window; yet she has walked *toward*—not down into—it only once, that about twenty years ago.

Another significant cultural difference was in our dissimilar modes of affective response. I already knew that area residents were taciturn, and friendly but reserved. This is not so immediately evident in those who are exceptionally loquacious, as are Sarah and various members of her family. But the reserve is still there: there is a we/they barrier that seldom lowers. Seemingly a product of this reserve, there are neither verbal nor physical displays of affection, no terms of endearment, no hugs, kisses, or even handshakes outside the confines of the family. But this is apparently a cultural behavioral difference beyond mere reserve, since this is true also *within* the confines of the family, both the Penfields' and a broad spectrum of area residents' families. Even understanding that, I had to struggle (subjectively, of course) to overcome feelings of personal lack or failure when, after all these years, Sarah still called me "Mrs. Joyce." Intellectually I knew that both she and I must be understood by the "ethical and social standards" of our own cultures;[47] emotionally I lamented the apparent barrier between us, we who shared so much: wifehood, motherhood, womanhood, all the joys and sorrows those roles entail—even the ultimate grief of losing sons.

Another example of cultural difference, not surprisingly, is Sarah's views of urban versus rural life. Though it is not within the scope of this work to record sweeping generalities concerning the region, I would state nonetheless that this is an attitude that also seems to move beyond Sarah: the city is, stereotypically, an undesirable place to live—great to visit, but... Country people are friendlier, more helpful, and probably more honest. (Traditional mistrust of the "city slicker" is alive and well.) The city is full of crime and criminals and is not safe to live in; it also has terrible drug problems. the impressive number of fifty- and sixty-mile-a-day commuters attests to these enduring beliefs.[48] City-country rivalry, a historic feature of America, continues here.

THE INTERDISCIPLINARY APPROACH

One of the goals of my life history research has been to supply a personal document with interdisciplinary value and utility. This is a hazardous venture. Each discipline has a different methodology, different concepts, hypotheses, and theories, different points of view and self-directed goals. For example, anthropologists have sought to analyze a number of cultural concerns in the narrower focus of the life history, such as culture and personality, culture change, and role analysis. Folklorists, although they have attempted a few life history–type studies, have been interested primarily in understanding a particular folklore genre and the process of its transmission. Sociologists and criminologists have applied life history research at varying levels, from the basic one of particular subject exploration to the abstract one of theory evaluation.[49] These differences create an enormous problem for achieving interdisciplinary kinds of research and research products.

In still another dissimilarity of emphasis, researchers in several disciplines—anthropology, sociology, and folklore—have sought to discover how social situations *appear* to their consultants. These researchers are seeking the subjective perceptions of their consultants, the relative "truths" of their lives. Historians, on the other hand, have instead been interested in determining the absolute truth, or facts, of individual situations, and they have pursued these absolutes through structured, rather than open-ended, interviews. Such emphasis was underscored by historians' choices until the late 1960s of only "significant" or famous persons; and those lives were of historical interest primarily as they illuminated the truth of those national or international events with which the subjects were closely associated.[50] Thus each discipline has looked for different elements within what is seemingly the same basic, biographical structure.

It is because of this tendency of researchers to reflect both professional and personal concerns in their research that there is new emphasis in life history methodology: on the collaborative aspects of consultant and researcher interaction, and on the need for detailed biographical information for the researcher as well as the consultant. For this reason, as I outlined earlier, I have included a number of my subjective feelings and personal history. As a woman, wife, and mother, I am particularly interested in—and can certainly "see" and focus on elements of—other women's lives and their views on woman's role. My personal and professional concerns thus indicated my choice of imposing form on this material.

Obviously no one can be all things to all people: I cannot "see"—or even look for—every discrete requirement of the combined academic postures. My contention is, nonetheless, that the life history is one of the few forms of research that offers a common denominator for interdisciplinary study.[51] My goal has been to make available a personal record as complete as possible, for as many disciplines as practicable, with this document.

Certainly there were few folkloristic models for presenting a woman's life history. And the classic method of organizing by genre was not applicable here. Sarah Penfield is an extraordinary bearer of tradition, but not in that generic sense: she is not a singer of songs, a teller of tales, a weaver of baskets. Material such as this dictates a different kind of treatment, an attempt at a holistic view of her expressive media and—in its total focus upon tradition—of her life itself as a genre.

There are, presumably, numerous ways to organize this kind of data, stylistically and thematically—for example, around the domain, the kinship structure, the nuclear family, or work. But, though the material is concerned with the cultural context of Sarah's life, it is not meant to be the ethnography of a culture. Instead it has been my goal to show the life and the perspectives of one woman in a specific culture, in a geographic space and a historical time frame; yet the book is meant to do more than evoke only a place or a period of time. Rather it is an opportunity to expand the little information we have on women's own viewpoints. Therefore, in order to show both Sarah's attitudes and her actions, both descriptive and attitudinal material are included, all in a contextual framework.

Neither is this a how-to book: how to make soap or crochet afghans or butcher hogs or quilt a bedcover. Rather the story itself is like a patchwork and appliqué quilt: Sarah's conversations are patched into a chronological description of her life; these are appliquéd together by my (sometimes forced) transitions so that Sarah can be the teller, so that she can speak for herself without duplicating the entire corpus of the transcriptions.

In this first chapter detailed methodological information has begun the book, and in chapter two Sarah is placed in a personal and a geographic context. Chapters three, four, five, and six put Sarah in a historical context as well, by reviewing pertinent Ohio and southeastern Ohio historical periods and by describing Sarah's life chronologically.

Chapter seven shifts from the chronological and more descriptive treatment to one which focuses on Sarah's attitudes, her judgments of her history as she sees it, her perspective on the world. Chapter eight, in addition to a summary of the data, employs Sarah's attitudes (with their interesting and surprising contradictions) to construct a paradigm for considering aspects of other women's lives as well. It then addresses the question, Does Sarah's life have pertinence for other women?

1. I strongly prefer the term *consultant* (after Basso [1976] and Farrer [1977]) to *informant*, with its negative connotations of *informer*. This seems to me not only more ethical but more practical, considering the problems in recent years of field-workers being seen as spies, intelligence agents, or agents of foreign powers (see Langness and Frank [1981:39]).

I have also followed the 1973 American Anthropological Association resolution on discontinuing use of the word *man* generically. Throughout this study I have used nonspecific gender terms, e.g., *person* or *persons* rather than *man* or *men*. (Quotations, of course, will not be altered to reflect this practice.)

2. Proverbs 31:10–31 (New World Translation, 1970).

3. All proper names are fictitious in order to ensure the anonymity of both the consultant and her family. However, to be in keeping with historical accuracy, the country of origin of all surnames has been kept intact, i.e., Germanic surnames have been replaced by fictitious Germanic surnames, Irish with Irish, and so on.

4. Langness and Frank (1981:10–13) and Mandelbaum (1973:177–80) provided excellent short historical reviews of the use of biography by the various disciplines.

5. See Langness and Frank (1981:13–23) for detailing of anthropological use; Frazier (1978:123–26) and Bertaux (1981) for sociology. Becker (1966), in an introduction to the reissue of Shaw's (1930) book, along with Denzin (1970), advocated rekindling life history use in sociology. See Benison (1965) and Morrisey (1965) for oral history interest; Erikson (1975:103–4) and Sundberg (1977:98, 880) for psychology; and Dégh (1972:77–80) and Tallman (1978:590) for folkloristics.

6. My bibliographic references, particularly in footnotes 6 through 10 are not meant to be comprehensive but rather indicative of pertinent literature. For rural Ohio see Ergood (1975:2–3); in McMillen (1974) the wife is at best a food-dispensing shadow; Santmyer (1962) did not deal with biography; see Hatcher (1942) for literary sources to that time.

7. Concerning rural women: a photographic essay (Lange 1967) hinted at the potential richness in studying the American countrywoman. Hagood (1939) gave brief biographical descriptions of sharecropper wives in the 1930s South. For a few comparisons, see Jorgensen (1962), Jackson (1970), and White (1975). Literary sources vary in both realism and in depth of portraying farm women or rural life, e.g., Garland (1899), the Dakotas; Scarborough (1925), Texas; Ise (1936), western Kansas; Roberts (1930), Still (1940), Arnow (1954), Ritchie (1955), Dykeman (1962, 1966), Marshall (1967), and Kelley (1972), Appalachia.

8. See Langness (1965) for an exhaustive bibliography of life history research to that time, and Kluckhohn (1945) for a critique of those up to 1945. For an excellent overview of anthropological life histories up to 1981, see Langness and Frank (1981:13–29). Their bibliography (pp. 157–207) is not comprehensive, they point out, because of the recent growth of life history research. Some important early works that did focus on women, though not using a life-history approach, were: in anthropology, Mead (1928, 1935) and Linton (1971); in sociology, Rossi (1964), Bernard (1964), and Epstein (1970); in history, Beard (1946), Lerner (1969), and Mitchell (1971); in psychology, Weisstein (1968). Some examples of literary and nonacademic sources: Gilman (1899), Woolf (1929, 1955), Atwood (1970), and, later, Kahn (1972), Morgan (1972), Howard (1973), and Friedan (1974). Early biographical-type studies in folkloristics were Abrahams and Foss (1970) and Ives (1964, 1971). For an early emphasis on artists as they affect genre, see Glassie, Ives, and Szwed (1971).

9. Since that time there has been an explosion of woman-focused literature. Some examples of works that were helpful to me were: in anthropology, Rosaldo and Lamphere (1974), Murphy and Murphy (1974), Reiter (1975), Ardener (1975), Friedl (1975), Weiner (1976), Jones and Jones (1976), and Chodorow (1978); in folkloristics, *Folklore Feminist Communication* (1974), Jordan (1975), and Farrer (1976); in sociology, Freeman (1975), Millman and Kanter (1975), Walum (1977), Wertheimer (1977), and Blumberg (1978); in history, Howe (1975), Carroll (1976), Kelly-Gadol (1976), Lougee (1977), Fischer (1978), Lerner (1977). *Women's Studies: An Interdisciplinary Journal*

began in 1972; both *Signs: Journal of Women in Culture and Society* and *Frontiers: A Journal of Women's Studies* began in 1975.

In the literary and nonacademic press a southern journal, *MAW: A Magazine of Appalachian Women*, began in 1977; several examples of individual authors are: Sheehy (1974), Cahill (1975), Piercy (1976), Rich (1976), Niethammer (1977), and Chesler (1978).

Some bibliographies were: Jacobs (1974), Rosenberg and Bergstrom (1975), Buvinic (1976), Oakes and Sheldon (1978), Diner (1979), cross-disciplinary; Astin (1975), primarily sociological and psychological; Farrer and Kalčik (1974), folklore of and about women in the *Journal of American Folklore* from 1888 to 1973; Bornat (1977), oral history in the United States and Britain; Lerner (1975), Rupp (1978), history.

10. In anthropology, Kelley (1978), Underhill (1936, 1979), both with women. In folkloristics, Dégh (1975), Pentikäinen (1978), with a woman, Rosenberg (1978). In oral history, *Oral History: the Journal of the Oral History Society*, (Great Britain), especially 5 (1977); *Frontiers: A Journal of Women's Studies* 2 (1977), Special Issue; Waserman (1975), Meckler and McMullin (1975), Hirsch and Terrill (1978), Thompson (1978), Raphael (1979). Several books in the nonacademic press were helpful: Carawan (1975), Baskin (1976); with women subjects, Gallagher (1976), Cooper and Buferd (1977).

11. Dollard (1935); Kluckhohn (1945:102–3); Angell (1945:227–32); Gottschalk (1945); Edinger (1964); Langness (1965:9); Greenstein (1969); Mandelbaum (1973:177–96); Barnouw (1973:273–77); Sundberg (1977:106–7); Tallman (1978:591–92); Langness and Frank (1981:chap. 1).

12. See Winkler (1982) for a recent discussion of the problems inherent in writing up an oral history. See also Shostak (1981). The quotation is Frank's (1979:89). Langness (1965:53) called for inclusion of "the other." Abrahams (1970:2–3) lauded "subjectivity." See Carpenter (1978) for an excellent review of the literature calling for "subjectivity." See Mintz, Watson, and Richardson (in Frank [1979]) and Frank (1979:esp. 85–89) for advocating stronger and more complete reference to the researcher. Langness and Frank (1981:32, 46–47, 60–61) emphasized the venture as complicated and collaborative. Based on her work in Africa, a Canadian anthropologist dealt primarily with how the researcher and the people researched affect one another (Cesara 1982).

13. Langness and Frank (1981:86). See their chapter 3 for a complete review of existing analyses. Until 1940 there seemed to be emphasis (though without overt analyses) on culture as shaping personality, a "bias" still present. The individual has seldom been the primary focus of an anthropological life history, though an increase in such interest has just begun, they point out.

14. Coles and Coles (1978, 1980); Lewis (1959, 1961, 1964, 1965).

15. A 1945 treatise by Kluckhohn remains a classic nearly forty years later. Langness provided new materials in 1965, which he and Frank updated and expanded in 1981. Unfortunately their excellent material was not yet available when I did the bulk of my research. Kluckhohn's work originated when, in the 1940s, the Social Science Research Council recognized the value of personal documents by enlisting prominent scholars for their expositions: Allport (1942) for psychology, Gottschalk (1945) for history, Kluckhohn (1945) for

anthropology, and Angell (1945) for sociology. In 1965 Langness noted virtually no change in problem areas for life histories since Kluckhohn. See Mintz (1979) and Brandes (1979) for further criticism. Langness and Frank (1981:13), though noting that such "gloomy assessment was not entirely applicable at the present," believed that much remains to be done, especially with problems of method and analysis. In 1973 Schatzman and Strauss detailed general sociological field research. Raphael's article in 1977 amplified oral history techniques, along with Baum (1974, 1977), Moss (1974), Thompson (1978) and Morrisey (1982). See also the translation of Vansina (1965), which dealt primarily with African materials. For folkloristic emphasis see Goldstein (1964), Brunvand (1971), Tallman and Tallman (1978), and Ives (1980); see Allen and Montell (1981) on using oral sources in local history research.

16. Comparable with the adoptive kin relationship Lurie had with her Winnebago consultant (1961) and the *patrona* relationship Kelley had with her consultants (1978).

17. See Kluckhohn (1945:117–22) and Langness (1965:38) on motivating the consultant. See Barnouw (1973:273) on finding "average" and not deviant individuals. See also Langness and Frank (1981:44).

18. See Wrye and Churilla (1977) for the enjoyment by, and benefits to, the elderly in a life review process.

19. See Kelley (1978:21) on direct payment's being inappropriate. Simmons (1942:4) and Lurie (1961:xiii) believed in payment, whereas Lewis (1961) did not; Lurie spoke of an "element of coercion" in payment (1961:93). Compare Lurie (1961:114), Kelley (1978:21), and Hagood (1939:75) on gift-exchanging. Langness and Frank (1981:37) contended there are almost always indirect rewards involved with successful ethnographies or life histories.

20. Kluckhohn (1945:124–27), Langness (1965:38–43, 46), Langness and Frank (1981:43–50).

21. See also Kluckhohn (1945:121), Dégh (1975:xi).

22. See also Langness (1965:41), Langness and Frank (1981:47).

23. Historically the directed interview was probably used most often, though lack of ethnologists' explanations of their field techniques precludes accurate judgment of either their chronology or their effectiveness. Kluckhohn spoke of the "blank-screen posture" (1945:122), the nondirected interview for personality emphasis (1945:106, 125). See also Langness and Frank (1981:48–50).

24. Lurie (1961:xvi).

25. See Langness and Frank (1981:58–59) on note-taking and recording. See Williams (1967), Collier (1967), Brunvand (1978:210–11) on electronic devices in interviewing. See also Edgerton and Langness (1974:52–54), Crane and Angrosino (1974:82).

26. Tuchman (in Raphael 1977:1) considered the tape recorder a "monster," whereas Benison (1965:71) considered it a "new kind of historical document"; Kluckhohn (1945:129), as "controlling the personal equation," and Goldstein (1964:100), a "mnemonic device."

27. Lurie (1961:xvii). Compare with Swain (1965:65–68), who felt taping and transcribing were fraught with problems and unnecessary.

28. Kluckhohn (1945:97). See Kluckhohn (1945:103) and Langness and Frank (1981:46) for criticisms of past research. For examples of texts in the first person, see Radin (1926) and Underhill (1936); for chronological texts, see Simmons (1942), Dyk (1938), and Lewis (1961); for omission of researchers' questions in texts, see Abrahams (1970) and Kelley (1978).

29. Kluckhohn (1945:152–54). Langness believed publication automatically meant deletion (1965:48). Yet in the first actual life history study in folklore, Dégh was clearly adamant that no editing be done to taped interviews, that they retain "the original tone, awkwardness and ramblings of the narrators" (1975:xi). Still, hers are four mini-life histories, designed in an inexpensive monograph series for rapid dissemination to "give a *sample* of the lives of four individuals" (my emphasis; Dégh:xiv). (Later, in a helpful personal interview, Dégh advised me to continue my plan for a chronological sequence of Sarah's life, but with the least possible interference—i.e., my nondirected interviews—to explore her personality and imagination, the order of her thinking, her identity, and values, for interpretation; Salt Lake City, 10 October 1978.) Though Finnish folklorist Juha Pentikäinen (1978) used "life history" in the title of his important and complex folkloristic study, it is actually the in-depth research of the oral repertoire of an idiosyncratic active bearer of tradition and its reflection of his subject's worldview. He wrote the biographical section (7 pages of 336) in his own words, with just one consultant quotation included, and he did not refer to editing policies used in the remainder.

30. Tallman (1978:591).

31. See Preston (1976, 1982) for lucid arguments for using standard written English for everyone. For several examples of well-known works using nonstandard English, see Dorson (1964), Montell (1970), Green (1972), Jones (1975), and Brown (1982). Raphael (1977:6) called for faithful reproduction of speech in history, as did Kluckhohn (1945:155) in anthropology. Thomas (1981:xv) pointed out that though she had been "reading about a black itinerant farm worker, my mind's eye had been seeing a white, educated woman. Because, although the *words* in the book were the woman's words, the *language* was not her language."

32. Mandelbaum (1973:177) noted that one could always derive new material. Consultants' inability to recall is dealt with in Barnouw (1973:277), Gallagher (1976:10), Swain (1965:68), and Frank (1979:86). See Langness (1965:49) and Collier (1967:45) on researchers' conscious withholding of material, and Langness and Frank (1981:119–29).

33. Gallagher (1976:335).

34. On preserving fields of inquiry for the future, see Festinger and Katz (1953:3–4), Langness and Frank (1981:chap. 5 esp. 134), Goldstein (1964:117), Williams (1967:30), Collier (1967:45), Schatzman and Strauss (1973:145–46), and American Anthropological Association (1973). On closed Indian tribes see Kluckhohn (1945:122), those motivated by profit, Kelley (1978:10, 24). *Folklore Forum* published a special issue in 1973 on ethics and legal considerations in archiving. Colleges and universities have instituted complex

Doing a Life History

policies and guidelines for any activities relating to "human subjects," originally directed to the biomedical sciences, then broadened to include the behavioral and social sciences. My research was approved by the Human Subjects Review Committee of the Ohio State University, and Sarah Penfield signed a complete consent form.

35. See Kluckhohn (1945:118–19) concerning detachment and objectivity, along with Paul, in Goldstein (1964:75), and Dundes, in Abrahams (1970:vii). Langness and Frank offer detailed reasons for *not* being detached and objective (1981:chap. 5). Becker pointed out: "We can never avoid taking sides. . . . Our problem is to make sure that, whatever point of view we take, our research meets the standards of good scientific work, that our unavoidable sympathies do not render our results invalid" (in Hadley 1982:46).

36. See Edgerton and Langness (1974:78–82) for refreshing attempts in recent anthropological literature to share anxieties based on the fieldwork experience. Carpenter's 1978 article listed a number of bibliographic references to such sharing; she also cited Malinowski's diary for the "pigs" quotation, along with Jeanne Guillemin's acknowledgment that the glimpses of Boas and Malinowski and Raymond Firth as fallible were "genuinely pleasurable. It was an assurance that the stuff of fieldwork, whatever the objective stance assumed later, was unavoidably a human experience" (1978:207).

37. See Talland (1968), Botwinick (1970), and Schaie and Griffin (1975) for discussions of the influence of aging on recall.

38. See Crane and Angrosino on using genealogies (1974:43) and (1974:160) on using photographs as gifts; Byers (1964), as clues to interaction; Collier (1967:1) and Williams (1967:35), as practice on complex detail; Collier (1967:47), for discovering new material.

39. A problem perhaps similar to Kelley's (1978:129); she found the age-dominance factor governing her relationship with her consultant, who soon became an "elder instructing a younger woman," often leading the conversations.

40. See Ives (1976) for a review of potential written resources.

41. Goldstein (1964:116–17) introduced the term "ethnographic dynamite."

42. See Langness and Frank (1981:65) for the quote on the problem of relating ideal and actual behavior. See Kluckhohn (1945:124–25), Spindler (1970) on there being no measure for omissions. See Kluckhohn (1945:131), Raphael (1977:9), and Kelley (1978:24–26) on problems of consultants' lying.

43. Concerning validity checks, see Langness and Frank (1981:50–53), Kelley (1978:15), and Raphael (1977:9). See Frank (1980) for a review of techniques to enhance reliability and validity of life histories.

44. Langness and Frank (1981:53) quoted Mead, and also stated sampling is irrelevant for a life history on a particular individual.

45. See also Moore (1957:passim; e.g., 17, 42, 48, 56) on the frontier settlers. As late as 1850, a delegate to the Constitutional Convention articulated that generation's thinking, which included official sanctions, stating that government was established for two great ends: (1) to protect the citizen's

inalienable rights, and (2) "The earth is to be subdued, the necessaries of life created, its conveniences and adornments secured; and the society's efforts for improvement are also to be encouraged." These are the "great operative duties of government" (Scheiber 1969:xvii–xviii).

46. Conversation with researcher, Appalachian Trail area near Robbinsville, North Carolina, July 1967.

47. See Niethammer (1977:xvii) on reminders of the "ethical and social standards" of each culture. Concerning an emic/etic barrier which seldom lowers, see also Strobel (1977), Pelto (1970:25), and Jansen (1965:45). Gallagher (1976:149, 163–64) found the same absence of physical affection in the Northwest in her study of six generations of women in a lower-middle-class family.

48. A study by rural sociologist William L. Flinn showed that some fifty-five Ohio communities completely disappeared between 1930 and 1970. However, in the last decade there has been a reversal of this trend, in what Flinn has termed a "rural turn-around," since nearly two million urban residents have moved to a rural setting. Since 1970 Ohio's metropolitan population has been outdistanced by its nonmetropolitan one. Younger people and retirees have both been wooed by "lower taxes, less crime, and relatively less expensive housing" (*OSU Monthly* 1981:43).

49. Concerning anthropological analysis, see Langness and Frank (1981: 12–13, and chap. 3); for folkloristic, see Tallman (1978:590); for sociological, see Frazier (1978:124).

50. Concerning how social situations *appear* as emphasis in anthropology, see Pelto (1970:99); in folkloristics, Dégh (1975:xi); in sociology, Angell (1945:178). In history, interest in and emphasis on determining the facts, see Raphael (1977:9). For examples of emphasis on famous persons, see White (1961, 1965, 1969), Dorough (1962), Miller (1974, 1980), Schulte (1978), Steel (1980), Fontenay (1980), Ewald (1981), Brodie (1981), Robinson (1982), and Barton (1982). There was a pronounced shift of anthropologists' interest in history after World War II, and work in a field of study termed "ethnohistory" burgeoned. The inclusion of a historical dimension was a recognition of the need to build change into their explanatory models; see Carmack (1972) for a review.

51. The same point is made by Dégh (1975:x–xi) and Langness and Frank (1981:10).

2. Sarah Flynn Penfield in Geographic and Personal Space

Ohio is composed of three distinct geographic zones: the Lake Plains of the northern end, remnants of a diminishing Lake Erie; the Central Plains of the center and southwest, rolling and then flattening into the western prairies; and the Allegheny Plateau of the eastern half. The plateau itself is divided into two distinct areas: the northern and western glaciated sectors and the eastern and southern unglaciated sectors. The southeastern unglaciated portion is marked by steep valleys and narrow ridges cut up by streams.[1]

Thus a region of twenty-eight counties in mid- and southeastern Ohio is similar geologically to its neighboring region of Appalachia. It is also considered politically and economically part of Appalachia by its inclusion in the thirteen-state-member Appalachian Regional Council.[2] This area is generally homogeneous culturally, and it tends to be treated sociologically as Appalachian (though little scholarly literature treats the region as an entity). Indeed, there are numerous similarities to Appalachian culture in value and attitudes, habits and preferences (e.g., emphasis on family, patriarchal dominance, and egalitarian status; close kin societal ties; a dislike of urban environments; and the popularity of square dancing, Nashville style country music, and numerous handcrafts). However, most native-born residents would probably not agree with being designated Appalachian. It seems obvious that Sarah Penfield does not consider herself Appalachian either, by the rather deprecating manner with which she refers to "West Virginians" or "hillbillies" or neighbors "from Kentucky": they are definitely "others."[3] Only further research can pinpoint actual similarities and differences between these Ohio residents and the southern Appalachians dealt with in existing cultural studies.

A Woman's Place

The significance of glaciation for creating complex, rich soils cannot be overestimated; for as a consequence, the eastern and southern unglaciated sectors of Ohio are valuable not for their agricultural products but only for their coal deposits. There is fertile land along the river bottoms, and on some of the more level uplands, but most of the remaining portions are suited only to more primitive types of agriculture, often referred to as "hill farming." Even so, industrious families have wrested a living from this less-than-hospitable soil since early to mid-nineteenth century, especially in the valleys and the less convoluted counties of southeastern Ohio.[4] It was in this center of "Appalachian" Ohio that both Sarah's and her husband Robert's grandparents settled around 1850.

Although farmers in the region originally engaged in subsistence farming, today they concentrate more on raising livestock and livestock products. Farms average about 192 acres—a somewhat misleading figure, since often large portions are steep, rocky, or wooded, and thus untillable.[5] Farmhouses of the region, many of them dating from the nineteenth or early twentieth century (and often replacing original log structures), lie approximately one-half to one mile apart. Each one is dwarfed by its cluster of outbuildings; many also date from earlier tenants: there is usually a large barn for storing hay and wintering stock, plus at least a smokehouse, chickenhouse, brooderhouse, tool shed, springhouse, corncrib, and machinery shed. (In fact, the more zealous early farmers would have left, in addition, an icehouse, a cider mill, a drying shed, a blacksmith shop, and a sawmill.)[6] Roads wind and curve and climb hazardously as they follow the contours of the land, and it is easy for a driver to understand why this part of Ohio is referred to popularly as the "foothills of the Appalachians."

Today Sarah lives on the farm to which her husband's ancestors emigrated. In all her seventy-nine years, she has resided in only two dwellings—her father's and her husband's—just three miles apart. The large white T-shaped frame house is located approximately a mile from an unincorporated village of seventy persons. Sitting on a high knob of the lovely countryside, it commands a view of hills rolling into the distance, with

Sarah Flynn Penfield in Geographic and Personal Space

Grandma Moses squares of farmsteads and pastures in the foreground, the whole picture dotted appropriately with trees and browsing cattle and an occasional horse or mule. The barn, where once hay was stored and stock wintered and cows milked, is gone. Gone too are the smokehouse, chickenhouse, tool shed, and summer kitchen. Gone are the children who played in the haymow, gathered the eggs from the chickenhouse, lugged the pails of milk to the springhouse. Instead the house now dominates the landscape. But it is no musty ruin of bygone days, no run-down-at-the-heels relic of another era. This farmstead speaks of a still vigorous presence: that presence, of course, is Sarah.

As a visitor you are greeted by close-clipped grass, extensive flower beds that bloom from early spring till late fall; a neat garage (complete with new posey-sprigged valance on its opening to match the car's flowered "bird-protection" cover); a hand-lettered sign by the gravel driveway admonishing "No Public Traffic"; and fresh white paint on, as the saying goes, anything that doesn't move—house, garage, flower urns, board fence, birdhouse, stacked beehives. Sarah's only apparent concession to age has been to get help with painting the house: on the third-story eaves from son James four years ago, and on part of the second story from a neighbor boy this year. Beyond the yard is still another huge flower bed, but this one is merely a screen for the *real* planting: an enormous vegetable garden—nutritional, emotional, psychological sustenance for Sarah, her pride, her joy.

As you are invited in—no doubt for coffee and at least one variety of fresh pie—you view the same sparkling, well-ordered interior that you did on the exterior. Despite the inconvenience of a narrow passage through the Pullman-type kitchen, the kitchen door is typically the entrance and exit for nearly everyone; the front door is seldom if ever used (fig. 1). The kitchen is embellished with a good refrigerator and stove, many of the latest gadgets—gifts from the children—plus a new countertop installed by son-in-law Adolf and carpeting installed by son Dennis. Beyond the kitchen to the left is the dining room. A new colonial-style table and chairs at the end of the kitchen

A Woman's Place

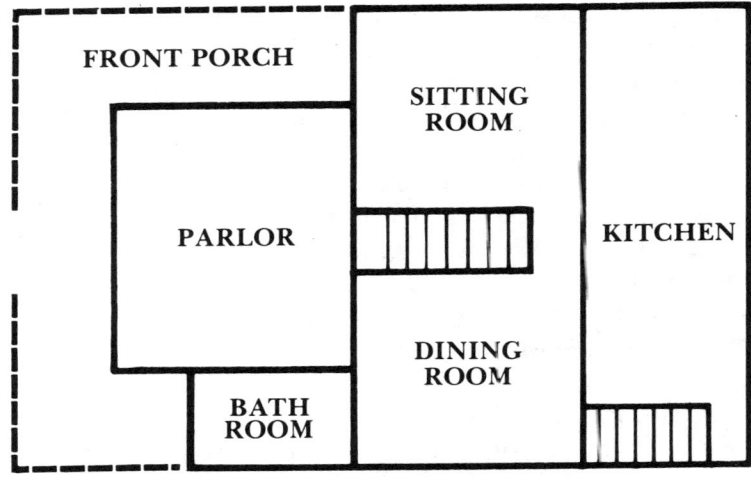

SCALE: 1" = 12'   First Floor Plan
approximately 40' x 30' without porch

Fig. 1. Ground floor plan of the Penfield house, 1900–1983. Three bedrooms occupy the same space on the second floor that the parlor, sitting room, and dining room do on the first. The house is white frame, with a slate-covered hip roof. The U-shape one-story front porch with railing is also roofed, although the rear porch was open. In 1950 husband Robert closed in that porch to make a new kitchen, and also opened up the inside stairway. Son James utilized a section of the front porch to add a bathroom, ca. 1965.

serve for all of Sarah's bountiful meals. Off the dining room is a bathroom, a relatively recent addition installed by son James. Beyond the kitchen to the right is the living room, and, in the very front of the house, the never-used parlor. The walls of both these rooms are hung with photographs: each child's high school graduation picture; the grandchildren at all ages, with now a special wall for the growing number of their high school graduation pictures; nieces and nephews of various ages. All the downstairs rooms are carpeted. All abound in memorabilia; for example, a carnival-type bronze statue of a cowboy and horse, pottery vases, crocheted doilies. Both living room and parlor hold comfortable chairs and davenports, recently reupholstered by nephew Teddy; small tables are decorated with flowers, fresh in the summer and plastic in the winter. A new television sits in one corner of the living room, and a new china cabinet in the corner nearest the kitchen, matching the dark table and chairs there.

A stairway from the living room leads to three bedrooms off a tiny center hall. The eight rooms of the house boast attractive wallpaper, all hung by Sarah. Another stairway, straight down as you enter the back (kitchen) door, goes to the basement, which is freshly painted and scrupulously clean; located there are the furnace, the freezer, a wringer washer, an auxiliary gas stove for canning, a playroom for the grandchildren, and a cold cellar (its shelves lined with glass jars of Sarah's home-canned fruits and vegetables and baskets of root vegetables).

In spite of her great love for growing, preserving, and cooking a wide variety of foods, Sarah has almost never experimented with culinary herbs. And she does not claim a large store of wild herb medicines in her traditional repertoire. Herb use is simply not traditional in her family. But then, Sarah spends most of her time in the house or its immediate vicinity. She is neither herb gatherer, bird watcher, wildflower seeker, nor even walker-in-the-woods. She does not share the love of solitude and contemplation or the opportunity for natural science observation that for some is an inherent part of living on the land. This reflects several cultural aspects of the area: nature is the enemy; women do not leave the confines of the domestic circle, except for the care of small animals; and their education, their reading materials, their whole upbringing omitted reference to a beneficent or a scientific "nature." (Certainly her knowledge far exceeds that of some: a car pulled into her driveway recently, and a couple leaped out with binoculars, excitedly asking if Sarah saw the two bald eagles in that tree in the field. She slowly shook her head and wryly commented, "No, I don't see any bald eagles, but I do see two turkey vultures." Without a word the hapless pair stepped in the car and sped away.) Her only interest in exploring the vicinity by car or on foot is tied to family, her own or a neighbor's: for example, finding the old foundation of her grandmother's house in Deer Creek Hollow; showing me the site of her parents' home, where the old barn still stands; seeing the land her sister Ellen bought;

making sure no neighbor's home was burning when we heard the siren of the volunteer fire department.

Her yearly income is probably modest enough to place her at the poverty level by government standards. Yet Sarah's lifetime has been spent stretching or conserving all available resources—money, time, labor, raw materials—so that her more-than-comfortable surroundings and life-style would not be described as "poor" by even a casual observer.

Sarah is an unflagging worker, and seems to embody the concept of perpetual motion. Even when she sits, her hands remain busy, picking nuts, sorting vegetables, mending, quilting. In her "spare time," she sews, crochets, quilts, bakes, cleans, wallpapers, paints, babysits, or whatever, for her seven children and twenty-three grandchildren! Her speech mirrors this incessant activity—machine-gun staccato with rapid-fire subject changes, which created some of the transcription problems referred to earlier.

Sarah is short, about five feet two inches, tan, freckled, and wrinkled from a life of constant sun and wind exposure; her blue eyes are always covered with glasses, her fine gray hair is slightly wavy, worn in an easy-care style, short with bangs. She is neither fat nor thin; perhaps "stocky" would best describe her build. The calves of her active legs are surprisingly lithe and muscular. She wears cotton print dresses at home, even in the winter, usually of "brunch coat" style (that is, short-sleeved, round-collared, with a pocket below the waist on each side, fastened down the front with grippers). She would not be seen in a pair of slacks: those are to be worn only by the men in the family. Thin white anklets and tennis shoes complete the outfit. Cold apparently does not bother her: on a bitter winter day, she added only a cotton raincoat and cotton head scarf (no gloves) to drive me home and to gather "nubbins" (corn the picker missed) for the pony. Although she appears to be in robust health, a childhood bout with rheumatic fever left her with a heart condition for which she takes numerous pills. She has problems, too, with "sugar" (diabetes mellitus), so she makes regular, but abortive, attempts to stop baking the cakes and pies so famous among family and friends.

Sarah Flynn Penfield in Geographic and Personal Space

Accompanying her speech patterns of rapidity and variety is a penchant for expressing her many strong opinions, often at the expense of hearing others' attempts to speak. Thus she dominates a conversation with her family and even, though to a lesser extent, with outsiders. All these outward expressions of energy and vivacity and strength, which indeed have characterized her life, would seem to indicate a happy, optimistic, cheerful person. Yet there is a grim, pessimistic, gloom-and-doom theme in Sarah's conversations that belies her brisk, positive, jovial demeanor. This may simply be an outgrowth of her somewhat recent involvement with a specialized fundamentalist religious sect, and a reflection of the normative for that group.

Though she does laugh at everyday "funny" things, she is not the joking type and has none of the sense of humor and fun so evident in her sisters and daughters. A Victorian sense of propriety rules out off-color humor, discussions of sex, and references to the body. On the few occasions such subjects have arisen, she has spoken in a lowered voice consistent with taboo subjects. Life is serious, life is hard, and her mien reflects that conviction.[7] Certainly she does not *act* sad (again, there is great contradiction here), nor is she a timid or passive person.

Sarah has a strong self-image and considers herself a happy person. She claims she would ask for no change in the life she has lived. "Your children are your life." And even the word *child* or *children* visibly softens her; nothing is too good for children, nothing too bad for those who would harm them in any way. Her relationship with all her family is very positive; most of them visit her often, not only children and grandchildren but a broad spectrum of kin: sisters (her brothers are all dead now), in-laws, nieces and nephews, cousins. All of them are concerned for her welfare, and she for theirs; she tries to maintain an extensive network of kin and ritual kin obligations. She makes a singular effort to be self-reliant: far from being dependent on others, Sarah tries always to extend a helping hand, especially to family, and usually in direct relation to the level of kinship. Her openheartedness was clearly demonstrated when she invited Martha, her elder sister, to come from Florida to live with her six years ago, even though her sister was in extremely poor health and they had not seen one another for thirty years! (The company and the care, interestingly, improved Martha's condition far beyond normal medical expectations.) Though her generosity is manifest especially with her family, it extends to everyone in the community, even to anthropological researchers.

Sarah "can't imagine" of what interest her humble life would be to anyone.[8] Yet her life, along with the lives of her parents and grandparents, and now of her children and grandchildren, *is* Ohio history, for it is prototypical of the development of the southeastern region. The region was settled predominantly by German and Irish immigrants in the early to mid-nineteenth century; Sarah's grandparents were German and Irish, and they settled there in the middle of the nineteenth century. Subsistence farming was supplemented by outside employment whenever possible; this was true of Sarah's grandfather, father, and husband, and is now for several of her children. In the twentieth century, especially after World War II, this pattern evolved to farming only part-time and commuting to full-time city jobs, even to urban flight; many of Sarah's children and grandchildren either commute to city jobs or have moved to town or city. One-room country schools gave way in the twentieth century to graded schools, then to consolidated school systems; Sarah's father attended a one-room school, as did Sarah, who also taught in one; her children attended a graded school, and her grandchildren attend the consolidated school.[9] Family size was modified from large to medium to small; Sarah's grandparents had eight children (Robert's had thirteen), her parents had eleven, she had seven, and her children have averaged three.

We begin to trace this history with the original Ohio settlers of both Sarah's family and her husband Robert's family: their grandparents. Though the editor's chronological commentary is the framework upon which the biography is built, Sarah's narrative is the substantive focus, painting a vivid scene of the social settings and portraying in small part both the lyric quality of the regional dialect and the expressive talents of Sarah herself. One must bear in mind that these are remembrances, and not always validated or recorded occurrences.[10]

    1. Roseboom and Weisenburger (1976:3).
    2. This is a joint federal and state venture founded in 1965 for the whole eastern United States' Appalachian region to combat the severe problems there, such as lack of transportation networks, lack of adequate medical facilities, and a large percentage of poverty-level families. (It is now being phased out, though more gradually than its political adversaries originally had proposed.)
    3. See Green (1978) for a discussion of "region," "regional," and "regionalism."
    4. Roseboom and Weisenburger (1976:3–4).
    5. U.S., Department of Commerce, Bureau of the Census 1978.
    6. See also Glassie (1968a:101).
    7. See also Kelley (1978:78).
    8. Strobel (1977:69) reported that women generally do not see their lives as having importance.
    9. Hicks (1976:4) found the same kinds of evolution in his Appalachia studies.
    10. There is still no satisfactory term in folkloristics to denote personal narrative of this type, except when—as in this case—it is part of a long text, and becomes part of the "life history." Dégh (1972:77–80) discussed "true experience" stories; Dorson (1971b:45) used the term "personal history." C. W. von Sydow coined the term "memorate," but it applies only to belief narrative of supernormal experience (see Honko 1964).

3. Sarah's Grandparents: The First Generation of Flynns in Ohio, 1853–1880

We have seen Sarah in her geographic and personal space. Since we are all rooted in a historical space as well, it is important now to understand how the generations of Sarah's family fit into the larger patterns of state and region. Therefore, an overview of historical developments, first for the state of Ohio, then narrowing to southeastern Ohio, introduces each of the following four chapters before focusing on Sarah and her family.

This chapter's first history section reviews the years 1803 to 1850 and sets the stage for the arrival of Sarah's Grandfather Flynn to this region from County Cork, Ireland, presumably in 1853. The next section develops Ohio and southeastern Ohio history during the period he lived there, from 1853 to 1880, the year of his death. After intervening biographical material, a short summary ends each of the chapters 3 through 7.

Ohio, admitted to the Union in 1803, remained essentially a pioneer state until well after the War of 1812. Settlers soon boosted population figures rapidly, and by 1850 Ohio was the third largest state in the Union, with a population of approximately two million.[1] These settlers were of diffuse origin (e.g., Pennsylvania Germans and Swiss in Lancaster, Virginians and Kentuckians in Chillicothe, New Englanders in the Western Reserve, Germans and Irish in Cincinnati, Germans in the rich northwest farming section, and, throughout the state, a rising black population). Their diverse skills, coupled with political events and geographical conditions, resulted in area specializations (e.g., manufacturing along the Ohio River, lively trade and government business in Columbus, dairying in the Western Reserve),

51

and by an importance of both agriculture and industry (e.g., orchards and manufacturing in the Miami Valleys, wool-producing in eastern Ohio and glass and clay industry around Zanesville, rich farming and trade areas in the north central region). Men, women, and children labored to develop the "western" state, which evolved socially as well as economically with the growth of churches and schools in a predominantly egalitarian society.[2]

Growth in the southeastern region paralleled that of the rest of the state. Counties were organized in the first years of the nineteenth century, and population more than quadrupled by 1850, since this area enticed the earliest settlers in the state. The majority of the settlers—from Germany, Great Britain, and the older states—were farmers, and they scattered throughout the townships. Coal and iron deposits were discovered, then developed and expanded near mid-century after the opening of the Hocking branch of the Ohio Canal and subsequent railroad lines. No good highway system developed, however, and no large cities grew.[3]

Family, church, and school were the mobilizing social forces here as in the rest of the state; an egalitarian spirit was maintained because of the need for cooperation and the dearth of large cities (with their usual higher percentage of affluent citizenry). Early circuit riders gave the Methodist Episcopal church numerical strength, followed by the Presbyterian and United Brethren churches. School funds were still limited in southeastern Ohio, where the average-length school term was only three months in the 1840s, and one county spent only thirty-six cents per pupil per year. However, a significant educational advancement was the establishment of Ohio University at Athens, with classes begun in 1809 and collegiate standards adopted about 1822. Agricultural societies provided further social contacts, especially with their yearly fairs.[4]

The years 1850 to 1880 were revolutionary ones for Ohio, signifying the transition from an agricultural to an industrial state. Although Ohio was still an important farming state, the rapidly developing prairie states were soon to end that primacy;

Illinois claimed first place, as the agriculture center of the nation moved to the west. Railroad lines expanded in Ohio and provided access to eastern markets, but at the same time they brought more competition from the developing west. The declining rate of population growth in 1871—only 13.9 percent as opposed to 62 percent in 1840—seemingly pointed to a subsequent stationary population. The general character of the population was little altered, with the exception of some European immigrants attracted to Cleveland industry.[5]

By 1870 Ohio had fallen even further in rank of farm production compared with other farming states. However, Ohio industry had quadrupled its dollar volume, and in 1880 the value of manufactures was more than double that of farm products. The crown of the "Queen City of the West," Cincinnati, slipped; Cleveland, in the center of Ohio's rapidly expanding industrial might, was on its way to dominance. Other strategically located urban centers grew, so that Ohio had twenty-six cities of over five thousand in population by 1870. Labor unions advanced during and after the Civil War as a result of the shortage of workers. Wage scales varied, but in 1871 Ohio carpenters averaged $2.73 per day and bricklayers, $3.37; yet farm laborers averaged only $1.28, and $1.00 in winter.[6]

The rapid industrial development of the state for this period promoted growth of the iron furnaces of southeastern Ohio, especially after railroads were built heading north and south from the region. However, the Panic of 1873 put most Ohio furnaces out of blast, and a difficult recovery period followed. By the 1880s the better quality of the Mahoning District iron, along with its proximity to industrial markets in the north, forced the iron production of the southern counties sharply downward. Agricultural output was declining as well (corn, oats, tobacco, hogs, butter, and cheese); only wool production showed any significant increase. Even some of the widely touted agricultural fairs were abandoned for a period from lack of general support. Population increased by only small increments, except in areas of mining and manufacturing activity.[7]

The log buildings that replaced early crude structures were

still widely used as late as 1862, though brick and frame buildings soon were prized for their aura of advanced status. Churches became involved in crusades against the liquor interests. A stricter law in 1853 for statewide school funding through taxation brought more children into the educational system, and Ohio University provided a teacher training curriculum. Communities offered Teachers' Institutes—often called Normal Institutes—for improvement of in-service teachers.[8]

Against this sociohistorical background, we are introduced to Sarah Flynn Penfield's paternal grandparents, her maternal grandmother, and also her husband Robert's paternal grandparents.

Sarah is the primary speaker throughout this chapter, but her sister Martha, who lived with her, and her sister Ellen, a frequent visitor, are also a part of the dialogue.

To aid in keeping the confusing recital of names and families introduced here straight, I have supplied a genealogical chart (Appendix C). Place-names will be found in figure two.

Sarah's account of her grandparents begins:[9]

> Well, John Flynn was my grandfather who came from Ireland. Direct from Ireland when he was a young man. And he was a twin and he—his twin we didn't keep count of, but his twin went up north someplace and settled and John Flynn settled around here. So his generation is here, but we got relatives if we knew where they were up in the northern part of the state someplace. They were Irish.... As far as I got this, well, they went to the recorder, the county court, and he wrote them a recommendation before they come to this country and I got the slip somewhere. Because Annie [a sister] went and had slips made for all of us. I don't know whether they needed a recommend or why it was they went to the officer of the county.... Yes and they were young men when they came to this country. [1]

Thus the first official information Sarah has concerning her forebears is contained in a treasured paper that has somehow survived three generations of housecleaners:

Sarah's Grandparents

John and William Flynn are now going to America. They belong to a respectable family and from every inquiry I believe them to be well conducted, industrious young men. They were bred farmers, and I believe they understand agriculture.

Horatio F. [?]
Dean of Cork
May, 1853

How the brothers came to Ohio, or why, is still a mystery.

> Why I don't know where Charlie—someone that knew told Charlie [a brother] about it, don't you remember, and uh, I don't know who it was around here that was old and remembered it and my brother is dead now where he could've told us. [14]

John settled in southeastern Ohio and was apparently the enterprising, hardworking young man advertised by the honorable Dean of Cork, for he bought or managed a large country hotel there (fig. 2, domicile a). A large frame building, the hotel was located in a wooded, hilly area of Bay township, several miles from the nearest village, Harrington, and fourteen from the county seat.

> They must've came [straight to this part of the country]. I don't know how he got the land. Oh, I'm sure he [grandfather] worked, you know, and bought it himself, because I'm sure he was a poor boy. [5]

He married a woman who was either German or of German descent, Heilbronn, though neither Sarah nor her sisters can remember her first name:[10]

> Martha: Esther, her name, her first name was Esther.
>
> Sarah: I might've, you oughtn't said that. You just said that so quick that you made me forget [laughing]. I might've thought of her name—now let's see what is it? Anyway she died years before we came to this world and there wasn't much said about—
>
> Martha: —One of those old-fashioned names—

A Woman's Place

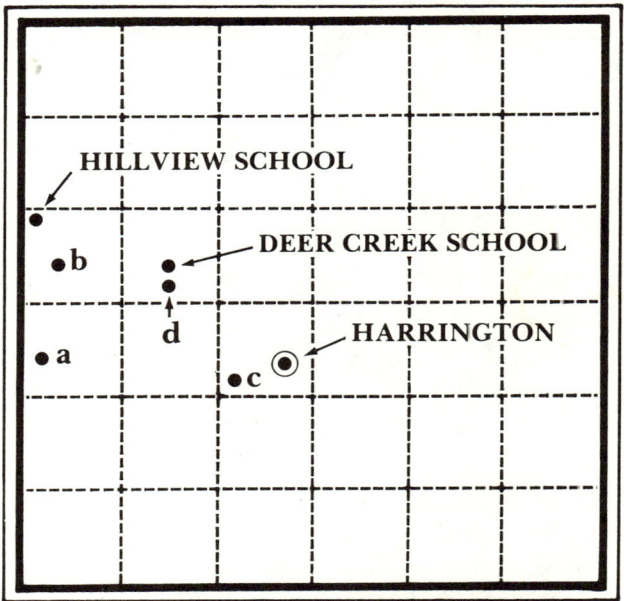

The larger square represents an approximate six square mile area.

Fig. 2. Residence proximities of the Flynn and Penfield families. This "map" is intended to clarify the relationships and relative distances between the family domiciles, but it cannot, in the interest of anonymity, be presented with cartographic accuracy. It still has a high degree of illustrative reliability, however, since the majority of Ohio townships are laid out in a grid system and tend to be nearly six miles square (see William E. Peters, *Ohio Lands and Their History* [Athens, Ohio: W. E. Peters, 1930], pp. 31–33, 41; and Thomas H. Smith, *The Mapping of Ohio* [Kent, Ohio: Kent State University Press, 1977], p. 123). (*a*) The domicile/residence of John Flynn and [?] Heilbronn, Sarah's paternal grandparents, ca. 1853–78. (*b*) The second residence of John Flynn and [?] Heilbronn, ca. 1878–80; the widow's residence, 1880–84; the residence of Sarah's parents, Joseph Flynn and Claire Rheinberg, ca. 1896–1938. (*c*) The residence of Harry and [?] Penfield, Robert's paternal grandparents, ca. 1850–1900; the residence of George and [?] Penfield, Robert's parents, ca. 1900–1908; the residence of Robert and Sarah Penfield, 1927–83. (*d*) The residence of Hannah Hewitt Rheinberg, Sarah's maternal grandmother, and her second husband, Henry Powers, ca. 1890–1908.

Sarah: —Yes, it could have been Hester. [14]

The young couple had three boys and five girls; four of the five girls (all, enigmatically, with the middle name "Mae") died as babies or as young children.

> Martha: It was three that died with what they call consumption.
> Sarah: Well, a couple died with typhoid fever I know.
> Martha: Consumption. I guess they call it walking tuberculosis, don't they?
> Sarah: They don't even have it—Ohio doesn't even have it—
> Martha: —Yeah, but we used to have a lot of it.
> Sarah: They got rid of the hospital even. See they found out that a lot of it came from cattle from Florida, and beef and milk and things and after they got to testing cows and treating them we don't have TB—it's very seldom a case of it.
> Martha: Of course they called it consumption then.
> Sarah: But then people died with it then an awfully lot. [14]

In fact, it was believed parents were "lucky" to raise half their children; the sad truth of such a statement is borne out by the disproportionate number of tiny headstones in local graveyards.[11]

Not only did the parents "work terribly hard," but their children too had a definite role in the family economy. The hotel, believed by Sarah to have been built before the Civil War, required significant labor, for there were no bathrooms, running water, or central heating.

> Sarah: And you know they sold them for a quarter apiece, those beautiful big pitchers, and whatchacall 'em, that you wash, they have to carry them by the rims, they had to take their hot water to their rooms to bathe. [6a]
> Martha: Well, I just wonder, that's a big building: I wonder if they had stoves in all those rooms.
> R: Where did they get all the help?

> Martha: Oh people didn't get any money for anything they did back in those days; they could get plenty of help. [15]

Encompassing at least thirty-six large rooms, the hotel also contained family living quarters upstairs that boasted "real good carpet," and a grocery store on the end.

Trains brought recreation-bent city folk to Cloverdale, thirteen miles distant, there to be met by staff—often one of John's three sons:

> Sarah: And my father said many times he had to drive horses to the railroad track to pick up these ladies that would come out there, and people that would stay over the weekend, and you see that was the only way of transportation they had, was to lead the horses and wagons and chairs and things.
>
> Martha: Where the people came to go there on Sunday and weekends there'd be buggy after buggy, going that way. [6a]

Heralding the popularity of the Great Outdoors in this century, the rough terrain of southern Ohio beckoned outdoor enthusiasts in the nineteenth century as well. Some were not so rugged, of course, and the long veranda of the hotel, overlooking oaks and pines and hemlock, was a favored spot for "rocking-chair generals." The managment provided other diversions as well:

> Well, they had what they called horse-drawn railroad tracks, and my father said he had to ride the horse all day, day after day, and these people would ride in these little, uh, miniature trains, of some kind, that were drawn by horses. And he—oh! he didn't like it! He got tired of it. [6a]
>
> They had ice cream socials, and had dances; they had old-fashioned musicians, and old-fashioned dances. Oh my! those people really dance, you know. . . . My father when he was young went. And he could really dance, I mean to jig or anything, he could dance by himself, he could really dance. But they had all that sort of thing, dancing, 'n ice cream, you know.[12] [6a]

Sarah's Grandparents

> And years before that they had what they called, uh, camp meeting, where the religious people would, they had, a nice, uh, it was really a pretty nice six-room house, out there in the woods from there [the hotel], where the colored, they always had, the gospel choir was always colored. They had the colored to come there to live. And they had, every summer they had what they call camp meeting, y' know. Colored come there and hold religious meetings.
>
> R: You mean a colored camp meeting?
>
> No, it was for white people, but the colored people came and did the entertaining.[13]

In spite of the work load, John's children did attend school, walking through deep woods in good weather, over longer roads in bad, to Deer Creek School in Deer Creek Hollow.[14]

> Oh, it's a mile across—you go across the hill. They would walk across it, it was an awful trip! [1]

> There was a little brook that went through this place and you'd cross this little brook on stones, stepped from stone to stone to get to the school. It's a pretty spot. [1]

Many years later some hint of the old school days was given when a new resident discovered a yellowed newspaper clipping (no date or author given) that reported the sixth reunion of the "folk who treasured memories of Deer Creek School." Some excerpts, paraphrased in the local newspaper many years later, focus on a mood of nostalgia:

> Following the picnic dinner, the program that followed found its inspiration in all that concerned the part that Deer Creek School had played in their lives. Even the hand bell was there that had called them to their noon meal and the Lord's Prayer spoken in unison made a fitting grace before their picnic meal.
>
> [Mrs. Nettie Carlisle] provided an opening song and then her husband joined in a duet. A little four-piece orchestra directed by [Henry Hunt] of Columbus made the woods ring with harmony and [Mrs. Jeffrey House] sang "The Old School House by the Brook."

A Woman's Place

> There was the period during which tribute was paid to the deceased members of the group, the secretary reading the names and the orchestra supplying the mood with soft hymnal music [eight names then listed].
>
> Two of the oldest members were present to talk of former days. Names of the teachers crept into the discourse. They discussed the incidents that made the primitive environment at Deer Creek so exciting. The daily carrying of drinking water from the spring on the [Shannon] farm and the history of the little school from the time of its construction on a plot of [Shannon] land. What an afternoon of wholesome reflection and reminiscence!
>
> The election continued the same officers.

As will be seen from the text and from figure two, the Deer Creek School is the unifying point for the three families who figure in this chapter, since both the Flynn children (Sarah's paternal grandparents) and the Penfield children (her husband's paternal grandparents) attended there, and the Powerses (her maternal grandmother) moved across the road from the school.

Although John Flynn probably owned "most of the land around the hotel," no one is certain about how many acres that would have encompassed. Little is known of his life, perhaps because he died as a relatively young man and did not live to enjoy his grandchildren.

> Grandpa might have owned it all—he might have owned it all up through there, I don't know.... He worked so terribly hard, and you know, he died so young. Dad's father. He died so young and Dad said what killed him was he dug these wells for people. They'd go down and you know if a lantern would go out they knew they had to get out quick. But you know instead of drilling wells, they dug these wells and walled them up. And oh! he was an awful hard worker. Said he worked terribly hard and he just killed himself. They would take a lantern and go down when they were digging these wells and if a lantern went out they knew there was no oxygen and they knew they had to get up out

Sarah's Grandparents

of there quick.... Well, they dug them about this big around and walled them up with rocks as they went—for water. They had to go down pretty high here some places. [1]

Sarah's sister Ellen believes that their grandfather sold the hotel before he died and that he was only about forty-five at the time of his death. At some point the family had moved to an adjoining farm (fig. 2, domicile b), living in a house that may have been on the land already. John's widow continued to live there with her three sons and one daughter. One comfort: after she sold a small piece of adjoining land to her brother, he built a house next to hers. She died only two years after her husband, leaving her eldest son, Harold, to become "parent" to his young brothers and sister and to keep the family farm intact.

Harrington, the closest town to the Flynn household, was approximately three miles away. It had been established not long before John settled in the hotel. Log cabins clustered on either side of the one street.[15] Commercial enterprises included a barrel factory, a gunpowder factory (just outside of town), and, at one point, two stores; by 1880 a blacksmith shop, a wagon shop, and a shoe shop had been added. The population in 1870 was about sixty-seven, dropping to sixty in 1880. The first sermon was preached in Squire Shannon's cabin, the same Shannon who had donated land for the first school in the township in Deer Creek Hollow. A Methodist Episcopal church was built there several years before the town itself, and a United Brethren church was built late in the century.

One mile west of the town lived another family of early settlers, the Penfields, paternal grandparents of Sarah's husband Robert (fig. 2, domicile c). He was both a farmer and a blacksmith. Sarah believes they were English, and had owned the land since the middle of the nineteenth century, their deeds tracing ownership "clear back to the government" [1]. Approximately ten years ago, a descendant of her husband's grandfather visited Sarah, in search of genealogical information. He gave her a copy of his work to that point, but, to her continuing distress, that link with the past was wiped out:

A Woman's Place

> We had this family tree, and my daughter let it get destroyed. So I can't tell you much about it. She had put it in the magazine rack, and George [the daughter's husband] took the trash out and burned it. It was a mistake, it was too bad. We didn't know the man, he was a stranger. I was teaching at the time, and he said he would come back, he wanted to see me. And he never come back, so we wondered if something happened to him and Paula didn't get his address. He was from up the northern part of the state. Just a bad situation. We could have gotten a copy from him, I'm sure. 'Cause he was coming back and didn't. I'm afraid something happened to him.... No, I really don't [know where the Penfields emigrated from], some say they come from the southern states, some say from this and that, I really don't know. I would have if that hadn't got burned up, it would have been nice. Such a dreadful thing for it to get destroyed, I felt terrible about it! [11]

Either her husband's grandfather or great-grandfather was the original Penfield settler in the area; the grandfather, Harry, and his wife—origin and name unknown by Sarah—raised eleven children (two more died as infants) in a log house;

> Not in this house. The old house down there. I helped to burn it up when we came here. It's down across here—the old house down by the spring. Years ago people built by the springs.... The old house sat right down there and the barn sat up here. The old barn was still here when I came here.... They raised their family in the little house down there. The road went there, do you notice the low place goes up across? [11]

> Mr. Penfield, he was my husband's grandfather—great-grandfather, no it was his grandfather—the *children's* great-grandfather. He had a very high temper, I guess he was a very honest man, and everbody liked him, but when he told somebody something I guess he run them out.... Um hum, that's what they say, he really did. He had, well, he had so many orchards here. There was even the old orchards here when Robert and I came here, but he would raise melons

and sell them and he made cider and things like that and he had a cabin. Ol' Eli hasn't been dead too long, but he would always laugh about it, 'cause he got drunk one day and crawled in the [grandfather's storage] cabin and was laying and went to sleep on Henry Penfield's onions and he hit him with a cane and said "I'll give you something for laying on mother's onions!" and he was always telling and started laughing about it. [2]

The Penfield children attended the same school, Deer Creek, as the Flynn children did, though it was an even more difficult journey for them, "more'n three miles; a long walk, a long walk, a long, long, walk" [14].

During this same period, a family moved from north central Ohio to the little house "just a few steps from the school" (fig. 2, domicile d). Henry Powers had married a widow with three daughters; this was Sarah's maternal grandmother, and one of the daughters was her mother. Glowing reports of the country there drew them south.

> Martha: She remarried and they knew of this little farm and they came down there and settled. Back then it's hard to underestimate what the conditions were.
>
> Sarah: Well, I think she got it through her husband she married before she came and he was the one that wanted to come. He told stories about them blackberries being—everything was so easily done that they could have such a wonderful living and everything. He found it out differently once he got down here. [17]

Hannah Powers was happy enough to leave her hometown, where tragedy had struck twice, first with the loss of a baby girl, and second with her first husband's unexpected death:

> He took care of race track horses. And then, shoeing a horse one day the hammer hit him on the knee and he got what they call "white swelling," and I'm sure that it was what you would call a form of blood poisoning today. Well, uh, the way the doctors doctored it, mother said, they would, this old doctor come out there and heat irons and burn his leg,

and she said the flesh just smelled terrible. I can remember Mom telling that.... She was just a little girl when he died, and that's the way that they treated it, and she said they called it, they gave it the name of "white swelling," which I've heard of it before. It's more like gangrene or something is what I've heard, probably a form of gangrene. [6b]

Grandmother, "tall and sandy-haired," was evidently a strong person, and stories of her made a lasting impression on her young granddaughters:

Martha: Grandmother must have been a widow for several years because she took in washing, I know, to make a living for her three children before she married. [14]

Sarah: I think that the people down around there told her life was so easy here. She was an awfully hard worker.

Ellen: Well, she did a lot of things for a livin'. For instance, she sowed the onion seeds and raised onion sets and that sort of thing for commercial.

Sarah: You can raise—from onion seed you can raise onions big enough to eat if you get them out early in the spring.

Ellen: But she raised the sets—she sowed the seeds. See it takes like your cabbage and everything else two years. She sowed the seed and made the sets and that, that fall; next spring she sold them. [17]

She even caught and sold cardinals:

Ellen: Well, I guess it goes way back, it answers my mother's mother she said she used to stand behind where it wasn't against the law behind the door and listen to red birds in the house and at that time you could sell them—that was before they were outlawed to have them as pets and she said she'd stand behind the door—

Sarah:—You know they say they are awful hard to catch.

Ellen: Well, that's what she'd do, she'd stand—and she kept one in a cage and that way then she'd open the door and they would come in and apparently they must have been more plentiful. [17]

Sarah's Grandparents

Grandmother also played a significant role in the larger community:

>Sarah: She had a horse and she rode this one—I wish we'd kept that—but she had this sidesaddle, something you never see today, and she rode all over the country all hours of the night and delivered babies. . . . I 'spect she was as good as a doctor at that time, you know, I mean the old doctor. . . . Yes, she went all over the country, everyplace. She rode this horse, and went everywhere and delivered babies. They couldn't even got a doctor then, we were so isolated. . . .
>
>Martha: In fact, mother had quite a lot of her children—
>
>Sarah: —Lots of them except Andy she delivered with midwives, except Andy.
>
>R: Was this *her* mother?
>
>Martha: Yes, it was her mother.
>
>Sarah: Her mother; my mother's mother. . . .
>
>Martha: But I don't think you ever thought of paying back in those days, did you?
>
>Sarah: Midwives? Oh no, it was—
>
>Martha: —It was all gratis.
>
>R: No kidding?
>
>Martha: It was never any impression of it being paid for.
>
>R: That's interesting; I wonder why?
>
>Martha: Now they have the visiting nurses in these outlying districts that go—a lot of places do not have doctors.
>
>Sarah: Well, see, doctors here would refuse—they wouldn't go to your house.
>
>R: Well why—how did they manage to become, to be a midwife if they didn't pay them?
>
>Sarah: They were very friendly people, helped each other, at harvesting time and everything, see they threshed and everything, neighbors, free gratis, they went back and forth.
>
>R: Did these midwives have any kind of training or just teach each other how?

> Sarah: Just by experience, by teaching each other, sure, by being with the doctor in some cases. They never lost a case that I—natural childbirth, it's just what you would call natural childbirth.[16] [3]

Of the three daughters, only Claire, Sarah's mother, remained in the area. Claire was a teen-ager when Henry and Hannah moved to Deer Creek Hollow, but she did not attend the Deer Creek School next door. Sarah was not sure how her mother and father had met.

> Well, they just lived within a mile of each other and they had dances and things like that; I don't know where she really met him, but they had social gatherings, you know, spelling bees and things like that in schools at night. . . . He's older than mother and he wasn't going to school when she moved there. But that's where he went to school. Well the family here, my husband's father went to Deer Creek School. All the children—there was eleven children raised here and they all went to Deer Creek. Long, long walk.
> R: What, in those days, what kind of courtship would your mother and father have had?
> Well, it would be a horse and buggy, I'm sure. . . . Horse and buggy. I think that they gathered at people's houses more than they do today. I think people were more—yes, they were closer. . . . They had what they called husking bees in the barn and flaying out beans and things like that and afterwards they'd have cider, you know, sweet cider, and things like that and then they'd dance in the barn, things like that. I think they enjoyed themselves—when I'd hear them talk about it I think it was greater than our day. [14]

Through whatever chance meeting, Claire was courted by Joseph, second son of John Flynn, and they were married; they assumed patrilocal residence with Joseph's two brothers (the one daughter had married and lived only a mile east).

SUMMARY

Southeastern Ohio's development nearly paralleled that of the rest of the state in the first half of the nineteenth century, in large measure because it was the most geographically accessible land for eastern emigration. Agricultural products were of primary importance, though the opening of a branch of the Ohio canal, and later several railroads, spurred growth of coal mining and iron manufacturing in mid-century. But lack of an expanse of fertile land led to agriculture's decline there in the third quarter of the century; meanwhile competition from better-located cities in the northern part of the state led to a decline in manufacturing; various economic problems beset the coal industry as well. Thus the southeastern region as a whole fell behind in Ohio's general surge of industrial prosperity in the latter half of the nineteenth century. No transportation network grew, and no large cities developed. Most of the region was typified by farmsteads, with villages dotted among them that served as community centers; only two or three actual cities evolved, those along waterways. Large families were the nucleus of social life, with church and school an important influence.

There is little direct information concerning the first southeastern Ohio generations of Sarah's and her husband's families. Yet this description of the region parallels descriptions of them: among the early settlers of their township, they were typically Irish, German, and English; involved in farming and outside occupations; living in a primarily agricultural community with one small town the nearby center. Children, though included in the pattern of economic subsistence, were also educated in a log school typical of the period. Work was difficult and strenuous, and life expectancy was often short.

1. Knepper (1976:58, 64); Roseboom and Weisenburger (1976:109–19).
2. Knepper (1976:61–64); Roseboom and Weisenburger (1976:110–15, 117–22, 137–39); Smith (1977:122–49, et passim); Peters (1930:372–75).
3. *History of Hocking Valley, Ohio*, hereafter referred to as *Hocking*, (1883: 179–86, 421, 816, 829–33, 859, 1148–49); Howe (1852:927–28); Randall and

Ryan (1912:439–70); Smith (1977:127); Roseboom (1944:73); Roseboom and Weisenburger (1976:22).

4. *Hocking* (1883:55–56, 181, 243–49, 837–44, 888–1150); Roseboom and Weisenburger (1976:114, 146); Howe (1852: 137); Gordon (1940:99).

5. Roseboom (1944:4–6, 73–86, 100).

6. Ibid., pp. 11–19, 32–43.

7. Ibid., pp. 95–98, 27–29, 14–15; Roseboom and Weisenburger (1976: 219); *Hocking* (1883:129, 179, 186, 829–33, 844, 859).

8. *Hocking* (1883:25–283, 837); Gordon (1940:92, 101, 109–10); Roseboom and Weisenburger (1976:146).

9. Since the conversation quoted is predominantly Sarah's throughout, proper names begin sentences only when persons other than the researcher are included in the interview. If Sarah alone is quoted, her name does not precede the sentence.

10. When Sarah and her sisters cannot remember genealogical entries, as is the case here, it is almost always a female's name.

11. See also Baxter (1978:19): "The loss of children... was a recurrent sorrow, and the photograph of the departed infant is a reminder that in the days before modern pediatric medicine the pregnant woman had almost as much to fear as to hope for."

12. See also Martzolff (1924:14–148).

13. Cf. Bruce (1974: esp. chap. 3) and Frary (1942:118–19).

14. See also Martzolff (1924:141–43).

15. A story-and-a-half log cabin, its construction typical of the period, was in continuous use until 1975 (part of that time as the post office), when it was torn down to make way, rather ironically, for a one-story prefabricated house.

16. See also Gallagher (1976:59), Hagood (1939:111–14). For a history on, and recent revival of, midwifery, see Wertz and Wertz (1977), Ehrenreich (1972), Gaskin (1978), and Arms (1975).

4. Sarah's Parents: The Second Generation of Flynns in Ohio, 1880–1951

The state of Ohio continued to be characterized by a diffusion of population origins, by area specialists, and by the dual importance of agriculture and industry through the nineteenth century. Farming remained Ohio's most important industry in the nineteenth century because of mechanization, but by 1900 business and manufacturing surpassed agriculture with the combined value of their products. The booming Industrial Revolution demanded the steel, oil, machinery (and later, automobiles, rubber, industrial glass, business machines, and soaps) produced in the state, thanks to its geographic diversity, urban centralization, and immense work force potential.[1]

Emigrants from central, southern, and eastern Europe flooded the cities of the state, particularly in the industrial north. In addition, there was intrastate migration of Appalachian whites and southern blacks, as well as internal movement of rural and small-town Ohioans to the cities, all of these groups swelling the work force. The resultant overcrowded cities soon experienced all the problems associated with urban congestion and Topsy-like growth. Yet big business, entrenched both economically and politically, would not support needed reforms.[2]

While machine and money culture dominated the city in the late nineteenth century, life in the country continued in much the same pattern as in earlier days. Yet the farmer felt caught between rising costs for what he purchased and dropping prices for what he sold.

Education made solid gains, and most children attended some school, even high school in a few rural districts. Teachers, trained mostly in five-month training schools ("normal schools"), did not command huge salaries: $38 a month for men and $24 for women was the average in township elementary schools in 1890. Higher education received continued support, supplemented in the cities by libraries, music halls, museums, and historical societies. Farmers were especially enthusiastic about education, through Farmers' Institutes, the Grange and other agricultural societies, and even the county and state fairs.[3]

Churches continued to exert social force, though in the city they competed—often unsuccessfully—with a huge variety of entertainment, sports, and other activities, especially after 1900. Country churches remained a significant aspect of the social as well as the religious scene.[4]

Progressives in Ohio, in reaction to government corruption, scandalous urban problems, and big-business abuses, mounted growing support, but achieved less than their national counterparts. Still there was great political significance for Ohio in Woodrow Wilson's election in 1912, a reflection of the progressive spirit nationally: not only did it deny a native son and citizen, William Howard Taft, but it also cast Ohio's electoral vote for another party for the first time since the GOP's birth in 1854.[5]

The dark shadow of World War I soon relegated domestic issues to a neglected back seat, though the state's heterogeneous population made for divided sympathies. After the declaration of war on Germany, Ohio contributed nearly a quarter of a million citizens—volunteers, National Guardsmen, and draftees—and lost almost seven thousand of them in action. After having long faced severe discrimination in the job market, women were given wartime jobs, though not with equal pay for equal work. Industrial cities expanded still further because of the urgent demand for war materials.[6]

After the war voters were idealistic for at least a short time, and finally ratified Prohibition and Women's Suffrage amendments, but only after a lengthy and confused series of struggles in both cases.[7]

Strikes occurred frequently in the difficult transition to a postwar "normalcy," but expansion of industry during the twenties, especially the auto industry, brought widespread prosperity in the state—except for the farmer. A drastic decline in prices in 1920 represented a virtual crash for him, and conditions—though somewhat improved by 1923—were not significantly better through the twenties. In the city phenomenal expansion continued, heralding, nearly all were convinced, a period no longer to be marked by "boom-and-bust."[8]

In southeastern Ohio coal mining and iron production continued to dominate the scene in the 1880s. But the iron furnaces were soon ghostly hulks; because of competition from the Cleveland-Youngstown area, most were "cold" by 1900, the rest by 1920. Mining of the region's rich coal deposits was spurred by industrial demand and by expansion of railway systems; yet prices were often too low for any profit, and the industry, plagued by strikes, was chronically "sick." The Hocking Valley strike of 1884 is still thought to be one of the worst and most violent in labor history; a fire started in a New Straitsville mine burns yet today as startling reminder. Coal mining did continue to expand until its peak was reached early in the twentieth century, when it experienced a steady decline in some counties after 1900, in others after 1920. Railroads pushed the canal system into total obsolescence as they were enthusiastically expanded to transport coal and iron out of the mineral-rich region.[9]

Neither urban centers nor transportation networks developed in the region, primarily because of the rugged terrain and, in circular fashion, the lack of industry. Ohio's major towns of the first half of the century (e.g., Marietta, Lancaster, Zanesville) were in the southeastern region, but they did not develop into major cities without the overall climate for industry offered in the north of the state. Instead many small farming and mining villages were formed as conveniently close service centers with fifty to five hundred inhabitants. These experienced population declines in the twentieth century, especially in the 1920s, when iron furnaces were shut down and coal production sharply dropped. Some virtually disappeared.[10]

A Woman's Place

Because of this distance from metropolitan hubs, no specialized types of farming developed, and farmers usually concentrated on cattle and cattle products and sheep raising. The years from 1900 to 1920 were probably the most prosperous ever for farmers in the rest of Ohio; but land values in the southeast did not experience the sharp rise typical in the rest of the state.[11]

World War I brought, besides its tragedies, a temporary boost in the economy, since all agricultural products and coal were wartime necessities. Camp Sherman, built at Chillicothe for Ohio draftees, was a virtual war-city, with as many as 1,378 buildings, and a capacity of 40,000 in 1917 (45,000 planned for in 1918). It made an inestimable contribution to the war effort; but the most tragic aspect of the camp's history was the force with which the Spanish influenza epidemic hit there in the fall of 1918: almost 6,000 cases of flu, more than 2,000 of pneumonia, and over 1,000 deaths, the highest rate of all the camps. (Among United States troops, approximately as many died in the epidemic as in battle!)[12]

There were few rural high schools until well after 1921, when passage of the Bing Act made attendance for all Ohio children mandatory between the ages of six and eighteen. A 1909 survey showed 76 percent of rural churches declining, due to rural out-migration and general financial problems in the southeast. There "overchurching"—many churches in a small area, dating from pioneer days of slow travel—was the rule. The postwar decade merely intensified rural church problems.[13]

The gap between city and country widened, especially in this area where transportation and communication were not advanced. Rural dress styles were not nearly so elaborate as those of city cousins, especially since wives had to make all the family's clothes themselves. A bewildering variety of entertainment was available to city folk; the farmer's recreation consisted mainly of church suppers, lodge picnics, and going to town on Saturday night. Architects were creating splendid castles for their city clients; carpenters, rather than architects, utilized a variety of styles in rural architecture, and what building there was—often only additions to the family homestead for a growing family—placed emphasis solely on utility rather than beauty.[14]

This is the historic setting against which we meet the next generation of Flynns and Penfields, Sarah and Robert's parents. Sisters Martha and Ellen contribute more to the dialogue in this chapter than to any other, since they were, of course, actively involved in the period (Sarah herself lived at home until 1927). Sarah's daughter Anne adds a few peripheral comments.

Young farmer Joseph Flynn, raised from age twelve by his brother Harold, brought Claire Rheinberg as his bride to the family home only a mile from her own (fig. 3, domiciles b and d), and another generation of Flynns was begun. The farm in the valley remained home to Joseph and Claire the whole of their married life—more than fifty years. Confined as the little log cabin must have been in those early years, it was a beautiful place to raise a family, for it sat on a small rise of the valley, overlooking a creek that cut through flat, rich fields and drained the high ridges guarding each side, north and south. Following his younger brother's wedding and subsequent move, Joseph purchased more land, first from his older brother, later from a neighbor, and the subsistence farm operation was gradually enlarged. The little house soon rang with voices—voices of frequent company, of brother Harold, who continued to live at home, and of babies: eleven were born, ultimately, to the proud couple.

Life was primitive, often rugged, sometimes rewarding. Yet Claire and Joseph provided models of behavior, indeed of all that seemed—and seems—right and good, kind and proper, to Sarah and to her siblings. There were few amenities: roads were scarce and often barely passable in bad weather; crops brought no money, since transportation to market was impractical or nonexistent; most stores were distant; cash was scarce; summers were hot, winters cold; electricity did not come to the valley until 1943. Free gas was a welcome perquisite when wells were drilled on the property about 1918, but Joseph, fearful of its explosive potential, refused to install a furnace and continued

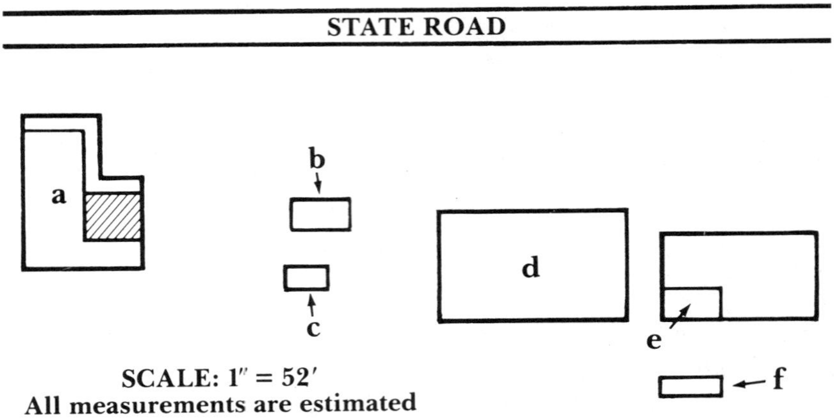

A Woman's Place

SCALE: 1" = 52'
All measurements are estimated

Fig. 3. Layout of Flynn farmstead, 1896–1936. (*a*) The house, approximately 40 × 42', was built onto the existing log structure (shaded area, approximately 16 × 20', typical dimensions for Scotch-Irish log houses; see Bealer [1978:24], Glassie [1968b:353, 355, 359], and Hutzlar [1972:33]). The house was white frame, with a slate-covered hip roof; the cellar, under the log portion only, could be entered only from the outside. The one-story porch had no railing; it ran across the front of the house, and followed the L-shape on around the corner. Sarah's father had the house built by a local carpenter (no architect, no plans, as was the custom) and his three sons ca. 1909. (*b*) Granary. (*c*) The spring house was unusual for the area in not having a projecting roof (see Glassie [1968a:10] for projecting roof types). (*d*) The bank barn (see Glassie [1968a:138–39] for replica; see also Hutzlar [1981]), which Sarah believes to have been 40 × 60', was unusual in that it was sided with close-fitting boards, probably pine, and painted white. Bank barns (i.e., two-level) indicated larger, more productive farms because of their extra floor. The barns in the area were—and are—almost always left unpainted; as the rough-sawn boards became seasoned, the resultant cracks allowed air to circulate and dry the stored hay. They were almost without exception side-opening, three-bay, and rectangular, some one-level and others banked (both are illustrated in Glassie [1968a:138–39]). The barns were covered with vertical siding of native woods (especially hemlock, oak, poplar) almost exclusively, with no battens; roofs were covered with hand-riven oak shingles (red or, preferably, white), which were later replaced with galvanized iron. (*e*) Hog house and pen. (*f*) Corncrib.

to heat with wood, free too, except for a cost high in human effort. All the cooking and water-heating were done on a temperamental wood stove. All water—for drinking, bathing, cooking, cleaning, laundering, or watering stock—had to be drawn from a spring each day; oxen, horse, and mules were the only source of power—except, of course, human muscle.

Farming was a subsistence operation.[15]

> Everything, you know, everything that we used practically was raised back in those times. We would have at least half an acre, an acre, of sorghum, and that would be made into syrup. And he [her father] butchered twelve hogs, and he had at least two beefs, two muttons at least a year, or more, whenever they got old he'd butcher a mutton. And we did practically *every*thing on the farm, and dad always raised a package—a field of buckwheat even—Martha was telling you about buckwheat for the bees, and we had our own flour that we'd take the wheat to the mill and lay it in for a year at a time. So really we were really self, you know, supporting. [4]

> Yes, we always had our own corn. We would always pick it out real careful, you know, the ears, and bring it in and let it set and dry real nice and take, we always had our own ground.... Greenfield had two, it was that close, Greenfield had two [mills] and Blufton had two if not more. [2]

> We always raised two or three acres of sugarcane [sorghum] and it has to be stripped before the frost comes and then that was run through big cogs and this had a great big—you had to hunt the woods over to find a log you could use for that beam and then you—it wasn't very long before that horse could walk around by himself, nobody would even— and it would take at least a barrel of this sugar juice, and they start the fire, oh, before daylight. [3]

> They have big pans made from galvanized, and they'd have to stir that all day long and keep straining it—they took a pie pan and made a pan of it and cut it full of holes, nail holes and they kept skinning that green off—well, it was a kind of

green from the sugar, it would boil up and they would keep skinning that off all day long and we would never take it off until about nine o'clock at night, and then the families, the country people, would gather and then we would make taffy, eat it too. [8]

Sarah: You know it was awful if the frost would come and strike those blades before you get the blades taken off because, see, if you didn't get those blades taken off they absorbed the water and then you wouldn't have any syrup—see you have to press this sugar water out of the —out of the stalks, so those blades all had to be pulled off before you run it through the—there's three great big iron—they're that long and there's two below and there's one comes and is automatically run together and this corn goes through that and you have a horse with a great big, oh, a beam, and this horse goes around and around and runs those rollers and then when you get a barrel of that juice you strain it into a big pan and you start boiling it and always took a day into the night to boil that off into a big pan of sorghum.[16] We made at least three or four of those every year and you pick lots of cane, so we kids had to all strip that and even after it freezes that would cut your hands so bad—it was awful after it frosted in the fall if you didn't get those blades all torn off.

Martha: I still have a scar on my finger here from those blades.

R: The juice is only in the stalk?

Sarah: Yes, yes, and the blades would naturally absorb some of it, the juice.

R: How did you take them off? Cut them?

Sarah: Pull them with your hands. And that's when you got cut. [20]

Cider was made the same way, at the same mill, and your apple butter was made pretty much the same way, except it was made in a copper kettle outdoors and they had to be stirred for hours and it was thickened with the apple—the juice of the apple was used.[17] [3]

You put your slices in and you always put three or four copper pennies in the pot to keep it from sticking from the bottom of the pot. The copper pennies when they moved around in the pot sorta scoured the pot from sticking. Wasn't very sanitary, but— [8]

We'd always make at least three big kettles of apple butter, you know.... You could only make apple butter in those copper kettles—they'd be worth a fortune today if you could find one of them.... Oh, they would hold thirty or forty gallon, and you took and scoured them with vinegar, yeah, you would scour them with vinegar water and things until they just glisten for you, and you boiled your cider, about three barrels of cider down into about a third of a barrel of cider and that was thickened with apples and it would take maybe ten bushels of apples peeled.... You stirred, stirred, and stirred that—you had to stir it all the time. You had to stand way back with a long pole and a stirrer, and that would take up into the night to take that off and have it come off in those big gallon jars and you would seal it. So people lived good. It was the food that done them good. Sorghum molasses on buckwheat cakes. They don't raise buckwheat even any more. [20]

And my father always put out an acre of buckwheat, for cakes and things. And there are bees that like that, so—and everything like that, we raised everything like that. [8]

We raised our own broom corn; we had a neighbor man that had a little factory, 'n he made the brooms on the shares, we'd take one and he'd sell his. You know the old-fashioned broom. [13]

Eggs came from their chickens, and milk, cream, and butter from their cows.

To supplement a scarce supply of cash, Joseph, like most farmers of the area, sought outside employment the few times possible: "Father worked whenever he had a chance" [13]. The gas company drilled wells throughout the area in the early twentieth century. Not only did Joseph receive royalties for the wells drilled on his property but he also worked in the gas fields, drove his horse and sled to meet workers at the railroad stop, and boarded drillers.

> The Gas Company came in, which helped the people. We got just as much for a gas well then as you get for your gas well today. They paid just as much royalty then as they do today. We had five or six wells, which helped. [4]
>
> I can remember my father taking the horses and sled and going to the railroad and meeting the people that were drilling when it was drilling season at that time.... And there was no automobiles, so my father had made trips to the train in Cloverdale and would meet the drillers when they would go home and come back.... They would just stay around and board with the neighbors. People would take them in and rent them rooms. We had a man, his wife, his daughters in our house. [1]

Money for taxes was a perennial problem. Work on the roads was an alternative to paying out cash for some tax, road tax, Sarah believes.[18]

> Martha: Sarah, what did they call that, when the men worked on the roads?
> Sarah: It was road tax, your road tax.
> Martha: They could either work it out or pay it; two dollars I think it was.
> Sarah: They had these heavy old graders, and it'd take six horses pulling them and they still didn't do nothing. Still with six horses they weren't able t' do anything.... I don't know how many days they had to work.
> R: So you could work it out. Did they do that?
> Sarah: Always!
> Martha [chuckling]: There wasn't any money.
> R: Did you sell the crops as cash crops?
> Sarah: No, not his crops, more pork, his pork that he raised, 'n cattle, 'n sheep.

Sarah's Parents

Martha: Sheep wool. Back in those days you couldn't get anything for anything.

Sarah: He always counted his wool for his June tax. He always sold his wool and figured that'd pay his June tax on his place. . . . Yes, just once a year. Then he had his lambs to sell later, so he had two profits. He always liked his sheep, 'cause he said there were two profits a year. But the profits weren't much at that.

Martha: See we were too far away; there was no way of traveling except by horse and buggy or wagon or sled. There was no way of getting produce to market. We couldn't sell it around home because everyone else had it too. So the only income you had—dad had some gas wells—the only income you had was from your cattle. [13]

Sarah: Everyone worked, yes, as much as they could, but there was not much to do. The Gas Company came only once. The road work was just for taxes, unless they were building a highway.

Martha: They built the highway, what was that, 75, by our house? They built that when we were young girls. . . . As the old saying goes, we were all pretty much in the same boat. They all [neighbors too] had to work if they could get work for extra money. They didn't have to have money to live on.

Sarah: Do you know you could go to the grocery store, well, ten dollars would be a fortune, you know. You could take two dollars and buy as many as you'd buy with twenty, thirty, fifty, today. [13]

The women, too, were dedicated workers. Their mother, Claire, raised a huge garden and canned hundreds, even thousands, of jars of the resultant produce to feed her growing brood.

Sarah: We had our own potatoes, we had all the vegetables we ever had [ate]. We didn't buy vegetables. Anything we had. Mother even raised celery. You can even can cabbage and keep it beautiful, you know. Cabbage, everything we picked, we canned.[19]

Martha: We had a cellar. We didn't have actually what they do today. They kept things good, and it was always full of things. Then dad he sometimes buried turnips and things like that.

Sarah: Well if you bury them they keep wonderful. They just keep like they're growing. [9]

They made their hominy, they made their soap. See, our parents did all those things. It was the only way you could get them. [3]

Some items did, of course, require cash, either out of necessity or out of desire:

Martha: Of course you had to have money for clothes. We were very fortunate, though, we had an aunt who gave us a lot of clothes. [13]

"Money for clothes" usually meant money for material, however:

The garments were all handmade. You didn't go to the store and buy, even the coats and things usually were made. [9]

I can remember mother making us the cutest little dresses. She sewed so much; she sewed real well. [7]

I can remember when mother gave three cents a yard for calico; we called it calico then, today I don't know what they call it. It'd be red with little white dots and blue with little white dots, but we were so proud of those little, she really was a good sewer, we were so proud of those little dresses. [4]

Obviously her mother's many talents included sewing and handwork:

She could just pick up anything, which I think back in those days women didn't do—they weren't interested; and she did lots of quilting. [1]

Sarah's Parents

> She was very industrious. Mother could just take a needle and thread and she could create most anything.... Mother could just, she could crochet anything. [1]

> I can't remember when they spun their own cloth, but I do know they made their own carpets 'n things. My mother did that even. Carpet rags. No [they are not braided] they have a loom. It is really pretty.... I can remember 'bout her covering a whole room at a time with them. Done by hand. Lots of work. [11]

Some material could be purchased at the small store that had been built next to them at the crossroads, where Mr. Black carried a "few pieces of dress material, but no hardware or anything." A larger selection was afforded at the General Store in Harrington, about four miles away, and still more in the larger town of Greenfield, about nine miles.

> Martha: So actually about all we bought was sugar, dad's tobacco—he and Uncle Harold both chewed tobacco for it didn't cost much then. There was one other thing—oh, coffee.... Oh, it was a big treat to my dad—he loved crackers and he loved cheese, and for him to go to town, as I said he and mother would go once in a while, it was a big treat on the wagon coming home to have cheese and crackers.... He was just very fond of cheese, as it was something he never got. And as far as fish is concerned, the only thing that we ever got was sulphur fish. [9]

Shrewd peddlers took advantage of transportation difficulties:

> Sarah: We used to have huckster wagons go through with groceries once or twice a week with horses....
>
> Martha: With fresh meat—that's how you got fresh meat in the summertime.
>
> Sarah: For instance, for years and years the old Harrington [General] Store, they'd run a huckster wagon all over the country. [14]
>
> Sarah: Well, we had lots of peddling wagons. For instance, we had a peddling wagon that came from Overlook, down

to Hillview then, for a long time. It was one of the Schneider's, wasn't it Fred Schneider's brother Peter? Ran a peddling wagon for years, a good one. He went all day.
Martha: Sometime he'd bring fresh meat, 'cause you had no way to keep it unless you had it canned, which wasn't so good. [7]

Farm and family required constant work, by parents and by children, too, as they came along.

My father would do any kind of work; he was a terribly, terribly, hard-working person. [4]

We really were, we worked hard, but then he worked awfully hard. He didn't lay around and tell us to do it. He was right there too. [9]

Sarah: Everybody at our house worked. I don't think anyone didn't help.
Martha: Yeah, everybody had to work.
Sarah: Everybody had to. We kept at least twelve cows.
Martha: Oh, in later years we had eighteen or nineteen to milk—by hand. [18]
Sarah: Everything was done the hard way then. We had no conveniences. We had lots of cows. We had to help dig out the barn. . . . We also had my father's brother living with us, too, so there were actually fourteen in the family. Three big meals a day, a lot of washing and ironing.
Sarah and Martha, in chorus: A lot of *everything*!! [4]
Martha: Years ago if a child went out and made a little money on the side, the parents usually took it.
Sarah: Yeah, you know we picked blackberries to get our clothes.
Martha: We certainly did!
Sarah: For twenty-five cents a gallon! or twenty. Carry 'em for miles. You can't find the blackberries today, can you? So don't think you can go out and make a fortune. You cannot find blackberries today.

> Martha: First teeth—first work I ever had done on my teeth I picked blackberries.
> Sarah: We sure picked gallons of 'em.
> Martha: People used to come from the city, and pick 'em up for wine.
> R: Did you have access then to money as children?
> Sarah and Martha, in chorus: It was very, *very* little!! [4]

With only one boy older, the first three girls helped outside as well as in:

> Martha: We had this one brother, then there were three girls in a line, then the next boys were too young. During the First World War, our oldest brother was taken into the service, and the girls had to work right out on the farm like boys. [4]

Turnabout was not fair play, however.

> Sarah: Oh, I believe girls have a harder time of it, don't you, because we had to work outside.... Yes, and the washing and everything had to be done by hand and everything ... and we milked lots of cows.
> Martha: We worked outside as well as inside.
> Sarah: We always had to get outside and bring the horses and things in from the pasture in the morning. [4]
> Martha: With my brother in the service, we [three girls] were the ones that worked in the field, the [younger] boys never did any work there.
> Sarah: Well, to tell the truth when they came along they just didn't do anything. They just didn't amount to too much.
> Martha: That's the truth.
> Sarah: Let's be honest about it.
> Martha: Our oldest brother, when he was home he did work in the field with dad, but after he—
> Sarah: He left awfully young.
> Martha: Well, he left young because he wanted some

money. And the only thing he could do was go out and get a job with another farmer. [9]

The disparity was obvious: both Sarah and Martha hooted at the merest suggestion that the boys might have also helped inside. "Never!" was their simultaneous reply. But their mother helped in the fields.[20]

> Martha: Whoever was in the family did the work. Like my mother, went out in the fields *all* the time. Oh yes, she did! [4]

This was probably unusual; they could remember no other families in the community in which the girls also worked outside. When queried as to whether the father then worked inside too, Sarah's reply was less positive, more defensive: "Yes, I'm sure he would, uh huh" [4].

But there was little doubt in the minds of either Sarah or her sister Martha that not only did girls work harder than boys but that, significantly, this carried through into later life, with women working harder than men in most families:

> Oh sure they did! They went out and worked in the field with their husband and they'd have the home all to do, too, to take care of.[21] [9]

> Her [housewife's] work is never done! They say man works from sun to sun but a woman's work is never done, which is right, you know—especially if there's children. You never get away from it. [11]

Even the memories of their mother's beauty were interlaced with those of her work.

> Martha: Mother had dark eyes, real dark eyes and dark hair.... I thought when I was a young girl coming home from school, see, we lived next to the schoolhouse, we had to come home—we never got to carry our lunch—once, didn't we? I think mother packed it for us once—
>
> Sarah: —She wanted to go to a sale or something all day and she packed ours too.
>
> Martha: And mother—of course in those days everyone

wore long dresses and we remember mother in a long dress with a tiny figure, and her hair, she always, I can remember yet her flinging her head over like this and pulling it all on top and putting it in a bun roll up here, and little tiny dark curls around here and around her forehead. I thought she was the most beautiful thing I ever saw! And she nearly always did the wash and she'd scrub the floor with lye, and that floor, that kitchen floor was white, just as white as could be. But I can remember so well, remember her that way. [15]

In spite of her grueling daily schedule, Claire always made time to attend to more than her family's physical needs:

My mother was especially education-minded. . . . Oh yes, she was interested in education. Of course she was raised in town. [1]

She loved to read. Mebbe she would read all night and work all the next day. She loved to read 'n things. She kept up on things. Yes. She was very much interested in getting us in school. Of course we had nothing but the little one-room school. [4]

Yeah, I saw her with my oldest brother. He didn't want to study and he'd cry and he'd cry and he'd fight and she'd make him study anyhow. . . . He hated school, but she sure did make him study. [1]

Martha: You know as hard as mother worked, you can imagine the wash, digging in the garden, digging in the fields, cutting corn, helping in the hay and all, and I know my mother used to read all night long—sit up till four o'clock and go to work. [15]

Certainly the school was physically convenient, for a new one, Hillview, was built just across the road from their house (see fig. 2), replacing the old Deer Creek School father Joseph had attended back in the Hollow. (In typical rural conservative fashion, lumber from the former school quickly became their neighbor's barn.) Martha reminisced about the social codes for teachers:

> Well, I can remember when the schoolteachers wore their dresses way down to the ground. Never seen a person on the ridge with a colored dress. . . . When I went to school. But the older girls all wore long sleeve white blouses and a long black skirt. All the older girls wore that. There was no variation. They wore long sleeve white blouses and a black skirt. Possibly taffeta—serge in the wintertime. . . . That was the uniform. They [the teachers] were awfully strict. They were more like nuns than people. [18]

Surprisingly none of the six boys were educated beyond the one-room school, but *all* five girls were! Two became teachers, one a store saleswoman (later cook/manager of a bank dining-room), and two were nurses.

> Well, she was for the boys too. . . . Yeah, but the boys wouldn't take it. . . . No, not to amount to anything. [5]

Though the family was unusual both in having their daughters work in the fields and in having them educated, the mother was traditionally conservative in wishing to keep her children close by, especially the girls.[22] Though seldom overtly stated, numerous conversations made it obvious that the significant difference was that girls could become pregnant:

> Sarah: You know a mother can keep the girls closer, and I think they watch over them closer. I think that mother watched over us closer than she did the boys, don't you, because she didn't have the control over the boys she did over the girls.
>
> Martha: The boys were allowed a lot more freedom.
>
> Sarah: They had the silly idea that the boy could do the same thing, be guilty of the same thing as the girl, but it didn't hurt him like it did the girl. And people forget that! But they wouldn't forget it if the girl did it. [4]
>
> Martha: It was mostly a home life, wouldn't you say so, Sarah? Mother never allowed us to go to other places. . . . Mother would, she would gladly have other children come to our place, but she never allowed us to go anywhere. [9]

Sarah: Well, she cautioned us, I mean, and, you know.
Martha: Didn't allow us to get out much.
Sarah: You know she didn't leave us go too much, she thought that we should have our entertainment right there.
Martha: Mother was very, very careful about us. [4]

Later, when the more volatile sister, Ellen, was sharing reminiscences, she discussed the enormous differences she observed in social regulations for nurses in training today.

Ellen: Now my land, they can live at home, they can do whatever they want to do. Don't make any difference if they go out all night every night of the week. Boy, not then [when she attended]! Of course, they couldn't be any more strict than mother was, so we were used to it.
R: Was your mother really that strict?
Ellen: Oh, humph! I went home when I was twenty-one and I wanted to go swimming and she said, "If you go, you stay." I didn't go. You call that strict or not?
Martha: Oh she would have had a perfect family if she could have controlled the boys like she did the girls. . . . Boys weren't supposed to be able to get into trouble, but girls were.
Sarah: No, if they got into trouble it didn't hurt them.
Ellen: No, I disagree with both of you. She would have been just as strict with the boys if she could have managed them and kept them at home—she wouldn't have allowed them to go either. They didn't go because she wanted them to go. They went because she couldn't keep them from going.
Sarah: Oh, she whipped Charlie when he was a great big boy!
Martha: They still would have sneaked out—and I was guilty of opening the window so he could crawl in—many a night—put a wedge under the window so he could get in late.
Ellen: But she just had control of the girls and didn't have of the boys and I wanted to know why.

> Martha: Oh, they are a lot more lenient with the boys in families, you know that.
>
> Sarah: You know if a girl gets in trouble you very seldom heard—they don't hunt a boy and rake around him and downgrade him—it's the girl that takes it. They don't worry about the boy at all. Don't you notice that?
>
> Martha [very ironically]: Because the girl, even though the snake tempted her, she was the guilty one.
>
> Sarah: Sometimes they don't even try to claim the boy—they just, uh—they rake the girl, now isn't that the truth? Lots of times maybe she has been raped—she wasn't guilty at all. In our community those things happen. [18]

Social life consisted, then, of simple pleasures, all close to home, within sight of mother's watchful eye: walking, climbing hills, berrying, nutting, swinging on grapevines, riding horses, swimming in the creek, sliding down haystacks in the summer and snow-covered hills in the winter. Simple, but apparently effective.

> I think your happiest period is when you are going to school. . . . It's a carefree time.[23] [4]
>
> There was more of a sociable life then. [9]
>
> Martha: Our entertainment was mostly walking and climbing hills, berrying, things like that.
>
> Sarah: Why, we would cut grapevine, and we had horses, horses to enjoy. We had the creek. It wasn't dangerous then, we could wade. But it wasn't dangerous. Today you wouldn't darst to use the water to wade in. We had lots of fun, we surely did. [4]
>
> When we were growing up, we practically made our own play. We always had a good long hour to play with the school children; we saw them every day. . . . We had a country store right across the street from the schoolhouse, and we used to neighbor back and forth with those two families. We took walks and went hickory nutting. We had a big grapevine up on the hill. We'd go up there and swing on

> that grapevine, and in the winter time we'd slide down the hill on a board instead of a sled. [5]
>
> And sliding down the haystack, going to the old hotel. It was just across the field, and we played there all the time. And then there was a fine little creek that run through over by the woods, we would be, go and get hooks for turtles. There's a sand bar there, believe it or not. [9]
>
> The boys were . . . almost two years younger . . . and we'd have to take the cow around by the store—we'd take 'em down around by the store and then around oh about a quarter of a mile to, you know, and we'd get on and ride and she would get scared or something, you know there's nothing to hold to—we always get up, all three, one would take the other you know, we would all go up on the road, but we had an old-fashioned buggy and we'd hitch her up to the buggy. [20]

At the nearby hotel (which had been their grandfather's) "old-fashioned musicians" still played then for "old-fashioned dances," but

> Mother wouldn't take us very much. But they had all that sort of thing, dancing, 'n ice cream, you know. But then we always got out and played a lot—games outside, like, well, different ones, like "Old Dan Tucker," you don't have to dance it you can play it, and "Down the Old Mississippi" was one, and "Down the Old Ohio" was one. . . . Oh we used to play out, we had gas jets, and usually lights outside with the gas. Then in those days we would stay out 'til three, four o'clock in the morning and play those games! You know, "Old Dan Tucker," and all those, we played them.[24] [6a]
>
> . . . In the evenings our mother would tell us stories, we would set by the fireside and toast onions in the ashes of the stove, and our mother would read to us. [16]

As they grew older, there was more exposure to the neighboring community:

> Sarah: Some parties were at Northfield, we went to Berry's,

and we went to all of our, each neighbor would have us, we'd have each other, we had the party at our place. We'd have it someplace. And we'd have Japanese lanterns if we didn't have anything else, to light up the outside.... The last one I think I ever went to Henry took me, Henry was our favorite neighbor, and it was in the house that James [her son] owns, and we danced in the little room there that she has for a living room today. And that's where we danced that night. That house has been changed quite a bit since then.

Martha [wryly]: That must have been after I left home.

Sarah: We had a wonderful time. But it was just older people. Just two young girls, probably a couple of young boys, 'n nearly all old families—but I enjoyed them because they were the old-time dancers that could really dance. You take Bud's sister, and you never saw anyone dance like her! She could just pick both feet up—and do you know my father could clap his feet together twice—what'd you call it, double shuffle? And she could do the same thing. And so they were really interesting.

R: Would they serve refreshments?

Sarah: Oh yes, always . . . coffee, pie, maybe sometimes be a lunch, 'n sometimes ice cream and cake. And you know we had what we call candy parties where you just took candy.

Martha: Yeah, make taffy, pull taffy—taffy pull. [6a]

The growing family required more and more space:

Sarah: They put a big room—they put a new room on and they saved that when they built the other house.

Martha: But we actually slept in a log cabin because I remember when mother had a baby, we always had a girl, one of our neighbors to come, 'cause the neighbors were cousins, and I can remember—the best thing I can remember—about her is sleeping in bed with two of us. I was in the middle and she'd tell such ghost stories that every night I saw things on the ceiling. I was years getting over that! She couldn't have been too much older than I. [14]

Sarah's Parents

Finally the cabin was replaced by a substantial new house, "saving" the addition on the log house for an addition to the new one:

> Sarah: [It was built] When John was a baby, and—how old would he be today—he was a year old. I can remember old Mr. Jenkins bringing him, picking him up to the house.
>
> Martha: Well, John died the year we went to West Virginia; he was twelve years old and we went to West Virginia in 1921.... The reason I know is we were on our way to West Virginia to the Montgomery Ward store and he had typhoid and he had to be buried. We stopped on our way and he was sick then and that was in 1921 and he was twelve.... He was born in 1909 then.
>
> R: Can you remember what the house looked like?
>
> Sarah: Oh yes. It was a nine-room house and it was a wooden house you know like this, yes, it had nine rooms, and had a—
>
> Martha: —had five bedrooms upstairs—
>
> Sarah: —and one, two, three, four—four downstairs—
>
> Martha: —and a large porch.
>
> R: That went across the front?
>
> Sarah: Well no it was rounded shape, round like this.
>
> Martha: One of the rooms extended out—the living room extended out like this and then the porch went here and here and here.
>
> Sarah [to researcher, sketching]: And you called it an L shape; no, that's it now, the house there, that's right, like that. [See figure 4 for sketch of floor plan.]
>
> Martha: It had a hip roof too.
>
> R: Do you have any pictures of it?
>
> Sarah: Oh maybe someplace. You know the house burnt and there's so many things, bibles and things, that burnt in the house—it just burnt down—there's no saving anything. [14]

Next to the home, two other institutions served as socializing

A Woman's Place

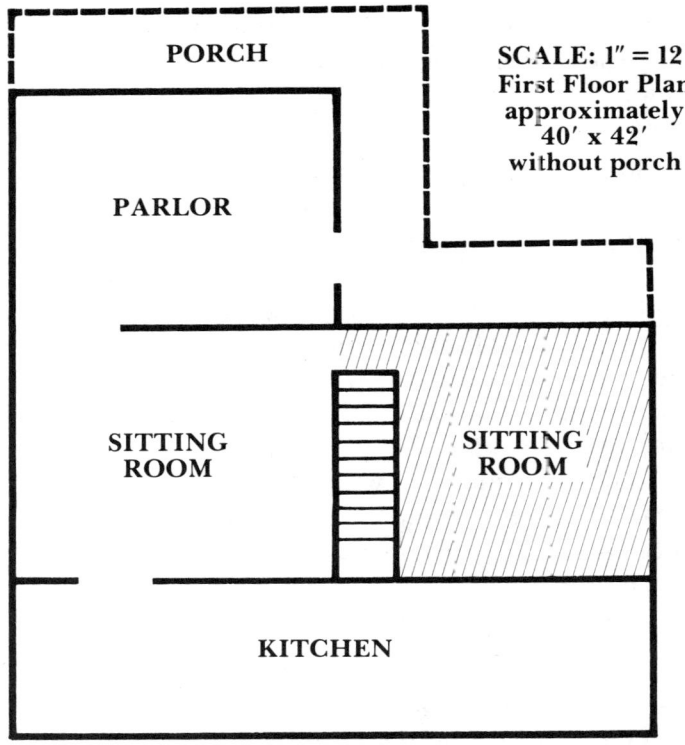

Fig. 4. Flynn house ground floor plan, ca. 1909. Similar to the Penfield house floor plan (chap. 2), this dwelling was also white frame with a slate-covered hip roof. The location of the five bedrooms on the second floor corresponded exactly to the location of first-floor rooms (two bedrooms occupied the space over the kitchen). The shaded area indicates the original log house, around which the new structure was incorporated.

agents: school and church. The school apparently served as a focal point, more so there than, as indicated in historical accounts, the churches did.

> The little country schools, township schools, were the center of the social life for the country people. You can just put it that way because that's the way it was. [9]
>
> Sarah: They [the older men] would go maybe in the winter when they didn't have anything else to do, you know. It was

Sarah's Parents

a kind of entertainment—they played ball, it was their social lives. They'd have box socials, and they'd have spelling bees at night in the schoolhouses. And really the schoolhouse was about the only place they had social gatherings. And they had old-fashioned spelling bees.[25] You know, they would choose sides and then they would have what they call—which was a lot of fun—they don't do that anymore—they had. They would choose sides and then they would take the subject, you know—

Martha: —debate—

Sarah: —debate. They had so many debates. And the older men, the lawyers, the educated people would come in and they would have those debates. Really to tell the truth I think they knew more about enjoying themselves than we do today. [1]

Sarah: Really the old educated people all were good spellers. We had spelling bees and things like that. At school. Pie socials, you know. And luncheons. And they'd bid 'em. I loved to go to those.

Martha: Learning poetry. I loved that. We had quite a bit. The teacher would write on the blackboard and he would find out who could, which of the pupils could memorize it the quickest. And we went off, we went to school with all the pupils from the first to the eighth grade in one room.

Sarah: We always got a little present for the one who had the most check marks; if you stood at the head of the week, then on Monday you'd go to the bottom again and start all over. And we'd get a pencil, which was quite a bit then. I knew an old farmer, and he'd really, uh, he got to be rich, and they said he'd take a pencil and cut it in three pieces, when he started his children in school. And those children started with a third of a pencil. I know Sally [Sarah's eldest daughter] would chew up a pencil a day [chuckling]. She had to have a pencil a day. [4]

I know I loved to bake a pie and fix it so nice and I know we'd always decorate our box and then we'd have a man to

A Woman's Place

> auction and naturally we'd let the boy know that we really wanted to eat with him and they'd bid those boxes off;[26] and then we'd play games outside at the old school, little old-fashioned schoolhouse, down here in the valley. One of them stands yet today, the schoolhouse down here on the other side of Harrington. [14]

As pointed out in the history of early education, the teachers did not always have lengthy training;

> Sam was an old-fashioned school teacher. Never took school training of any kind, he just went through the grades, but he—you know they went three, four, or five years maybe in the grades.
> R: How do you mean?
> Well, they all went in the eighth grade, they just go to the one-room schools, and they just go on until they were pretty good, you know, and he was wonderful—oh they say he was wonderful in math. . . . No, he never went to college, but maybe he was equal to some of those that did—he was really smart, you know. . . . No, he didn't, didn't have a chance to go to high school—he could have got it, but, you know they got pretty good old-fashioned teachers, and they were pretty well versed on the things that a child really needed to know, you know. He was like Abraham Lincoln—pretty self-educated—he was a very intelligent man. Children that went to school to him liked him so well and said he was a wonderful man. [19]

The church, too, was a social force in the community:

> Church, really church was the center next to the school. They went to church for entertainment. Then they had what you called protractive meetings, and had church singing.
> R: What church was it?
> United Brethren and Methodist. Nearly everybody went to church. [5]
> Martha: And we never did anything on Sunday. [4]

R: Your family was United Brethren?

My father and mother was a strict Baptist. And I'm sure that if either were living my dad's people would be Catholics. I'm pretty sure of that.

R: Because they were from Ireland?

Yes, uh huh, but we were raised up here near the Methodist church. [20]

R: Was your father, uh, did he have any part in the church? Was he an elder or anything in the church? Did he go to church?

Not very often. And he almost got a church in our community one time, and, uh, there was a fight among the people. A couple of Indians had a fight and that broke it up. We would have had a church close. So we didn't—we don't have a church here [United Brethren]. [9]

Martha: You didn't go regularly. You didn't go every Sunday like most people do if they go to church, because there was no way of getting there. You couldn't hardly walk all that distance; we did walk that way in the wintertime when they had the revival services.

Sarah: Revival. Revival in the wintertime. Oh yes, it'd last two, three weeks at the church, revivals and things like that.

Martha: Old-time religion, you know.

Sarah: Yeah, some of those old people could sing s' pretty. [9]

Similar to revivals were another kind of religious meeting:

Sarah: Do you remember the Chautauquas used to come around?

R: What was that?

Sarah: I went, and I think they had music, it was on the religious line. Yeah, they would put up a tent, and be out in the open.

Martha: They'd have a lot more music then.

Sarah: I believe it is a kind of a religious, I don't know if they have them any more or not.

> Martha: Have you been down to Blufton on the old road? They're building the new road, a shopping center.... Just this side of it there's a building and they have a tent up. But Chautauqua's about the same thing as a revival but on a bigger scale is mostly what it used to be—hymns, maybe a speaker or two. They used to have shouters all over the place. We were out in the open; it was summer. You never heard about Billy Sunday or Amy McPherson. Well, now that was Chautauquas.
> R: Did they come around here?
> Martha: They came to Columbus, but Billy Sunday was the greatest, I suppose the greatest revival minister ever.
> Sarah: They said that he really had his downfall, though, one Sunday. I guess it happened in Columbus. A girl got sick and she got up to go out and he said for someone to kiss that young heifer and put a halter on her, and they said that the people were so down on him for it. They have their come and they have their go, don't they? [14]

Sarah's father, Joseph, was not an elder in the church, and neither her father nor, certainly, her mother moved in the public sphere often.

> My dad never belonged to the Grange. [9]

> My father was always at home at night—never away at all. [9]

If their father was always at home at night, no doubt their mother was too. In fact, she must have been home almost all the time, since her children came home every day for lunch from school across the road, and it was a signal occasion when she was not there to greet them:

> I remember once mother wanted to go someplace all day and she fixed our lunch and I thought that was a little bit of heaven. I can remember yet today what she put in my lunch. I know she put chicken in a sandwich and one roll, and I can just remember that, taking our lunch.... And she packed it in one of those little buckets. Remember those little buckets? [18]

Sarah

Lack of transportation was undoubtedly the most significant factor in their isolation.

> Martha: The only way in the world you had to getting from place to place was horse and buggy; maybe if you were fortunate you owned a surrey or a buggy. Some people never owned one. And they still used oxen, at times, not as much, but I can remember when they used, Daddy used oxen, particularly for lumbering. You never got to go any place. There was no place you could go. The nearest church that we went to was the only place I ever remember going was Northfield.
> Sarah: Harper's Chapel.
> Martha: You had no way of getting there, Harper's Chapel, which is even farther, I believe, isn't it? [4]

It is easy to understand why work, omnipresent as it was, was turned to a form of socializing whenever possible—barn raisings, bean hullings, corn huskings, butchering, harvesting. Neighbors or kin, often one and the same, developed a relationship of mutual dependency through sharing: heavy tasks were thus possible, lonely isolation was thus eased. Wheat threshing, for instance, was a grand occasion, hot, dusty, difficult work for all, but laced with an air of festivity, a feeling of community;[27]

> And there were thrashing days, and we would always have people overnight. [5]

> Martha: Mother would always save her last ham, smoked ham. Dad had a lot of smoked ham this way. For the threshers, remember? The table they usually set out in the lawn on a, it was made on a, saw horses they called it, not boards. And the farmers came from all around to help at each farmhouse. And all—
> Sarah: —So you changed—worked back and forth. You didn't give them money, you went to your neighbor and worked, and then he'd come to your place for—
> Martha: —And some of the women in town . . . they cooked all day. Then they stayed two or three days. And the men would sleep in the hay mow and work the next day. [9]

And then they gathered their beans—you know you never had bean beetles then. They'd bring their own beans. Well, they'd get out in the barn at night, and they would thrash them out or hull them, and husk their corn together. They'd go back and forth for miles, families would.... Then they'd dance later in the evening, in the barn 'n things. So the country people did have their ways.[28]

Martha: It was a big event in the country when I was growing up for the harvesting to all be done by the neighbors . . . and the butchering.

Sarah: Our family when we butchered, our family would come over and have a house full all night.... My father always said, butcher a hog for each one in the family, and then one for the company. So that would be several in our family. Oh yes, we butchered a lot. [13]

And like when my father built his barn, you had what you call barn raisings, and it takes as, mebbe fifty men to, these barns are all cut out and laid out, you know, and you have to have mebbe as many as fifty of your neighbors. They come from *miles* around! And you have to have a big dinner for them, to, uh, put your barn up, and that barn down home—was a big job. That's the way it was put up. It's a pin barn. See those are a pin. Now they're put together with spikes. They're lots better if there were pins. See they never rot off, but if it's got spikes, those spikes'll rust and break off, and you don't have as good a barn. But if you have, the wooden pins are made out of oak, 'n they last through eternity.[29] [12]

Relatives, too, cooperated, of course. Joseph had "built-in" help from his brother Harold, who continued to live with them all his life (it was his home place as well). And Claire's mother, Hannah Powers—who lived only a mile away in Deer Creek Hollow—was always a great help to her. Helping was reciprocal: Martha moved in with her grandmother when the latter became ill.

Martha: They took my oldest sister—older than I—and she

cried and wouldn't stay and she got homesick, so they took me over and I stayed with my grandmother [at age seven]. [3]

Before she died, Claire's mother, Hannah, delivered Claire's first six children. A local midwife delivered all but one of the last five.[30]

Martha: It runs in my mind that one of those children were born when there was no midwife there and dad cut the cord, yes. Which one of us was it?
Sarah: I don't know. I don't remember, but I remember he did. [3]

Such physical isolation apparently led to a sense of enclosure in a world of their own.[31] Sarah, the booklover, retreated into the world of literature as well. She can remember few titles, but remembers the "classics," Zane Grey's western books, and *The Last of the Mohicans*. Since she often speaks reverently of "the pioneer women," she may have read of them often:

R: Can you remember any favorite books that you had when you were a girl?
Well, you mean in school? You mean classics and things?
R: Well, at school, at home, whatever.
I read so many, but you know we had to read so many classics in high school when I went to school—they don't make kids do it today. I studied, our high school teacher had—she was a woman and we had so many Shakespeare books—I think you like it because I think it's like studying Latin, you just have to take it a line at a time.
R: Yeah, it's a challenge. Well, do you remember what your favorite, what some of your favorite books were?
Oh, I had lots of favorites. The novel that I liked better than any other'n was *St. Albans*, did you ever read that? Well, there's a sequel to that and I never got to read the sequel. If you have a chance and you want to read that, because that's the story about an Irishman. If you can get *St. Albans*, and let's see, what is the sequel to that? Oh I've read all those, just practically name them—an awfully lot. I read nearly all

of Zane Grey's books. . . . He lived those places you know—that's nearly all western books I have read. But I just don't read so much anymore. . . . I like Washington Irving's books, and *The Last of the Mohicans* is one that I liked, but I can't remember now the characters without going back through the book—that's one I liked. And of course I read the *Merchant of Venice, Robinson Crusoe,* I've read all those old stories.

R: Any books about pioneer women?

Some, yes, what is his name that went to Kentucky, what was his name, Daniel Boone; that would be one good one, and the life of Abraham Lincoln would be a good one, and—their life wasn't too much different from our early life, and everything was done by hand. [20]

The same sense of enclosure is reflected by the fact that international, national, or even statewide events are not mentioned in these remembrances by Sarah and her sisters, with the exception, following a direct question, of one account of World War I:

R: Do you remember much about the first World War?

Sarah: I can just remember—yes, I was just old enough that mother and I, I remember that my brother was in the service and he went as far as New York. He didn't cross—the Armistice was signed at the time and he was in the camp, at Camp Chillicothe. Like they remember about the Spanish flu breaking out and so many people died.

R: Do you remember, Martha, that time?

Martha: Yes, I remember that no woman that was pregnant escaped the flu. She just died.

Sarah: Oh yes, they all died.

Martha: That was in 1917.

Sarah: I don't think any of them that was pregnant lived. The doctor didn't know how to manage. He just didn't know how to take care of them. . . . It was just a new thing and they just were not up on it.

Ellen: The truth of the matter was, they had no idea what it

Sarah's Parents

was. There were wooden barracks and they wouldn't do a thing but open the windows and give 'em fresh air. It just killed them like flies. Diphtheria back then, our brother died when he was eleven, not quite twelve; they didn't have anything for—it had just come in—now the rest of us had shots is what saved us. He died before they knew what happened. That is, I mean, he took sick and the doctor came that night and gave him a shot, but eleven o'clock the next day he was dead. But the rest of the family all had immunization.

Sarah: But with this Spanish flu, it, the doctors did—

Ellen: —It had just come in, Martha, Doc James told dad when he went to pay the bill, "Joseph," he says, "when due," he says, "your bill will be only half of what it will be if you have that to pay" and the state did. The state picked up the bill.

R: Why?

Ellen: Well, because it was new—that was when they first had found the vaccination. You know, diphtheria vaccination today in schools is more or less free.

Sarah: Antitoxin, it came from the mare, it was pretty...

Ellen: It was just developed.

Martha: I was just nineteen when the war was over; I was nineteen years.

Sarah: It came from horse, you know.

Martha: ... Kaiser, you know, it started when an Australian king was killed; it started the World War, and there was a Spanish diplomat that was killed it started, actually started it.

R: How did it affect you here; how did it affect people here?

Ellen: Well, everything went up.

Martha: Girls got out and worked like men. For instance, my older sister and myself, we helped try to put the hay in. We couldn't pitch the hay onto the wagons, and by the time the farmers took their hay and started, most of them, some of them stacked it in big ricks, what they call hayricks, and

A Woman's Place

others took them to the barns, if they had barns, and we would get up in the haymow and take the hay, and dad would pitch it up to us, and we'd do the best job we could do as, as kids and girls.

R: 'Cause your older brother was gone?

Martha: Yes, and the other three was too young, you see. Sarah and I were both in between any boys, and dad kept us out of school in the fall until the corn was cut—we would have to cut the corn, rick it, and, uh, that's all the help you had. Now *some* of the boys were exempt. If the fathers wanted to go to bat for them because they were farmers—

Sarah: —I just happened to think of it—

Martha: —but some of the boys didn't want to be exempt; they wanted to go and serve—

Sarah: —Kaiser Bill went up the hill to get a shot at France,
        He came back down again with bulletholes all through his pants.

Do you remember that verse?

Martha: No. But you know Kaiser Wilhelm, I think one of his arms was withered. He was not—he was a very small man to start with, and he was not a complete physical man.

Sarah: See, the war ended in France. That's where, oh! the gas was the worst thing, you know. They used gas and that was what destroyed the boys.

Martha: There wasn't any real bad, there wasn't any [?] in that war like there is today.

Sarah: The worst thing was the gas. When the boys came back gassed they were never right afterwards.

Martha: Oh, they would step in a mine and the mine would blow up.

Sarah: Well, the gas was the worst, after they were in those trenches and got gassed they were never right afterwards.

Ellen: We had a lot more mentally—

Martha: —That was like all the wars, they had parades, and people went wild; they lost their equilarium, or whatever you want to call it, and you know what happens when people

go into a riot, for instance, they don't think, they act; it was pretty much—
Sarah: —I can remember going down to Chillicothe, you know to—that was Camp, you know. And, uh, the Wright Brothers was out there trying to fly one of those old-fashioned airplanes, and a woman was running along trying to hold them, whatchacallit, wings—
R: —You saw what?
Sarah: —wings down. Yeah.... Their planes were—
Ellen: —They were Ohio boys.
Sarah: Dayton, they were from Dayton.
Ellen: Didn't you see the story of them on TV yesterday?
Sarah: They were from Dayton, weren't they?
Ellen: I didn't see it, but I read the press story—
Sarah: —They were born and raised in Dayton, weren't they? Dayton boys.
Martha: Yes.
Ellen: It showed the, the last two or three minutes in the air, I think the first flight that they made—
Sarah: —Wilbur, and what's the other's name?
Ellen: Wilbur and, uh, Orville.
Martha: Now they did use some airplanes like, uh—I don't know how to pronounce the word—reconnoisance, is that right? I don't know how to pronounce it. They did use some—
Sarah: —renna, reconn, reconnaisance, I'll get the word after a bit. It takes me a—
Martha: —For instance, we had a friend that was, well, that was a friend of ours in later life, that was a partial Egyptian and partially French, and he was a linguist. And he acted as a linguist during the First World War, and he was one of them that went up in these planes to see what the other army was doing on the other side; but there was no real planes as fighter planes used in that war.
Ellen: Naturally, because it was over with in 1919. [18]

Politics were mentioned briefly, but again only as the result of a direct question:

> R: People around here, were they mostly Democrat or Republican?
> Ellen: Most of them voted Democrat—a community of Democrats, really—actually back in that day dad was a strong Democrat. Mother I guess held more to it. I married a Republican and became a Republican.
> R: So you would say the country generally speaking was Democrat. Did people tend to always vote?
> Ellen: They did, didn't they? They had a pretty good turn-out, didn't—
> Sarah: —Oh, I think so.
> Ellen: Yeah, the country people were the trustees, governors, and that sort of thing in the community, I think, as a whole. [17]

The War (as they refer to World War I) signified the beginning of change for the close-knit family. Martin left the farm to work for the gas company following his discharge from the army not long after the armistice. The two youngest girls were born just before the War (but the youngest son was not born until 1921). The second child, Hannah, named for her grandmother, left to teach in a nearby town; Martha left to marry in 1919. And Sarah, the fourth, attended high school away from home, first by living with her maternal aunt in Greenfield, eight miles distant, later with her schoolteacher sister in Northfield, only three miles from home;

> I stayed with my aunt down in Greenfield, where Ellen my aunt lived, and I stayed with her two years; then I came back to Hillview [home] in my third year, and they divided—they petitioned—the school off and had a teacher down from Madison, and there was about ten of us that started in, I think there was five that finished the year, and he was able to give me my third year and then I went to Northfield. My sister was teaching and I went to Northfield and stayed with

her and went back—there was a group of children back and forth to Bay Creek [Greenfield High School], and graduated that year. [1]

Her oldest sister, Hannah, had paved the way for her to attend college in Athens for teacher training.

> Sarah: Did you know then when I took my training it was just done away with, but when my sister took her training at Athens it was a little subdivision of Athens, and they had this rural school and we would go out there and get our practice teaching under rural schoolteachers. Then they done away with that when I went. I had to take mine in the city schools.
> R: You were pretty unusual not only to have finished high school, but to go on to college.
> Sarah: Then it was because you couldn't hardly get a school.
> R: You were probably famous in the countryside, weren't you?
> Anne: Ellen and Annie went to nurses' training too.
> Sarah: Yeah, but there is fourteen years younger than I was so that makes a little difference in time.
> R: Were your parents just education minded?
> Sarah: Yes, my mother especially. [1]

When a question was posed concerning the difficulty of going away to school—the researcher's thought directed to problems of separating from her beloved family—Sarah's answer referred only to the physical complications: a buggy to the railroad stop at Cloverdale, then a long railroad trip to Athens. It was unclear from questions during several interviews if it was Ohio University she attended there, but later on our trip to Athens I discovered it was:

> Yes, I went summers [three] and then I went one winter, and I got what you call a county, a Rural County College. I got a diploma for it, for teaching in primary grades. And I had to take practice teaching and all those things. It was a two-year course at that time.
> R: So then did you go back home? And teach from there?

> Um hum. Yes, I taught three years in one little country school there. [4]
>
> R: Did you teach all the grades?
>
> Oh yes, we didn't even have a music teacher. [7]
>
> R: What was it like being at home when you were teaching?
>
> [Laughing] Just about the same as always.
>
> R: How many were still at home?
>
> Three, four of us gone, be seven, father, mother, and uncle. There still would be ten at home altogether, mother and father and my uncle and seven children.
>
> R: And it didn't seem any different?
>
> No, huh uh, about the same, I think.
>
> R: Glad to be back home, probably.
>
> [With wry laugh] I think that it was something that you went through, that you didn't even question, you know, just a matter of existence. [4]

Sarah ventured into her first entrepreneurial experience sometime after she began teaching: she bought a small parcel of land, approximately thirty acres, that adjoined her uncle's property (just south of her father's farm). In only a few years, she sold the piece to a timber contractor and realized a tidy profit.

During that same period Sarah met a neighbor who also had lived all his life in that same township—except for several short periods of employment in Columbus. She does not remember when or how she met him, but she believes he was a friend of her brothers.

> Well, he was in that community a long time. I don't know, he was with my brothers quite a bit, so I suppose that's how [I met him]. . . . Of course people don't get around like they do today you know. They didn't travel for miles like they do today in a few minutes. [20]
>
> R: Martha, where did you meet Perry?
>
> Martha: I met him at the Greenfield fair.
>
> Sarah: That was a good place.

Martha: And the schoolteacher introduced me.

Sarah: Our schoolteacher, he was a young man, he was real nice.

R: What was he doing at the time, was he working?

Martha: No, he taught.

Sarah: He was in high school, wasn't he, when you first went with him?

Martha: I think it was his last year, and he taught an extra one year after that, after I met him, and then we got married; he taught, he got $50 a month for teaching.

Sarah: That was a good wage then.

Martha: And we got married on $400; he saved $400. [14]

Plays and programs at the school and Friday night spelling bees were courting fare in the early twentieth century, with only an occasional movie:

Sarah: Yes, we'd go to the movies. And mother and father, they didn't have a car 'n they'd go with us. We'd all go as a family, yes. Neither one of us cared for that sort of thing—pictures. We went visiting, you know, family sometimes. It's been so long ago.... But there wasn't too much, if we didn't go to church or something at the school. That was all the social thing of the community. If you went to a little picture show you had to go as far as Blufton [fourteen miles].

Martha: To start with, mother didn't want us to go.

Sarah: We spent a lot of time going to church; we walked in groups. We went to church and often we'd maybe meet up with somebody and walk with a certain one or something and to tell the truth, I don't think that we brought too much company home.

Martha: I can't ever remember ever bringing anybody home.

Sarah: Mother would let us have a party if we wanted.

Martha: How often?

Sarah: Well, as often as the rest had ...

Martha: I can't ever remember having a party.... I think

they did more of that after I left home because I can't hardly recall anything like that. I recall going to a couple square dances. That's it. I think after you [Sarah] got out and then the younger children got going out—I never got to do anything like that; Mother never allowed us to.
Sarah: Oh, we had lots of those—it was right there at the Hillview school—we had what they'd call—
Martha: —spelling bees—
Sarah: —yes, and debates, they were fun! [14]

Along with the revival-like Chautauquas, medicine shows plied the circuit and provided welcome diversion.

Sarah: We'd drive the horse and buggy down to Northfield, watch the medicine shows. Well, they sold medicine, I don't know what kind, snake—was it made from snakes or something?
Martha: Sort of like a carnival in a small way.
Sarah: Yeah, they'd have, probably somebody'd play a guitar or something, a little music, tell some jokes with it.
Martha: Usually a man, usually a girl, the girl would get up and sort of dance.
Sarah: And the man'd tell stories—
Martha: —The man'd tell this particular medicine would cure anything, snake bite or anything else. I think it used to sell for a dollar a bottle.
Sarah: It was a cure-all, I know that. [14]

Weddings were fairly simple affairs, usually at the church, with family present.

You could go to the minister's house; you could have it in the church or you could go to the parsonage.
R: What did you do?
I went to the parsonage. It was really a snowy day. My! The snow was about knee deep. . . . I had a pretty dress, it was blue crepe, I still remember what it was like. . . not real long, but just about, I think that about that time, about half way

Sarah's Parents

between the knees and the ankles—I think it was about half way. They weren't real short, you know. No one wore real short dresses in those days.

R: Did you wear a hat?

No, I was married, it was real, it was early in the morning; no, aw, it was awful! . . . It was in February, it was real cold.

R: Did you have any kind of party?

Belling. They called them bellings. Yes, we did have a, you know, belling; the neighbors came in and we had all kinds of lunch, you know. . . . I don't remember what we served, we always had something.

R: Do you remember any other weddings you went to? What might they have served?

Well, they would usually have drinks, er, no hard drinks or anything, but they would serve, you know, sandwiches and cake and maybe fruit and pie, you know, regular things. And then they had—you know they get out and make a lot of noise. And they have a captain and he calls the bride and groom out and then they go around and shake hands with them and wish them a lot of happiness and things. That was the old-fashioned way; and then sometimes, now I think when Edna Jones up here got married, they had a buggy and they took them a buggy ride, you know, a couple of them pulled it, they do different crazy things you know.

R: And did they do that to you?

No, humph, it was too cold.

R: Did they have a belling?

Yeah, kinda a belling. They have kinda quit that, they don't like those old-fashioned ways.

R: I thought the belling was when they came to the couple's new home and called them out.

No, not necessarily.

R: So this was at your parent's home. And who all came?

Well, our neighbors. I don't remember who they were all now.

> R: And then did you take any kind of trip?
> Oh no, it's right in the wintertime, and I was teaching too. [20]
>
> Martha: I think I had a wedding with a preacher—
> Sarah: —You'd better had!
> Martha: No, you don't have to have a preacher to marry you.
> Sarah: No, you can go to the justice of the peace, but I'm sure that Perry wouldn't have been married with a justice of the peace. His family wouldn't have allowed it. Why they marched him to church every Sunday, he never failed to go to church.
> Martha: Guess he went to church too often as a child, and then he didn't care abut it after he grew up. [14]

Marriage was a central factor in rural society:

> R: Your sisters all married, too, didn't they?
> Um hum, the whole family was married.
> R: And were the husbands all from around here?
> Yes, uh huh, Sally's [Sarah's daughter's] husband is from over near Blufton . . .
> R: No, I mean your sisters.
> Yes, oh, yes, Junior [Ellen's husband] was raised practically—his mother had to go to Columbus when her husband died—she went to Columbus and he was in Columbus part of the time, but then he had a place out here and he always came back to it and then, Annie she met her husband in Columbus. Hannah's was raised down here across the creek back of the graveyard—it was a big white house then, the house, I don't know whether it stands there.
> R: Where did Martha meet her husband?
> Oh yes, he was a Northfield boy, too, and went to church with them. She went to church in Northfield.
> R: So Annie is the only one that married someone away from here?

Sarah's Parents

Uh huh, she met him after she went to Columbus to live. See mother and the girls [Sarah's two youngest sisters] went to Columbus after they were through nursing training and she met Sam up there.

R: What about your brothers? Did they all marry someone around here too?

Well, Charlie's wife was up here, and Jim married, married in Columbus, but she was out here on the ridge, she was raised out here, and uh, Andy's wife was. Elmer's wife is from close by at New Hope—Elmer is an awfully nice person [actually deceased for several years]—Elmer has an awfully nice wife.

R: What was the oldest's name?

Oh yes, uh huh, he's the oldest of the family. I forgot about him. And he married a girl just right close to home, just about a mile. Went to school with her.

R: So the pattern then was to marry someone who was from around here.

Pretty much in those days. I think maybe it still is—seems to be—seems to be quite a bit. . . . They kinda come back.

R: Was it kinda taken for granted that women would get married?

I suppose sometime or another. I think everybody, I think everybody themselves looks forward to having their own, don't you think? I think that's the normal thing.

R: But by having a home of your own . . .

You never, I don't think people ever accumulate anything that amounts to anything, do you, until they get responsibilities or have responsibilities.

R: By getting married?

Yes, and have something to live for, you know, that's something you really live for 'cause they know their parents aren't always going to live and be around and they need roots. [20]

With these strong, traditional attitudes as background, Sarah agreed to marry her brother's friend, Robert Penfield. It was to his father's and his grandfather's (and possibly his great-grandfather's) farm that he took her, just three miles "up the road, and over the hill" (fig. 2, domicile c).

Of the thirteen children born to Robert's grandparents, Harry Penfield and his wife, eleven lived: five boys and six girls. George, the youngest boy (and Robert's father), ended up with the family farm of 120 acres because, according to family legend, he promised to take care of the parents and build them a new house. (There is little record of the other children's whereabouts, except that one boy became a preacher.)

There are almost no remembrances either concerning the parents' generation, other than that George did build a new house for his parents to replace the old log cabin;

> Sarah: That was a trick to build those houses then, because if they wanted a little plain lumber, they had to hitch up the horses, and in the wintertime they went knee deep in mud to Blufton and back and to get, you know, a little plain lumber.... Lot of hard jobs had to be done with a saw and hammer.
>
> R: What year was that?
>
> Sarah: Well, it's been built about seventy-two or seventy-three years [she was very close: it was seventy-four years, or a little more].
>
> Anne: It is in nice shape.
>
> Sarah: It woulda been, but Robert's father never put the right foundation after we came here, and if you can put the right foundation ... [2]

Unfortunately, George's parents were not destined to enjoy the spacious new dwelling, for just before the long-anticipated move, Harry died, and his wife followed him in less than a week.

Tragedy was to strike soon again: George and his young wife (name not remembered) lost a child. They had two boys; but when they were only three and five, their mother died. She was only twenty-six. Despondent, George moved to Columbus, where he worked until his death twenty years later.

Sarah's Parents

> Robert lost his mother when he was about three. His father went to Columbus. He had an aunt moved in there and took care of the two boys. . . . Yes, he came back and forth to see the boys often. The aunt was a sister to Robert's mother. [11]

An old sepia-tone, slightly out-of-focus photograph, shows the two little boys posing self-consciously with their handsome pony and cart in the farmyard; it is the only memento of a period of gradual erosion, both for continuation of the traditional large, extended family and for the prosperous small farm. With the advent of Sarah into the Penfield family, however, the old patterns were soon to be revitalized.

SUMMARY

Ohio continued to industrialize in the last quarter of the nineteenth century and by the twentieth century was one of the four leading states in the country in manufacturing (the northern regions of Ohio were predominant in this growth). Agriculture, increasingly mechanized, maintained its importance in the dual economic structure.

The southeastern region also focused on industrialization, particularly in iron manufacturing and coal mining; but its increasingly noncompetitive status—from labor problems, geographic distance from market centers, diminishing natural resources—brought a steady decline in production in the early years of the twentieth century, a marked decline in the 1920s. An absence of large areas of rich soil also prevented its competing agriculturally with those regions of the state—southwest, northwest, northeast, and central—that were able to mechanize large holdings of arable land.

The second generation of Flynns, Joseph and Claire, carried on a subsistence farming operation on land that had been his father's. The primitive conditions meant onerous labor in the house and in the fields for the parents and their eleven children, including the girls. Though little outside employment was available, any such opportunity was utilized to add cash to the family economy. Education was prized, and all the girls were educated beyond the available one-room schoolhouse, all had some type of career before or after marriage; yet none of the boys availed themselves of educational opportunity. The girls were, traditionally, kept close to home, and social life was simple. School and church provided almost all available social activity besides work-sharing parties. Sarah's life was characterized by stability and continuity: she was born and raised in the same house; she attended three years of high school away from home during the school week, but lived with relatives; she returned home after three summers and one winter fifty miles away for teacher training; and she lived at home again for three years of teaching before leaving to marry and reside only three miles away.

1. Knepper (1976:165, 125, 130–34); Roseboom and Weisenburger (1976:235, 218–19); Dubofsky (1977:24).
2. Knepper (1976:154–61); Jordan (1943:263–77); Dubofsky (1977:23, 26–27); Roseboom and Weisenburger (1976:255–58, 230).
3. Jordan (1943:3–5, 14, 388–97, 290).
4. Ibid., p. 281; Pershing (1942:355–59, 364).
5. Knepper (1976:174, 176–78); Roseboom and Weisenburger (1976:316, 322–25); Ohio Writers Program (1940:31).
6. Roseboom and Weisenburger (1976:334–37, 342) Knepper (1976:158, 162, 192); Ohio Writers Program (1940:33).
7. Roseboom and Weisenburger (1976:343–49).
8. Ibid., pp. 359–60; Lindley (1942:132).
9. Ohio Community Development Division (hereafter referred to as OCDD; 1974:unpaginated); Roseboom and Weisenburger (1976:219, 241, 247); Knepper (1976:154); Fess (1937:55); Roseboom (1944:15); Jordan (1943:124, 243–46, 309); Havighurst (1976:142–44).
10. OCDD (1974); Roseboom and Weisenburger (1976:221); Fess (1937:18, 55).
11. Falconer (1942:131).
12. Lindley (1942:427, 431).
13. Jordan (1943:390); Pershing (1942:378–80).
14. Jordan (1943:343–45, 335).
15. See also Faber (1982), Deitz (1981), Gallagher (1976:47, 48) and Hayes (1920:74–80). Glassie, in discussing the subsistence farm, reminded that the pioneer relied not on an idiosyncratic self but on collective traditions brought from across the Atlantic—new combinations but with Old World antecedents (1968a:195–96). Roberts described the subsistence farm as characterized by

the extended family in European folk society (1972:235). He discussed subsistence crafts and stated that they covered a wide range of activities, each requiring considerable skill and a knowledge of the associated traditional lore (248).

16. Glassie noted that both the acceptance of Chinese sugarcane (sorghum) in Ohio, Indiana, and Illinois (where sugarcane could not be grown) and the use of southern sugarcane machinery could be seen in the 1858 Agriculture Patents Report (1968a:156–57). He also included a clear diagram of southern syrup-making machinery, with a description and a long bibliographic note (107–8).

17. See also Frary (1942:35).

18. "Local officials, such as justices of the peace, sheriffs, and coroners were chosen by popular election, which permitted the participation of virtually all whites of male sex over twenty-one years of age, for, although the suffrage was limited to those who paid a state or county tax, work upon the roads was considered a fulfillment of that requirement" (Roseboom and Weisenburger 1976:70).

19. See also Gallagher (1976:67).

20. See also Cooper and Buferd (1977:125), Hagood (1939:86), White (1975), and Lozier (1975).

21. See also Hagood (1939:159), White (1975), and Lozier (1975).

22. See also Underhill (1936), Chiñas (1973:54), Niethammer (1977:xiii), and Gallagher (1976:110).

23. See also Baskin (1976:72) and Gallagher (1976:47, 48).

24. Noted also in Newell (1883), Botkin (1963), and Ise (1936:22); music and words in Seeger (1961:52).

25. See also Frary (1942:49).

26. See also Gallagher (1976:117).

27. See also Gallagher (1976:57), Frary (1942:44–47), and Riley (1981:174).

28. Note, however, that Hutslar (1981:235) quoted an 1837 Ohio newspaper as referring to a quilting frolic, apple-paring, and husking party as those "customs and pastimes of our ancesters"!

29. See Hutslar (1981: esp. 230, 236) for detail on barns.

30. See also Hagood (1939:111–14).

31. See also Baskin (1976:46) and Gallagher (1976:7).

5. Sarah and Robert: The Third Generation of Penfields in Ohio, 1927–1946

In 1927, the year of Sarah's marriage to Robert, the urban areas of Ohio were still enjoying the famed prosperity of the twenties. Industrial and construction expansion was phenomenal, and shorter working hours meant flourishing leisure activities. The dizzying rise in stock market prices led to a new model for success: shrewd maneuvering instead of painstaking effort.[1]

Notwithstanding a history of markedly different life-styles between city and country, radical dissimilarities underscored this period. The whole decade of the 1920s was a seriously depressed one for the farmer, in spite of an urban boom. There were some improvements to note: in livestock quality, introduction of new crops, increase of total farm products, development of farmer-owned buying and selling cooperatives, and upgraded agricultural research and education. By 1939 half of Ohio farms had electricity; many farmers used machinery. An improved road system, rural mail delivery, the telephone, and the radio abolished complete isolation. Local communities tended to disintegrate with these changes, and county-seat towns often became new social centers.[2]

The crash in 1929 ended the dream, in industrial and financial circles, of prosperity forever. Tens of thousands of workers were laid off. One hundred and twenty-five Ohio banks failed in 1931. Farm income dropped 42 percent, and the years 1930–33 were agriculture's worst ever. Tax revenues nose-dived, so by 1932 relief measures were collapsing; the state was unable to cope with the financial strain, and local governments had exhausted their funds. President Hoover, reluctant to use federal funds nontraditionally, moved too late.[3]

Voters reacted in 1932 by giving Franklin Roosevelt a plurality (albeit a modest one) and electing the first Democratic majority in the Ohio General Assembly in fifteen years. Major relief assistance came from New Deal "alphabet agencies," such as the Works Progress Administration (WPA) and the Civilian Conservation Corps (CCC), which employed young men and gave part of their income to their families.[4]

An economic recession in 1937–38, caused in part by a decrease in federal spending in the state, was a blow to the slowly reviving economy. It took the eruption of World War II in Europe, and subsequent spending for defense, to bring an upswing toward prosperity.[5]

Ohio responded quickly to the great demand for food and for war materials. Agricultural production increased 30 percent, coal production by 82 percent. Ohio ranked fourth in value of industrial war contracts. Wages rose 65 percent for industrial workers; women and blacks were employed in unprecedented numbers; and labor unions grew more powerful. The cost of the war was, of course, high in human terms: more than 800,000 Ohio men and women served in the armed forces, with 23,000 killed or missing. Such statistics can reflect only a small part of the social "expense." Yet there was also a sense, however temporary, of national accomplishment toward a noble cause.[6]

The fact that there are but few references in the literature pertaining to eastern and southeastern Ohio tells a story in itself. Most of the existing references are negative ones. Large areas of hilly land were abandoned because of erosion and poor cropping systems. The population of Appalachian Ohio did not grow as the rest of Ohio did through the 1930s, and it declined in the 1940s. The iron industry there declined, and only coal mining remained after 1916. World War I's coal boom turned to bust in 1929, with only a slight upward trend by 1935, and that marred by mine disasters.[7]

A lack of improved roads in southeastern Ohio retarded transportation development; in a familiar circular pattern, this inhibited growth of industry and urban centers, which in turn constricted transportation development.[8]

Sarah and Robert

Sarah and Robert began their married life in 1927 in this historic context. Life then for our country people was difficult—and soon to be more so. Sarah is the primary speaker in this chapter, with more comments this time from her daughter Anne and only a few from sisters Martha and Ellen.

After their mother's death, Robert Penfield and his younger brother were raised on their family farm by a maternal aunt, and they attended school in Harrington. Several times in his teens and twenties Robert attempted working in Columbus as a conductor on the streetcar lines, where his father worked, but he always returned "home," to the country.

After his wedding to Sarah Flynn, the newlyweds lived with her parents until the cold winter spent itself, for the Penfield farm—once sufficient to raise generations of large families—had fallen into severe disrepair through the years.

> [We stayed with my parents] till spring and we moved up here.... This house was so open then.
>
> R: What do you mean by open?
>
> Well, some of the windows, when we moved here, some of the windows were missing.... Oh it was *awful*! [20]

With the energy and determination she displays yet today, Sarah stormed the run-down farmstead (see fig. 5 for farm layout), cleaning up trash, weatherproofing the house, painting, setting out flowers, planting a garden. With characteristic practicality she also began to build her own herd of milk cows, bringing several from home, buying more at auction.

True to rural and family mores, Sarah and Robert welcomed their first child the following March. Their road was in extremely poor condition, Sarah explained: "You see, we were knee deep in mud in the winter" [3]. Therefore, she moved back to her parents' home—on an improved state road by then—and their family doctor from Johnstown delivered Sally.

The following winter Sarah and Robert were persuaded to move to Columbus to escape the rigorous climate in a house not yet habitable enough for the baby:

A Woman's Place

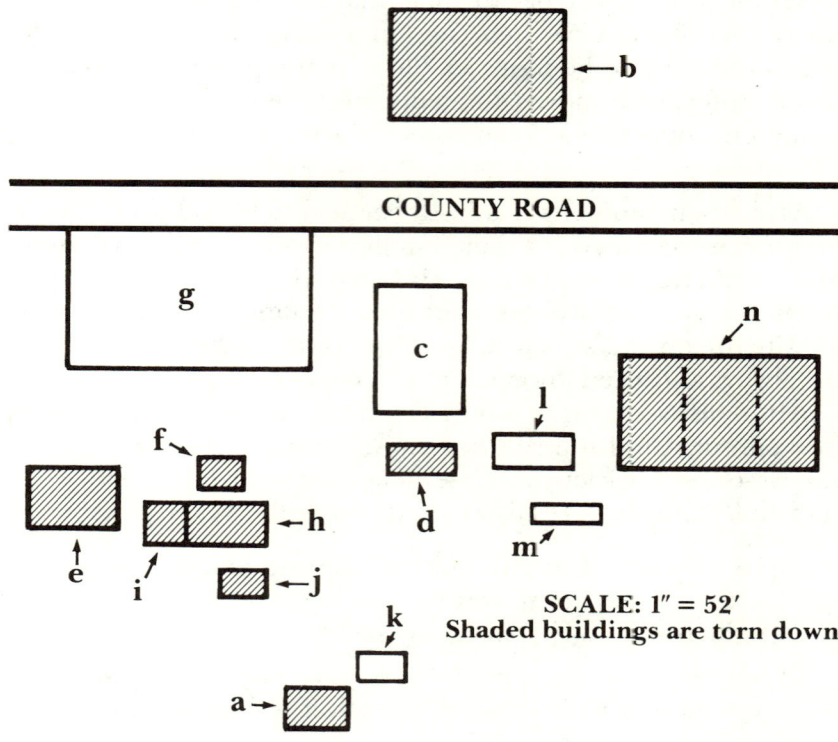

Fig. 5. Layout of Penfield farm, ca. 1900–1983. (*a*) Site of the original Penfield log cabin, built ca. 1850. Sarah helped burn it down after she married Robert. (*b*) Site of the original one-level barn (also still standing in 1927 when Sarah came to live here), unpainted, with a slate roof. (*c*) In 1900 (eight years before Joseph Flynn had his house built), George Penfield, Robert's father, had this house built for his parents by the same local carpenter who built Flynns' (with no architect, no plans, as per local custom; "You just told them what you wanted, and they built it," Sarah explained.) (*d*) Summer kitchen, torn down in 1950 when back porch was enclosed to make a new kitchen. (*e*) Hog house and pen, loading ramp. (*f*) Workshop. (*g*) Garden. (*h*) Chicken house. (*i*) Brooder house. (*j*) Smokehouse. (*k*) Springhouse. (*l*) Garage. (*m*) Corncrib. (*n*) Bank barn (see fig. 3 for description of barns of the area), built presumably at the same time the new house was. It had double doors on both sides of the upper floor (center) and a granary in the corner. The lower level was divided into a milking shed, hayracks, and horse stalls. James tore it down in about 1965.

Sarah and Robert

> The house was so cold and Sally was little and my father and mother thought that it was so cold that maybe we would get sick and they thought we ought to leave. The house was so open, you know . . . it was awful run-down. We even put the foundation on it . . . and the basement, [there was] nothing but an old cellar that's fell in. . . . The porches was rotted and fell off—they put a new porch on it. [19]

The move to Columbus was not a happy one. Robert's father had just died; work as a conductor was monotonous and confining to farm-bred Robert. Sarah remembers nothing of the stay, except that within six months they had returned:

> He didn't like it. I don't know whether I did or not, but he didn't. It was such a short time. Didn't much more'n get moved till we moved again. . . . Aunt and uncle of Robert's lived here. Of course we owned it then, see, his father had died in the meantime and the places were settled. Frank [his younger brother] took the place in Columbus, and we inherited the farm, my husband got the farm. [11]

> We didn't like it and we came back and then we lived here all our life. [19]

It must have been discouraging to begin again, cleaning, repairing, rebuilding the nucleus of a dairy herd, but Sarah is stoic and impassive in glossing over that period.[9]

Times were always hard for the farmer, so that those long, difficult years of the 1930s disastrous depression do not seem to stand out for Sarah. She mentioned it only in a historic—not an economic—sense. Her comments also mirrored feelings shared by many rural people: near-reverence for Franklin Roosevelt because of his dramatic gestures of aid to them.[10]

> Sarah: There was one [CCC Camp] at Camp Marengo, and it contained colored. It was called Camp Marengo. Don't forget that. And Camp Vernon was here [for the white soldiers] pretty close. And each camp contained 200 boys and they'd come from the bigger cities. Now Roosevelt did that for our country. And families that were on welfare they would send their sons there and it was a help to the families

at this time. Three C boys cleaned out the forest and replanted, they just planted and planted acres of trees. They reforested. . . . Oh yes. Oh yes, my brother who got killed helped to plant all those trees.

Anne: Oh, those great big spoons they would throw away in the garbage! [One of her father's jobs was hauling the camp's garbage to feed his hogs.]

Sarah: I think I have one, but I was gonna say I gave the last one—didn't I give you another?

Anne: The nice thing is these spoons would go down in a can [glass canning jar] so when you were canning—

Sarah: —They were nice and big, but they would fit into a can. Back then you couldn't, I would find them out here in the field. But then you couldn't hardly get [any like that]. Now you can get plenty of them. [1]

And later:

I just remembered lately about my brother was working there [Camp Marengo] with them; he was one of the bosses and he was telling about them growing this plant and these Negroes getting out there and smoking it and crawling around and laughing and cutting up you know and carrying on, and it had to be marijuana, I imagine, but they were using it back in those days! That'd be forty years ago, and they brought them in from Toledo and Cleveland—it was all Negroes—about 200 Negroes over there and about 200 white, a big part of them came from the big cities, Roosevelt did it to get the kids out and then you see their parents got a part of their salary to live, people were on welfare and things. Oh, just about everybody pretty nearly then.

R: Did that Three C thing work out well? Did they do good work?

Yes, oh, I don't think they ever bothered anybody. [2]

Again later:

He's the one that made the banks safe, and he put the Three C boys out in camps and got 'em off the streets, 'n so you know those bigger cities where they were getting in so much trouble and things like that. Gave 'em a salary and then he sent so much of their salary home to their parents. And he did *wonderful* things! I said we didn't know just what Roosevelt did till we stop and think of the good things that he did. 'Cause the banks were jist a mess, you know. He closed them down for a few days, and then he brought them back. Made them safe. Now you see if you've got money in the bank it's insured. [11]

Sarah referred to Roosevelt again when discussing instances of community work/socializing combinations (see below). Direct questioning about the depression's economic implications elicited comment from only sister Ellen, in her usual robust and straightforward style:

Ellen: Many people in town today go to bed hungry, and I can say this for my dad and mother's hard work. I don't think we ever went to bed hungry. And back during the Depression, I don't think anyone can realize what it was like. I graduated from high school in '34 and I went to Madison and walked the streets and asked for housework at $3.00 a week. Three dollars a week—50¢ a day! And I worked in the house, took care of an eight-room house besides working in a small grocery store besides, and was tickled to get, believe me I was tickled to get it; took that 50¢ a day, most of it, home because my dad was about to die.... There's no doubt about it, everybody, we probably had more than most and still it was rough, mighty rough. Daddy kept 200 head of sheep and the sheep, the wool in the spring paid the spring taxes and the lambs from the fall paid the fall taxes. The taxes was *that high*. They paid and sometime they couldn't pay. Sometimes they didn't have the money to pay, the wool went to nothing and the lambs went to nothing.

Martha: Wouldn't surprise me at all if this doesn't happen again. That's the history of the country.

Sarah: Just remember when it comes, you will lay down and go to sleep one night and get up the next morning and find it's here.

Ellen: My daddy took a basket of eggs down on his arm and

walked to the store there at Hillview. We lived there, oh, closer'n from out at the corner. George told him he couldn't get him three cents a dozen. He had no price. Took them back home and threw them to the hogs. Oh, it was that rough for the farmer, it was that *rough*.

Sarah: It isn't so bad—it's those people that's got themselves swimming in debt that it's gonna hurt when it comes.

Ellen: Yes, but if you don't have [land]—*we ate!*[11] But where was the money coming from to buy two girls that was in high school clothes? Where was the money coming from to buy a little coffee, a little tobacco, a little, a few of the most essential things in life? There wasn't any. There was no way of making. It wasn't relief, my dad had too much pride, I don't think he would have gone on relief, these people that sit on their behinds and don't want to work as far as I'm concerned, I'm tired of keepin' them—I'm tired of keepin' them. Carter can go and do all the keeping he wants to. He is absolutely doing everything he can against the middleman, the working-class people of this country, and he's gonna throw—he'll never get reelected I don't think. I thought he would help. The people that needed help. All he has done is help the rich bum. [17]

Life changed little thereafter: stability and continuity were maintained; the patterns of living grounded in childhood were perpetuated. Six children—three males and three females—followed the first girl in the next eighteen years. (Sarah's family of seven was closest in number to her mother's large one of eleven: Sarah's ten siblings averaged only 1.4 children, though Ellen had several miscarriages and stillborn infants.)[12]

Sarah's mother, Claire, a practiced midwife as *her* own mother had been, was with her for the birth of each of the seven, though not as principal attendant.[13] That was one tradition that Sarah did not continue.

I was never with anyone when they gave birth to a child. I had seven, but I was never with anyone.

R: Weren't you?

Sarah and Robert

No, they at that time convinced them to get to doctors. I was at the doctor. My Jim was born here in the home. Sally was born down home, that was because the roads were so bad—it was March—and she was the only one. The rest were born here. As I say, with Jim they come here with this new highway.

R: Sally was born where?

Sally was born down at Hillview at mother's. It's the first house on the other side of the store down there.

R: And did she deliver her?

No, no, I had the family doctor from Johnstown, he delivered all my babies until the last three, then I had a Doctor Farquar. That doctor is still living in Greenfield, but he had a brain operation and all and he's blind in one eye. I don't know whether [he still practices], he still has his office, I don't know— [3]

Though a concession was made to have a doctor in attendance for the births, Sarah did not go to a hospital for the deliveries.

Sarah: See a mother isn't exposed to anyone's germs [at home]. In a hospital you're exposed to the other germs and there's a lot more danger—[14]

Martha: —lot of staph.

Sarah: So much now, infection and these, and at home you're not exposed to it. Mine were all born in the home, I never went to the hospital for any of mine. Paula [the youngest] was born in this room up here. I never—she was easy—I always thought I was getting a pretty good age, "Oh! this one will be terrible." You know she was the easiest child at birth I had.

Martha: You were so used to them—

Sarah: —Yes, I took, well, I raked this whole hillside that day—I always wanted everything just spotless you know, and I came in that evening and I had ate my supper and helped do up the dishes and everything and I said to Sally I'm goin' on upstairs and I don't think I'll be down for awhile, and she said, "You said that several times," I think

> she said that to me. I didn't wait. I, they called the doctor at seven and she was born at eight.
> R: What did she mean, "You said that several times?"
> Sarah: Well, you know the little boys were playing in the yard, and, uh, Robbie was pretty good size—I think Sally must have been thirteen or fourteen, and anyway when the doctor come he said, "Is this where it is?" and the boys said, "Oh yes, they thought it was." You know that just tickled them, the boys, when they realized that was what he was coming for. That was Doctor Farquar, that's the man that has had the operation. [3]

Subsistence farming was pursued in this generation as well:[15]

> It was probably a follow-up of my parents' life, because we lived on a farm . . . you really provided nearly all of your living. . . . We've always been people that's raised lots of our living—self-sufficient. [11]

However, the complexion of agriculture had been changing, with farmers throughout the state forced to mechanize and specialize in order to compete nationally. In the southeastern region this was impossible, since large holdings of arable land and capital for machinery were not available. Robert and his neighbors, even more than their parents had been, were forced to seek available outside employment through the ensuing years;

> My husband, he owned two of the old-fashioned threshing machines. He threshed up till lately [he had been dead eleven years at the time]. . . . My husband, this man took him clear to New-ark and he built three cabins out of— [wood] picked up out in back here. You could get just plenty of them [trees] 'cause they were here when we came here; they had been growing for years. And he built one of them right in the city of New-ark. You know New-ark is a pretty big place today. [2]

> My husband worked on the highway at times, he worked, he worked for the state, and he done an awfully lot of work at

Sarah and Robert

these state parks. A lot of the work you see at these state parks, he got a team of mules and a team of horses and he did an awfully lot of that work. There were no tractors when these parks were built. . . . And then he worked on the, worked for the gas company and the pipeline. So besides farming, he did a lot of work. He was a state highway man, he worked, he operated one of those big graders sometimes. In politics I said we're right. Whenever the Republicans got in, my husband was a strong Democrat [meaning if the Democrats were in office he had a job; if the Republicans were voted into office he did not]. I don't know if he actually knew what they stood for or not. [9]

Anne: My dad was central committeeman [for the Democrats] so he had a little pull. When the Democrats were in he had a job. But we had a neighbor, dad'd always get *him* a job. He had a big family, no education, dad'd try to help him. Again, when the right politics were in, they had jobs. Dave finally committed suicide; I think that [tenuous employment] had a bearing on that. [II, 1]

Sarah contributed steadily, determinedly, to the family's subsistence and maintenance, her work providing large percentages of their cash income.[16] She raised cows to sell milk and cream, chickens to sell eggs.

Anne: We had about ten, twelve, or more milking cows at a time, and we all milked some, but mom did most of the milking. And [chuckling] she said dad always found something else to do at milking time. . . . I can remember holding the cow's tail for mom when she milked when I was just little [in rereading this account later, Anne laughed aloud as she recalled, "That's the only time I ever got smacked, the one time I let go the tail!"]. . . . We'd take our eggs 'n sometimes mom would clean chickens, we'd help with that, 'n we'd take them to town and sell them and buy groceries.

R: The eggs or chickens or both?

Anne: Both. Eggs, chickens and eggs. . . . One time I can remember we separated cream, had a cream separator, did it that way. That was quite a job! It's not hard to separate it, it's cleaning that separator after you get through. [II, 1]

Sarah contributed further to actual cash flow by teaching three different times: before her first child was born, before her third child was born (the oldest was in school; her mother kept the second one), and later when the last three were in high school. Anne remembered her making significant purchases for the farm with those monies, a "hay rake and other large equipment." Though Sarah was the one who handled all their money, it was not a position of great control, since extra cash was earmarked for necessities anyhow:

> I never gave it much thought, we just, you know, when we—'cause if the children needed clothes, they needed clothes. If they needed food, they needed food. That come first. That's what you worked for. That's what we live for, isn't it? That's what money's for. [11]

> Really to tell the truth, if either one of us had money, if we needed it, well we just never gave it a thought, really, to tell the truth. We just go one to the other. . . . I usually got my milk checks 'n we used 'em for whatever we had, you know, and our egg money 'n things, and more or less all went in one—whatever we needed for. . . . I would help pay some, I would pay so many of the bills out of them [milk checks], you know, the children's clothes. Sure, the clothes and things like that. . . . No, it wasn't my money. If there was any left over then it went for whatever we needed. . . . Yes, I don't think we ever had much money—or trouble over that, over finances. I mean we used what we had, and if we didn't have it we didn't use it, that's what I mean. [11]

Still there was a little leeway. Anne confided that if one of the children *really* wanted something for a special occasion, they knew where to go.

> Anne: Yes, she always had it [laughing], under the carpet! And she had a little change purse she carried around in her pocket. I don't know how she did it, but she always had a

Sarah and Robert

little money—from selling her eggs, people'd come to the house and buy eggs, 'n milk. [II, 1]

And at one point sentiment completely overruled Sarah's stringent frugality:

> Anne: When Sally graduated [from high school] she saw a coat she wanted *so bad*! It had fur on the collar. So mom said she gathered up every chicken she had [selling them to buy the coat]! Sally had her graduation picture taken in it.

And tears rolled down Anne's cheeks at the poignant memory of this extravagant gift—a modern day demise of the "golden goose."

Mountain Wolf Woman, the Winnebago grandmother who worked with Lurie in Wisconsin, implied that men are the providers in her culture, and spoke approvingly of her husband as "industrious." In plain fact, like Sarah, she too had always contributed large amounts to the family income; furthermore, she too exercised primary control over family finances.[17]

As the children grew older they also were expected to contribute to family maintenance.[18] The boys helped in the fields, plowing, planting, and harvesting; they fed the stock and gathered the eggs. The girls worked in the house almost exclusively, though Anne remembers riding the horses when they "took in hay," that is, unloaded it from wagons into the barn. But Sarah stood firm that her girls would not work in the fields or at any job requiring heavy lifting, determined to spare them the physical problems that she believed had resulted for her from those activities. On the other hand, jobs were circumscribed for the boys: they never worked in the kitchen or inside the house. The whole family "broke spruce" in early winter; that is, they cut hemlock branches from the woods, bundled them, and sold them to city florists for Christmas decorating;

> Jennings always broke spruce and took it to Columbus to the greenhouses . . . broke the twigs off [the hemlock]. I think they use it maybe to put in their baskets, don't they kind of pack it, but he hauls, he just made a fortune at it. He hauled truckload after truckload. . . . Oh yes, we used to just

love it; we would go out in the snow and break spruce back there on the back of the place over there. Whole bunch of kids together. But they don't buy it anymore. [2]

In order to keep bills for coal as low as possible, they burned wood primarily;

> Anne: I remember all one day we were cutting wood, that's how we used to heat our house, 'n cook, with wood, and some coal; and Dad fixed up a buzz saw onto the tractor, one of these Farmall tractors, and we sawed wood all day long, all of us kids and some of the neighbor kids, we had quite a time cutting wood. That night it caught on fire. We think it was a spark that fell down in the sawdust. I can remember mom and Jim and Bobbie and I think I helped some too, we'd go out and cut brush and pile it and burn it, mom and Jim and Bobbie mostly, cleared that field below the house, that's in corn now. It was all trees then.
> R: That's a huge field! Your mother's always been a worker!
> Anne: *Very much so!* [II, 1]

Martha, though she had never visited the Penfield family during those busy years, volunteered that it was an *extremely* difficult, arduous life.[19] Based no doubt on her own girlhood recollections, she described it as:

> Martha: Up at dawn, feed the animals, get a huge breakfast for the family, clean that up, get the children off to school, take care of the little ones, wash, iron, clean, haul water, keep the heat going, or else work in the garden, can, and so on. [8]

This was a simple, straightforward statement, but Martha often used irony and veiled sarcasm to covertly inform me of her complete disagreement with, and bitter amusement at, Sarah's romanticizing their early girlhood years. Only once, as Sarah described spelling bees and box socials, did Martha state quietly, grimly, "I never liked it. I never liked *anything* about the farm."

Anne added another realistic note:

> Anne: As far as I can remember, we had electricity, but there was a time when there wasn't any electricity in the

house, so mom did all her washing on a washboard, 'n then she'd have to carry her water up over the hill to wash![20] [II, 1]

The weekends were not much different. Ideally, Sunday is a day of rest, but, as Sarah confided, chuckling, "My husband, his hardest job was usually saved for Sunday" [13].

Much of the work revolved around feeding the ever-growing family. They butchered their own meat, at least two steers, two lambs, and up to ten hogs, as had Sarah's parents—"we still followed that out" [11]—with Sarah herself canning the meat and sugar-curing and smoking the pork hams, shoulders, and bacon. She planted and tended an extensive garden, using an old hand cultivator for planting and cultivating, and time-honored "signs" to guide her (gardening was considered a "woman's job"). Of course, the always bounteous harvest was preserved; every autumn the fruit cellar shelves boasted row upon row of gleaming jars: fruits (apples, applesauce, peaches, pears, cherries, rhubarb, blackberries, grape juice); vegetables (beets, broccoli, cabbage, corn, peppers, carrots, tomatoes, tomato juice, green beans, wax beans, lima beans, soup beans, spinach, brussel sprouts); pickles and relishes (corn relish, tomato relish, catsup, dill pickles, bread-and-butter pickles, watermelon pickles, mixed pickle, garlic pickle, sweet pickle, chili sauce); and jams and jellies (strawberry jam, elderberry jelly, blackberry jam, raspberry jam, apple jelly, peach preserves). Potatoes, apples, onions, winter squash, butternut squash, and pumpkins were stored in the cool cellar, as were crocks of sauerkraut and sausage.[21] Wheat was taken to the mill to be ground into flour, an important item in a household where baked goods were a staple item;

> I'd never leave Saturday go by without baking at least two cakes. I never baked one cake at a time. I always kept baked things for my children. They never were without jelly on their table. [9]

Anne corroborates later:

> Anne: One good thing I can remember when I was young, coming home from school, mom always had homemade hot

> bread 'n fresh churned butter and homemade jelly. Boy, that was good! And on the weekends, when she'd bake, she always baked two cakes, six, seven pies, at one time. And back then when you baked a cake, you always had to cream the shortening and the sugar together. We didn't have a mixer. And so it was quite a job to get that creamed. [II, 1]

One can safely hazard the guess that it was "quite a job" to do most anything.[22]

Another family necessity provided in large part by Sarah was clothing. Her flying fingers kept sewing machine, knitting needles, and crochet hooks busy.

> Sarah: They used to put the chicken feed in such pretty sacks—
> Anne: —You used to make towels and underwear and dresses 'n everything, prints—
> Sarah: —Yes, I've made beautiful pillowcases, I've got them with lace like this, I'd crocheted lace, and I've got a drawerful of them with lace on yet. As long as I live I'll have them. [18]
> Anne: Pillowcases, curtains, my clothes, my pajamas, clothes I wore to school, all from feed sacks. . . . I got so later on I made them myself, still feed sacks. Remember the pajamas you made me and Denny—
> Sarah: —to take you to the doctor to get your tonsils—
> Anne: —were great big—
> Sarah: —beautiful flowers, sunflowers. . . . Uh huh, dressed you good to put you in bed, when I brought you home, and dressed them in their pajamas before you went to the doctor to have your tonsils out.
> Anne: I had m' tonsils out and Denny had his tonsils out and was circumcised and [laughing] he thought a bee had stung him! [12]
> Sarah: No, I never wove any cloth. I did lots of crocheting. I have sewed carpet rags and had them wove, but I never wove any myself. Sewed carpet rags, you know.

Sarah and Robert

R: In a long strip?

Sarah: Yes, uh huh. But I never made carpets. My mother did, I can remember 'bout her covering a whole room at a time with them. Done by hand. *Lots* of work. [11]

Little cash, then, was mandatory. Sugar and shoes were purchase items, as were some school clothes—though not many after Sarah utilized the ubiquitous feed sacks. Harrington, less than a mile and a half away, boasted a general store that met many needs for their family, as it had for Robert's parents and grandparents: hardware, nails, needles, thread, corsets, shoes, bolts of material, canned goods, bologna, wheels of cheese, and her husband's great treat:

> My husband could hardly wait till Jack got them salt fish, they came in the keg. And he'd usually buy a keg of 'em. Well, I always took all the bones, I always yeah, I always boned them, you know, and then soaked them overnight. He loved the salt fish! I don't think you can hardly get them.[23] [9]

Harrington, Greenfield, Northfield, the store at Hillview—these were all a part of living in the farm community;

R: Sounds like you went to Harrington more.

Sarah: Yes, because, because that's our school there. . . .And we went to the United Brethren church there, the children went every Sunday. We usually had Dr. Farquar, as long as he was able, from Johnstown.

R: Is he the one—

Anne: —No, he lived in Harrington—

Sarah: —right beside the church.

Anne: Who's he related to, the Mains?

Sarah: No, he's, uh, Dr. Weaver is the father of Jack Klapp's wife, Donna's mother.

Anne: Oh, Donna's mother. I thought it was some relation there.

R [after discussion of their kin]: Really a lot of towns served you a little bit.

Sarah: Yes, and Harrington because they had a pretty good general store, you could get just about anything there, you know, not like now today, now Bertie keeps lettuce and vegetables and things like that. They didn't keep anything like that.

Anne: Did they keep dry goods?

Sarah: Not to amount to anything. Kept women's corsets, I know that after he died they just had scads of 'em [chuckles] to get rid of.

R: What other kinds of things did he have?

Sarah: Just everything you could think of back in those days, stored in there, they never got rid of anything. See that store went clear back, they've cut it off now, its not as large as it used to be.

R: What other kinds of things did they have besides corsets?

Sarah: Horses? Corsets! Ohh, everything, name it. Oh, I imagine they had clothes, they used to, those old stores, to keep shoes.

Anne: He kept hardware, nails and stuff like that. They used t' have a big round ring of cheese—

Sarah: —Oh, they kept the best cheese in the world.

Anne: He'd cut off a big chunk o' cheese, whatever size you'd want, he'd cut it off.

Sarah: Yeah, you could cut it off and Jackie'd weigh it and sell it to you, but you could cut off what you want. Well, Jenny [his successor] was cash and carry. It was cash and carry when Jenny, well, just lately, you know, when she died. . . . Oh yes, yes, Jenny'd keep plenty of thread 'n needles 'n things like that. . . . They kept a few bolts o' material. Always they kept a pretty nice line of materials [at Hillview]. . . . They [at Harrington] didn't handle meat. Cheese it wasn't perishable. Baloney and canned, all kinds of canned goods.

Anne: How could they keep baloney without spoiling?

Sarah: It's so highly seasoned. It's so highly seasoned, Anne. It's cooked, baloney's cooked, and it's so highly seasoned.

Anne: I don't care, I can't keep it.

Sarah: Well, you think it'll mold, but they'd just scrape the mold off and go ahead 'n sell it. The mold is s'posed to make it good. Yeah, and cheese molds, cheese, you know, molds. [12]

The children were taught the same survival skills that Sarah was taught by her parents, with one cardinal virtue overlaying all: work!

And he [her father] *should* teach us to work. Keep us out of mischief! You know they say an idle brain is the devil's workshop, and it's so true![24] [4]

They'll be lots happier that way [sharing work]. That's what keeps a family close together, is to work together. [4]

Anne: It seems that work was our—fun time, I guess. If we weren't working—that's just it—we just worked! [II, 1]

Oh, I don't [work hardest on Sunday as she had said Robert did]. I think we need a day of rest, but I do, I do work on Sunday, a lot. Just depends on the way I feel, if I'm miserable setting around I get busy. [13]

R: Don't you wonder when you got it all done?

I expect that I always—I think that's the reason I still keep busy. I, I trained myself properly. [9]

Work, then, was the hallmark of their family, even of their community, of their life. Though there was little occasion for simple visiting, still neighbors were friends-in-need; and, as in her parents' day, even work times were potential fun times as well. Threshing, butchering, and quilting still provided such dual opportunity.[25]

Anne: You always had your thrashin' back in those days, too. A big day.

Sarah: And butchering. People kind of stayed on butchering day.

Anne: A lot of people to feed that day. A lot of the time the women would come and help. [12]

A Woman's Place

Memories of one particular butchering day often elicit one of Sarah's favorite personal experience stories (see Appendix D for two other versions of this happy memory):

> I can remember one time we butchered and Robert's aunt, the aunt that raised him, came and stayed all night. I think about, uh, maybe six or seven of us slept in one bed, I know Evvie [Sarah's sister-in-law] and I and all the kids slept in one bed—we just had the three bedrooms, we had to pile up. Yeah. But anyway, you know, oh, it was such a dull day, and Evvie's brother, well, Frank [Robert's brother] told him he had to scrape the hog's hair off of the ears, and not leave one on, 'cause they always used the, the ears too. So he was, I went to the barn to milk, and Percy was sitting out there, and oh! he was just, oh, getting so cold and miserable and he wanted to know if he really had to do it, and I told him he didn't. And so he, he got hisself, "Well, I'll get it back on Frank," so he went and got a kidney, and a couple of slices of bread and he made him a sandwich out of the kidney. And just goofin' around like that, we did have fun. [12]

> I know that we as neighbors used to gather in and we'd quilt or something, you know, and have a big dinner 'n things, which we don't do any more.[26] [11]

Roosevelt's name is again linked to aid, this time involving a work-socializing incident:

> When President Roosevelt was president, down there was so much flood down on the Mississippi Valley, and the cotton got so wet 'n everything and it didn't sell good, and they gave us a project, and we made mattresses and they were *wonderful*! Oh, handmade! They were just marvelous! . . . No, I don't have 'em any more, but they sure were nice. Well, church basement's where we first made 'em. And then we finished the comforts [they were for themselves].
>
> Anne: I remember goin' with you up there to the election house.
>
> Sarah: Yeah, well, we made 'em in the yeah, the comforts in the election house, and we made the mattresses in the

church, and I don't know why that they moved 'em up into the election hall, but they did. And we'd take our lunch.... But there weren't too many that made the comforts then later. See we give $1.25 for our mattress and it was this hickory, like this, this hickory. Oh, they were beautiful! The mattresses were *wonderful*, because they were all cotton, just as soft as could be, and Mrs. Benton went and learned how to do it. So it was just like a little factory, really, that were just like they were factory done. We learned how to tie them 'n everything. We even went to the shoe shops and got white suede to tie the knots through, they made 'em so purty. Instead of using balls of cotton we got white suede. And then, after each one, if you made three mattresses, you could have three comforts, and you have a quarter for the comfort, and they were five pound comforts when you got through. Five pounds of cotton; and they were green and blue, plain green and plain blue, they were very pretty.

Anne: I can remember those green—

Sarah: —green and blue, green and blue, uh huh. And now that was Roos—that was one thing that Roosevelt did, that was the project that Franklin Roosevelt—all right, wasn't that in '32? [11]

Anne later explained that it had to have been after 1939, as she was born in 1936, and could remember it well [II,1].

Barn-raisings were mostly past history, since baling machines precluded the need for the old-style large barns.[27]

Sarah: Oh, they haven't been building barns, it seems as though they aren't able to. There's not enough money. Humph. They aren't building barns anymore, they're just putting up little galvanized sheds.... See, they started to baling, they started to baling the hay and they didn't need as large a barns. They weren't putting up those big barns. 'Cause they could put three or four tons where you—

Anne: —We still put hay up; I rode the horse.

Sarah: Yeah, uh huh. Yeah. But then it wasn't very long till dad [her husband] had a baler, and you can put several bales, several tons of hay where you couldn't put one of loose. Yes. So that done away with the big barns. [12]

Though life was generally characterized by work, still there were some institutions that answered a need for socializing, and, concomitantly, for building necessary foundations of community and reciprocity. Farmers' Institutes, the Grange, and the Odd Fellows Lodge were popular;[28]

> Well, there were fairs, they had fairs and carnivals and things like that . . . and we always had an Institute, now we always had a township Institute, Farmers' Institutes, where farmers got together, you know, for three or four days every year . . . and things like that that they don't have any more. Well, they were interesting. We always had an Institute, and things like that, little things like that.
> R: What happened at the Institute?
> Well, you bring into this place and show them the quilts and display fancy work, and, and your grain, and different things on display; it was to be like a little family fair.
> R: So all the time you were married they had them?
> Yes, uh huh. It's called Farmers' Institutes, they had speakers, and they'd have speakers to come; they'd have good speakers usually. And as I say they displayed things. Sometimes they'd have what they, they'd bring even corn in and have a contest, who could husk corn the fastest, you know, and little contests on things like that, like they do any place, you know, for entertainment, different forms of entertainment. I just happen to think that was kind of nice.
> R: What about the Grange?
> The Grange has been very successful here. We have a Grange right here in our community. I'd never joined it, but it is here. . . . Yes, I think that the country people enjoy the Grange very much, it's a nice organization.
> R: Still?
> Oh yes, we have one right on the other side of Cloverdale and we have one right here [at Hillview]. And they had one

at Greenfield; I don't know whether they still have it or not these days. [9]

Robert joined the Odd Fellows Lodge, Sarah the ladies' auxiliary, but,

> I forgot what the ladies' organization was. We weren't very good, weren't very good. We didn't do very much. [9]

There may have been another lodge as well:

> Sarah: And as I say, he belong to this lodge; he went to that years ago . . . Red Mans. Red Mans, I believe it was.
> R: Now what, what were one of those lodges for?
> Sarah: Well, they're supposed to be re-founded on a religious form, but I don't think there's any religion about 'em, do you?
> Martha: I didn't think they were founded by a religious form.
> Sarah: Oh yes. They go to religious rites when they take them in. [9]

Many social events were associated with church; the Evangelical United Brethren church at Harrington was a center not only of worship but of social life. Nearly everyone was a churchgoer, Sarah claimed, and the children all liked to go to church. Her husband was baptized and converted to the "EUBs" and liked to sing in the choir; so did the boys. Anne, however, had a slightly different perception of that religiosity;

> Anne: Yes, my dad was baptized, but I sure don't remember him *ever* goin' to church! Us kids always went; they always sent us off with a nickel or a penny. And [giggling] lots of times we came back home with 'em still in our pocket. One time when Denny got caught, he said "Well, God's got more money 'n I've got!"

The various ministers were popular and often dropped in. Sarah would invite them to dinner whenever that happened, and she invited them specifically on Sundays or after special events, such as "one of the kid's graduations" (he would preside at the baccalaureate service).

A Woman's Place

Still other activities were associated with school—4-H club, PTA, basketball games:

> Yes, and then there came the clubs then; now the 4-H Club is a great thing for the country boys and girls. The boys all played basketball tournaments and basketball games and [we went to] things like that with 'em. [9]

Once she and Robert chaperoned a boat trip on the Ohio River for the local 4-H group.

> Sarah: And then we took a few little trips, like taking the children for the 4-H down to the Ohio River for a boat ride and things like that.
> R: Things like what?
> Sarah: Well, we took a boat ride, on the Ohio River, and things like that.... This was a big boat. It had, it had an orchestra and everything else. Oh, you couldn't take them down the Ohio—or the Hocking [River]—it wouldn't be big enough. This was a big boat.... It had two or three, it had more than one, it had a nice orchestra.... This one had at least three decks that we were on. One of the boys that played in the orchestra was an albino, and that's the first time I ever saw one. He was a perfect albino. Oh, it was such a hot day!
> R: What town did you go to?
> Sarah: Either Portsmouth, or, uh, we got it at Portsmouth or some place.
> R: Did you drive down and back?
> Sarah: Yes, we drove down through that heat—that was terrible. Clear down to the Ohio River, and then we went two, three miles up the river. It wasn't fast.
> Martha: Then you went up the river?
> Sarah: Down the river. It was for the 4-H Club. [13]

The word *segregation* was not in common usage, but the practice was subtly present. Sex roles were unconsciously circumscribed, beginning at a young age. Sarah's daughters, like other girls in the community, were kept literally close to home. Anne recalls that when they rode their bicycles it was to go only "as far as the corner" [II, g], a distance of just a few hundred feet from mother's watchful eye (Sarah was even more strict than her own mother had been; see above, chap. 4).[29] The beautiful forests, the unusual flora, the outstanding cave formations were not for them to explore—and they did not. Their brothers, nonetheless, ranged the countryside at will. Sarah's son James, a skilled raconteur himself, thoroughly enjoys recounting tales of his boyhood. In one remembrance he and brother Denny had "borrowed" a neighbor's watermelons, and were evading relentless deputies by tearing through the woods at night—no mean stunt when cliffs with 75- to 100-foot drop-offs lay somewhere in that darkness. Obviously he knew the country, as the expression goes, "like the back of his hand." When questioned as to why the girls did not have similar knowledge, Jim's answer was simple: "Girls just didn't." He then added:

> James: The girls never went out with us. Ever Sunday we would spend ever minute in the woods, playin' cowboy and Indians most of the time. We'd take a big sack of old corn cobs and those'd be our ammunition. If we ran out of those [chuckling], we'd just use rocks. [III, a]

His wife, Susan, raised in the same community, broke in with:

> Susan: It wasn't proper for girls [to go away from home]. I never did any of those things. In fact, it wasn't till after I was married and had children that I ever saw any animals [be born, presumably]. And then I had to help Jim pull some lambs. [She made a face of near revulsion; yet she works as long and as hard on the farm as any man.] Why it was just last week I saw the first egg laid! My childhood was *so dull*! 'Bout the only thing I ever did do was skip school for one hour—not one day, mind you, but one hour! And then I hurried and told my mother about it, and I don't think she spoke to me for two weeks! Why, I was furious just last week 'cause I come home and found out Shelley [their daughter] had been to the barn when the vet was there. I guess it's my upbringing, but it just doesn't seem right for a girl to go to the barn. Shelley teased me and said, "Some can just take

A Woman's Place

more than others, mom." I guess girls do more nowadays than they used to. [III, a]

In the larger community, the same situation held true with adults. At threshing and butchering, the men formed a tight circle of workers outside, and the women stayed close to their traditional domain: the kitchen and dining room. They prepared and served huge meals to the male "workers"—inferring that they themselves did not work. The women then ate after the men were through. Men were usually the officers of the clubs and chairmen of the various committees, with women again in their traditional role.[30] Sarah described two such examples:

Well, another thing that we had quite a bit ... was the Parent-Teachers Organizations and things like that and we'd always have suppers and serve; the families would go together, especially the parents. [9]

In the churches they'd have what they call Ladies Aid; the ladies have their meetings, and they do things at Christmastime, make baskets for the poor children, and make quilts and things and send them across [overseas]. There's a lot of different things they have for entertainment.[31] [9]

Women were not involved in politics, or in discussions of such matters;

Anne: Dad was pretty much involved in political things. He was a central committeeman, and a township trustee, and he went to a lot of meetings about that, some in Blufton. He also spent a lot of time around the old pot-bellied stove up in Harrington at the General Store. All the men did this. But the women didn't! They stayed home and watched the kids.[32] [II, 1]

Funerals also brought families and neighbors together again, with women playing a predominant role:[33]

Sarah: I can remember back years ago when a couple o' the neighbors went and laid, they called it laying them out, and they bathed them and got them ready for the grave, instead of the undertaker taking them in and doing it, see. And the women would usually go in and bathe—

Anne: —You didn't embalm them?

Sarah: No. . . . At funerals, at funerals two or three of the ladies would always come in and help get a big dinner after the funeral. They still do that.

Anne: And set up all night.

Sarah: They don't any more though. They used to always have what they call "wakes" you know, when people died. Yes, it's been kind of done away with. You see, the older houses, years ago—of course mother was in the family is the reason [there was a wake, the last one, for her], they didn't want to go to bed, they wanted to visit—but *rats* they tell me, it was on account of rats 'n things, they were afraid something would disturb the body, and that's the reason they had those wakes and set up at night;[34] that was the beginning of it. But with my mother, you see there were so many relatives, they really didn't feel like sleeping sometimes. [12]

Sarah remembers her neighbors as being good friends;

I know that we as neighbors used to gather in and have, well, mebbe ten or twelve of the ladies would gather in and we'd quilt or something, you know, and have a big dinner 'n things, which we don't do any more. . . . Yes, even when the children were little. Uh huh. [11]

In discussing her father's jobs on the highway, Anne was reminded of a neighborhood tragedy. The story illustrates both the interdependent quality of area relationships and the large part rural telephones played in improving local communication (whether intended to or not: the ringing bell signaled not only the person who was being called but also his or her neighbors on the same "party" line, who also enjoyed the conversation, albeit surreptitiously).

Anne: One night dad was working out on the roads, there had been a terrible storm and many of the roads were blocked by branches 'n things, and I can't remember just how it happened, but Frank Dresden, Sammy's father, was

> killed. I don't know if a car came along and couldn't see them, and hit him, or what. Anyhow my dad—we had party lines back then and crank phones. We had a certain ring, a long and two shorts, or two shorts and a long, all different kinds of rings. When you'd hear the ring you'd know who was being called, so everyone [on the various party lines] would pick it up and listen. One night late the phone rang and it was my dad, calling the Foxes to tell them—they were related—to have them go and tell the family, it was late at night, that Sammy's father was killed. It often happened on other things too [listening in on the party line]. That's the way we found out what was going on. Do you 'member Ma and Pa Kettle? That's what they always did. [II, 1]

When Sarah named the various families whom she referred to as neighbors, she included approximately fourteen, in a geographic area roughly two miles west, one mile southwest, and one mile south; about eleven families in or on the way to Harrington, one and a half miles east, were also added:[35]

> R: Now of all those people that you told about—which ones did you know the best?
> Well, I knew the one as well as the other. We just all, you know, went to the same school, same church, same gatherings, you know, together and things. [20]

In discussing those neighbors, she again mentioned the Odd Fellows Hall and Red Men's Hall, the school meetings, and Farmers' Institutes that "everybody attended and that you met at those places."

> We had those things that we don't have any more that people attended, that they don't have any more.
> R: So people don't tend to be as close?
> No, they just kinda moved away from it.
> R: Did you get together with the women?
> Well not too often after that, huh uh.
> R: No, I mean before.

Well, the church had a Ladies Aid. They still have. Yes, I used to go to that.

R: What did they do?

Ladies Aid? Nothing much; sing a few songs and have a little Scripture or something maybe, and that's it.

R: Did the women get together, like did you ever go over and have coffee at somebody's house?

Well *they* did. [20]

And Anne does not remember her mother "visiting around with the neighbors."

Interestingly, she almost always referred to her neighbors as "John Doe and his wife." When questioned, she could often recall the woman's name, however. It was always, as with her own forebears, the woman's name she did *not* know. For example:

R: Where did the Foxes live [pointing to map]?

Right up here, next neighbor up, up there, the next house right up there. Peter, he's dead and his wife is dead, but Clyde, his son is living there.

R: Oh yeah. Peter and—what was her name?

Ellen.

R: Who else?

... Dan Klapp.

R: What was her name?

Maude. And then on down to the next house—her name was, uh, well, I never did see the—the old man died before I moved here, but that old lady was living, but I can't think of her name down there next to the house. I can't think of her name. On down to the next house then was Jerry Kirks'. They were good friends of ours. Now is that as far down as you want? ... Now you go out this way and there has been so many changes in that house, but I think Harry Little and his wife lived there when we moved here. Their name was Little and his wife's name was Christina [and so on].

And, sadly: "They're all dead. All the folks that I knew" [20]. When questioned as to whom she would call on, family or neighbors, if she ever had any kind of problems, she was quite emphatic about her answer of "family," but, afraid that that reflected on her trust in her neighbors, she quickly added:

> Oh, I wouldn't say that I'd just—because my neighbors are wonderful, I mean—but, uh, I think that's what families are for, don't you? Yeah, I think so, that's what families are for. [12]

Family, relatives, kin: most often these formed the nucleus of both work and social groups.[36]

> We were always having company.... Oh, we had lots of company. Lot of it, lot of it would be relatives. We had company, you know, like my husband's brother would come on Sunday and we'd spend the day together or some of my family and little things like that.[37] I think we were always happy when we had company and went places together. And there would be programs at church and we would all get ready and go to and the basketball—we went to the basketball games; we'd take them when there was basketball in other places. Things like that. [14]

> My sister-in-law, Evvie, was... just someone you could depend on. We always had a bushel of fun [laughing]! She come one time and stayed, and we decided to go down to Middle Fork Church to a Protracted Meeting, they called it, you know?
> R: A what?
> They had what they call Protractive Meeting,[38] and the minister will give the sermon and they try to call people to the altar. They call it the Altar Call, 'n everything. Well, anyway, Evvie had a pretty good voice, and we talked her into singing. Well they had nothing but old coal-oil light, you know. And oh, we really, had some awful good times. And I know when we got there we didn't think that they'd have anyone to sing, and the Allen family, from over by Valiant, had come, and they were good singers, y' remem-

Sarah and Robert

ber [laughing]? We got up there and Evvie couldn't see the words [hard laughing]! She'z so embarrassed, remember? And we just laughed and laughed after, no harm, but I mean we just got so tickled! Because, um, the lights were so poor they couldn't see [laughing] the words—and these good singers were there, y' know. Things like that, we had lots of good times. [12]

Mebbe we'd get up in the middle of the night and visit; and I know that one night [during a butchering party/visit] Dick's aunt, she had something she wanted to tell us and she woke us up at two o'clock, and she said she knew when morning come she'd forgit to tell us. So she woke us up at two o'clock to tell us, whatever it was. [12]

Travel held no great fascination for Sarah. The few trips they did take, other than the 4-H boat excursion on the Ohio River, were not of the sightseeing variety. (Of couse, as Anne pointed out later, it was a large deterrent that no matter where you went or what time you got home, the cows, at least twelve or more, had to be milked, all by hand—several hours' work.) Columbus was the northernmost destination when they visited back and forth with Sarah's sisters, or with Robert's brother, Frank, and his wife, Evvie;

Oh, we went to Columbus lots. Oh yeah. . . . We had relatives in Columbus, we'd just go up there to visit, you know, and talk. That's as far north practically as I've ever been. I don't care if I ever go any farther or not.

R: How about south?

It's all right either direction, I think [meaning that *no* direction is good, for her]. [13]

To the east they visited Martha and her first husband several times in West Virginia, about 140 miles:

Sarah: We've been down to West Virginia, Martha lived down in West Virginia, and we went down there several times when you were living down there. Was it there? We went beyond the Ohio River. You lived almost close to Maryland, didn't you?

149

> Martha: Oh no!
>
> Sarah: About 35 miles [from Maryland], wasn't it?
>
> Martha: Grafton, West Virginia, one hundred miles Parkersburg south.[39] [13]

To the west she had been near Dayton, to visit her son in the Veterans' Hospital (see chap. 6, below). And to the south, she drove with her husband and two youngest children in a nightmarish trip to accede to the man's dying wish to see Florida. (They drove down in two days, arrived in Jacksonville, he looked around from the back seat of the car, and they drove straight home. The two daughters argued the whole time. They had left on Sunday and were back home on Wednesday.) Thus all her trips, too, revolved around the hub of life: family.

One family member who was a great source of help and companionship was Sarah's mother, Claire, who continued to live in her own home at Hillview until after all Sarah's children were born. Supportive of all her ten living children and twenty-one grandchildren, she presumably felt special empathy for Sarah's position of having the only large family. One son also lived close by, and the others remained within a fifty-mile radius except for Martha, who left the state after marriage. Several years after her husband's death, Claire moved to Madison so her two youngest daughters could attend nurses' training school there. She rented the farmhouse, which proved to be an unfortunate decision:

> Mother rented to a minister, and the house burned down.... Well, he had insurance on his—it was just one of those one-horse preachers. Lot of people thought he collected insurance on everything. I don't know whether he was careless or whether he intended it. Anyway he was smart enough and I wouldn't have ever thought of it, he had sent his wife and he had a child or two to West Virginia and he jumped out the window, but he had thrown a mattress out to jump on. Isn't that unusual? Because Wayne Souder is a neighbor there was the first person there and he said that's what happened.
>
> R: So did they ever find out how the fire started?

I don't think they ever tried to. I don't think they ever do much about it.

R: Was he farming?

No, no, he just moved there. He was just preaching around here and I don't know whether it had a circuit or not. I just didn't know too much about him. Just where he could get a sack of flour and things around his field. [19]

With Martha nodding agreement, Sarah described their mother as remaining exceptionally alert and active throughout her life:

She stayed well, mother stayed well, until she practically had a heart attack and they [the youngest girls] took her. She stayed pretty well most of her life.

R: How old was she?

Well, she was seventy-one, wasn't she, or was she seventy-two? I think she'd have lived to be a *great* old lady, but she took asthma, which was bad. She got a heart condition; but she was a *very* healthy woman, very much well throughout her life, she was very seldom sick. [4]

The seasons' changes were marked by work changes and holiday celebrations: Valentine's Day—mostly recognized at school—and Easter and Christmas seem to stand out.

Anne: Well, we used to take, before we had artificial dyes, we would make onion skins and color some of the eggs that way—it makes a pretty reddish brown color. I can't remember what else we used for color. Then go out and gather grass, well it wasn't actually grass, it was out in the field, spring wheat is what it was. Pretty 'n green. Looked like heck when it wilted. Then about the time Denny and Helen and Paula came along we had the baskets boughten from Murphy's 5 and 10, and artificial dyes. I can remember when they'd thrash, and put the wheat in the bins, it was so sweet and good. We'd chew it, probably the closest thing we had to chewing gum. Had a real good flavor. We had some little aluminum pans that the Three C Camp used. Dad hauled their garbage to fatten his pigs—it's against the law t' do that now—and they'd throw silver and pans away.

> Mom's still got some of them. Little pans about this tall [indicates about four inches] and about this round [about five inches]. We used 'em for cereal. I think we used those for Easter baskets.
>
> R: Did you have candy?
>
> Anne: Jelly beans. We always all wanted the black ones. The baskets were hidden, just out around the yard. [II, i]

The house was decorated for Christmas:

> And then we usually had Santa Claus for the children.
>
> R: Who was Santa Claus?
>
> Oh, their father or different ones. Robert would usually pretend that he was going someplace maybe and come back, or somebody in the family.
>
> R: You mean someone would dress up—
>
> —Oh yes, uh huh.
>
> R: We never did that.
>
> Oh, didn't you? Oh, it's lots of fun!
>
> R: Then what happened; did Santa Claus supposedly come during the night when the kids were asleep?
>
> Well, sometimes and sometimes we had him—he came in person. But I had a set too of the manger, you know, the camels and so on and so forth. I have a set of those too. And I had candles for the windows.
>
> R: Did you use cranberries strung on the tree?
>
> No, they do that [fall off] so quick after you get them on those little—make kinda a mess too, especially if you had carpet or anything . . . but we did use popcorn. [21]

Christmas was a double celebration, since it was also Robert's birthday:

> Sarah: And at Christmas, sometimes, we'd be so excited over Christmas that, one night you [to Anne] and Janie stayed up all night, and, what was it y' did? Christmas, y' know, you never went to bed? Well, you—
>
> Anne: —the time that I bought dad's cigarettes? I bought him a carton of cigarettes—which I wouldn't do today—for

his birthday. He knew by the way it was wrapped what it was. He takes it and unwraps it and takes all the cigarettes out and filled it with paper. Mom told me what he'd done. I got the package and put the cigarettes back in. When came time to open it, he thought he would have a joke on me. I had a joke on *him*. I can still remember [laughing] seein' his face! [12]

Thus life continued, its rewards and its demands a counterbalancing daily seesaw. The days hurried, and Sarah ran to catch them.

SUMMARY

Ohio continued to diversify, and improved both farm and industrial output, until the depression hit every sector so hard that only New Deal federal relief measures forestalled disaster. World War II, with its tremendous social costs, did bring economic upturn, though not to Appalachian Ohio, where population decline reflected continued unemployment problems.

Sarah and her husband continued the subsistence farming operation carried on by previous generations of Flynns and Penfields. Sarah carefully maintained the patterns of living established in her childhood. She and Robert raised a large family, and everyone—husband, wife, and children—contributed to the family economy. Sarah considered her parents, particularly her mother, a model for living and for supplying necessary physical, spiritual, and emotional needs to her own seven children. Close-knit neighbors traded work chores and socialized at school and church activities, but the extended family remained the dominant base of social and work groups.

1. See Roseboom and Weisenburger (1976:359–60) and Knepper (1976: 192–96).

2. See Roseboom and Weisenburger (1976:359–60) and Falconer (1942: 120–21, 123–32).

3. See Roseboom and Weisenburger (1976:360–62) and Knepper (1976: 196–97).

4. See Garber (1942:471), Roseboom and Weisenburger (1976:361–70), and Knepper (1976:199).

A Woman's Place

5. See Roseboom and Weisenburger (1976:369–71).

6. See ibid., pp. 371–73, and Knepper (1976:205).

7. See Falconer (1942:134); OCDD (1974); Weed (1942:185–90); Ohio Writers Program (1940:35).

8. Falconer (1942:125).

9. See Hagood (1939:75–76).

10. See also Gallagher (1976:144).

11. See Frary (1942:34) for similar details.

12. The issue of birth control is considered so personal that there is no general knowledge of methods used by individuals in the community. Mothers do not pass on information on this subject even to their daughters. Some do discuss menstruation with their daughters (though Martha related that her mother did not tell her *anything* [as in Gallagher 1976:126, 169]). Anne believed that all the women in her mother's generation relied only on nursing their youngest child to prevent conception. "I know they always said Zulu [a neighbor] nursed Betsy up until she went to school!" [II, 1]. See Gallagher (1976:88–89, 170–71) and Hagood (1939:118–27) for similar belief. See Bourguignon (1980:3–4) and Harrell (1981) for cultural perspectives; see Friedman (1982) for scientific underpinnings.

13. See also Hagood (1939:111–14).

14. See also ibid. (113) on birth practices in the rural south in the 1930s. See Romalis (1982) and Kitzinger (1979) on a return to the philosophy of having the delivery in the home.

15. See Glassie (1968a:196) and Gallagher (1976:47–48).

16. See also Hagood (1939:84–88) and White (1975). Riley (1981:87) noted that the census category of "Not Gainfully Employed" was clear and official illustration of societal views of "woman's work"; it reflected a moneyed society that tended to equate useful work only with paid work, a condition that still exists today, even when, as in the case with many rural women, there is cash money involved.

17. Lurie (1961:102). See Leghorn and Parker (1981) for a multi-racial, multi-ethnic view of women's work and the resultant economics, e.g., chap. 5, "She who sows does not reap." Thomas interviewed 56 farm women across the United States, and found they would always say they "helped" on the farm, when clearly they, too, had "managed the dairy herd and the poultry, raised all the family's fruits and vegetables, and participated fully in planting and harvesting the field crops. To call all this work 'helping' serves the useful social function of keeping male pride intact" (1981:xiii).

18. See also Cooper and Buferd (1977:39, 46, 81), Hagood (1939:106), and Hicks (1976:45).

19. See also Hagood (1939:107), White (1975), and Lozier (1975).

20. See also Frary (1942:27).

21. A far greater number and variety of foods there than reported in Hagood (1939:103–4).

22. See also Hagood (1939: chap. 8).

23. See also Ise (1936:275).

24. For similar kinds of statements, see also Baskin (1976:74) and Gallagher (1976:80). See Baxter (1978:24): "Industriousness not only led to a happy life [in the 1920s], it was a virtue in itself. And the work ethic is still with us."

25. See also Hagood (1939:175–77), Jorgensen (1962:45), Frary (1942:42–48), Hicks (1976:23), White (1975), and Lozier (1975).

26. See also Frary (1942:47–48).

27. See Hutslar (1981) for barn history in Ohio.

28. See also McMillen (1974:153, 161, 163) and Frary (1942:70).

29. See also Underhill (1936), Chiñas (1973:54), Niethammer (1977:xiii), Gallagher (1976:110), and Hicks (1976:44).

30. However, McMillen (1974:153), in discussing his parents' membership in the Pleasant Hill Grange Number 598 at Huntersville, Ohio, in Hardin County, said the Grange was the first secret organization to admit women on an equal basis with men because of men's and women's partnership in farm affairs. Since, as I stated earlier, the only woman (his mother) mentioned in his book is at best a food-dispensing shadow, one could assume the "equal basis" meant they were permitted to cook and serve the dinners for the combined membership. See also McMillen (1974:passim, esp. 152, 157), Lurie (1961: viii), Underhill (1936:53), and Hicks (1976:42–46) on circumscribed sex roles. See also Gallagher (1976:57) on threshing segregation.

31. See also McMillen (1974:156).

32. See also Hicks (1976:42).

33. See also Baskin (1976:45).

34. Evans (1957:289–94) described traditional Irish wake customs.

35. See also Hagood (1939:170), where "community" meant a two- to three-mile area in the South of the 1930s.

36. See also Jorgensen (1962:45) and Hicks (1976:35–36).

37. See also McMillen (1974:150), Hagood (1939:175), Chiñas (1973:48), and Jorgensen (1962:44).

38. Or Protracted Meeting, that is, extended, drawn out. See Lee (1892: 789): "In those early days [1830s] of grace and power protracted meetings did not run into the length of weeks and months that they do now [1892]. People were less accustomed to hearing the Gospel, and they acted more promptly."

39. Even though Sarah did not often travel, she was quite accurate. Grafton is almost due east and only thirty miles from the eastern border of Maryland.

6. The Years of Change, 1947–1983

Ohio's population increased rapidly in the postwar years, 22 percent in the 1950s. But the trend toward suburban living, begun in the 1930s, further exacerbated financial problems of the cities by removing tax income bases without a corresponding drop in service demands.[1]

The farm economy lost importance, and the state's rural population stabilized. Ohio's national standing had dropped substantially: from first place in value of agricultural products in the 1870s to only fourteenth place in the 1970s. Agriculture accounted for only 8 percent of the total value of all Ohio production, whereas manufacturing accounted for 89 percent. Farm life evolved, and, because of transportation and communication advances, was no longer isolated or self-sufficient.[2]

Losing its early industrial leadership as well, Ohio became less and less competitive with other geographic locations: at least 21 percent of its plants were obsolescent; traditional urban industrial centers had no expansion potential; and labor unions had boosted wage costs. The transportation network continued to be important: though rail traffic was modest, water transport flourished, the interstate highway system was excellent, and air facilities became widespread.

Education leaders faced increasing problems, for example, financial pressures, racial integration, and recognition of discrimination against females. Although there was new emphasis on vocational education, public college and university systems catapulted in size.

Religion, always difficult to report and then to assess statistically, apparently experienced an increase in church membership in the 1950s, which leveled off in the 1960s. Fundamentalist Protestantism received heavy support from the southern migrant population centers, such as Cincinnati, Akron, and Cleveland.[3]

A Woman's Place

In southeastern Ohio, farms have continued to go out of production as farmers commute to town and city jobs. Many of the remaining farms are marginal: though occupying 33 percent of the state's total land area, Appalachian Ohio received only 15 percent of farming income in 1977. Population figures for that area again showed a decrease in 1950 as a percentage of the larger Ohio populations, with an actual numerical decrease in the 1960s. Projections for the 1980s do show a stabilizing trend. The reflected outmigration indicated both a lack of job opportunities and a lack of large urban centers with their attractive kinds of services. In 1970 Ohio's Appalachian population had a lower median income than other Ohioans, with twice as many below the poverty level.

A national shortage of energy resources finally brought a revival of the coal industry, though poor mining practices of the past have not yet been completely ameliorated, for example, unreclaimed strip mines, polluted streams, acid runoff. Other mineral resources still hold promise of development. Poor cutting practices have hurt a potentially valuable timber resource, though remaining forests have encouraged a number of small-scale wood products industries.

Natural features—rugged topography, deep valleys, woodlands—are being developed as recreation attractions to overcome their negative impact on other aspects of progress; for example, a highway transportation network. Rail facilities are nearly abandoned, and air facilities are minimal, the least covered area in the state.[4]

In Sarah's own area, too, change took place, gradually but inexorably. World War II factories had introduced a whole new spectrum of employment opportunities in distant towns. Commuting began to be a way of life for many local residents, a compromise between forgoing rural life for better money or fighting poverty to preserve family land. The natural beauty and open country of the region attracted a renewal of recreation and leisure-time devotees, and "summer people" began to bring rural residents into further contact with different customs and viewpoints and life-styles.

The Years of Change

With this sociocultural background, the story of Sarah's middle and later years unfolds. Most of it was volunteered by Anne, since little could be recovered from Sarah herself. It is difficult to assess the reasons for this: they are undoubtedly very personal ones. The fact that it was a time that included transition and painful, traumatic loss is certainly one aspect. Sarah included *no* vignettes of individual children in the interviews, with one exception—after questions posed about their schooling—which concerned her eldest, Sally:

R: Which of the children was the best student?
Well, if they had a first place it was always Anne, and the boys none of them liked school. None of them was too good because they just didn't want any part of it. But Sally was valedictorian and Anne was valedictorian.
R: After Sally graduated from high school, did she go to work?
Well, I think she worked at the restaurant in Blufton a little while. . . . She went to Washington and she typed for the, was it the Coast Guard? Anyway, she typed for the government in some project and a lot of these girls—they lived in big hotel places like, you know, but she didn't stay too awfully long. She got awfully homesick.
R: How long was she there?
I don't remember. A year or something like that. At that time Robert's brother had a little boy, he was fourteen, and he took awful sick and he died at that time and she got so homesick that I think it made it worst for her. Frank had a boy that—Robert's brother had a young boy and he took sick, and that bothered her an awful lot at that time, and she got really homesick and didn't stay as long—she went to really stay—she didn't stay anyway and she came back and she wanted to take this beauty course so she went to Columbus and took a beauty course, and she met Will there. She—he lived right across here [in their township], but they met in Columbus. They ate lunch at the same place. He had

worked at a Kroger store, I believe, when they were eating lunch usually at the same place and they got acquainted.

R: How did you feel about her going to Washington?

I thought, well, she was going to back out after she got to Columbus to take the train that night, and we encouraged her to go on and practically forced her on, because if she backs out it won't be good for her, because she wanted to go so bad. And when we got there and saw this little child—we didn't know how sick it was—and she went on. Anyway she didn't stay too long. She's pretty much a home girl, but she had good experience anyway. [21]

Sarah was apparently nondirective with her children's vocational choices.

R: What did you want your children to be? Did you have any particular ideas for them—

—Well no, because they really selected what they wanted to do anyway.

R: Did you hope that one would be something special?

A doctor, a lawyer? No I didn't hope for that because I didn't think they'd get that really that far, because I would want them to be whatever they, you know, they thought they could be. Now George and Paula had Billy to sign, the boy they're raising, he isn't capable of it. They had him to sign up for, what, high school chemistry, and that's such a hard one, and I said, "For land's sake, if he doesn't get it don't criticize him for it," because maybe they couldn't get it themselves right now. They have been out of school so long. He's having a terrible time with it. He's got a woman teacher and every bad thing—I think, I think it takes a man maybe for that—and he didn't like her to begin with even before he went into the course, so he's having trouble. He hates school you know. He'll probably never use it. I think George wanted to at least send him to agricultural college. [21]

Vignettes concerning the other six children had to be provided by Anne. Robbie, the second child and Sarah's eldest son, quit school to work on the farm, probably after his sophomore year.

The Years of Change

The horses—Anne referred to them as a "good team, especially for logging"—were considered his, "he was so good with them" [II, 1]. After marrying a local girl, he lived in an apartment in Blufton for a short while, then was drafted into the Korean War.

Anne: I can't remember him too well. . . . He was never much to leave the place. If we would go to Columbus for the day he would never go along. In fact he had never been anywhere much until he went in the service.
R: Why did he go in?
Anne: Drafted.
R: Bet that was hard.
Anne: It was. I think that's what happened to him—homesick. He come back, really sick, and was sick from then on, so I don't know. . . .
R: Wasn't it a stomach problem?
Anne: Colitis, ulcerative colitis. . . . They said he'd gotten a germ in Korea, from maybe the water or somethin' and they couldn't clear it up. I guess this happened to a lot of the soldier boys there. Rob was in the marines.
R: So he was just enough older that you really didn't ever do much with him?
Anne: Never.
R: Which one did you seem mostly to pal around with, of your brothers and sisters?
Anne: Well, probably Jim, mostly my brothers [Jim and Denny]. 'Cause he played basketball, and I would go with the school team to basketball games 'n things like that. Helen and Paula was so much [younger] that, that—there's just too much age difference there. [II, 1]

After Robbie left, Jim, three years younger, became the "leader."

Anne: In the evenings when we'd come home from school we'd go out and gather in the corn, and then we'd go hazelnut hunting.

161

> R: You say you don't think there are any hazelnuts around any more?
>
> Anne: No, I haven't seen any hazelnuts in years. On weekends we used to go up on the corner from our house, and set up a stand, and we'd sell pumpkins, 'n Indian corn, cider, eggs, anything we'd have. We used to make quite a little bit of money, and we were quite pleased. Sunday evening, and Mom and Dad would let us, that was our money, share it.
>
> R: Share it? How would you know who got it?
>
> Anne: Well, Jim usually took care of the business part of it [chuckling]. He was the one that went around and gathered the apples and had the cider made.
>
> R: Was he easy with you little kids?
>
> Anne: Oh yes. I remember a funny incident happened with him, one time he was up at the general store, and there was a man by the name of Klapp, Dave Klapp, lived in Harrington, he was in there—they would get their oil in bulk, in big drums—and it had a pump, and handle like on it, and people'd take their containers there and get their oil that way. And he was standing, this Dave Klapp, was standing up next to this barrel, and he had a, a newspaper folded up in his pocket, and [laughing], and Jim didn't realize what he was doing, he was messing around with that handle, and crankin' it, and that oil started coming out of it, it was *right* so that newspaper was under it, a faucet, and all that oil [laughing hard now] goes down that newspaper right down into Dave's pants [more laughing]. Dave just about—! [II, 1]

And her voice trailed off into laughter. Obviously Anne has a delicious sense of fun, and chuckles joyously over the humor in everyday life. Generous and helpful, Anne is an exceptionally fine person. She is also shy and quiet, even passive, and talks little as a rule to most people. But her ability to perceive comedy overcomes her normal reserve—and is undoubtedly a saving buffer from the less-than-happy aspects of daily living.

The Years of Change

Recounting grade school experiences in Harrington brought to mind a funny memory of her first teacher:

Anne: I can remember Sam [a neighbor] was my school bus driver. . . . I can remember some of the kids. Bill Samuelson, Beth Durk, I graduated with Bill, went twelve years with him. Beth dropped out and got married in her sophomore or junior year.

R: How many were in your graduating class?

Anne: There was another one, Frankie Heilner, started with him, too. There were, there's five of us, six [graduated in that class].

R: Was that the normal-sized class, five, six?

Anne: Uh huh.

R: Did you always have three classes or more together?

Anne: Yes. In high school too. There's [first], second and third in one room, fourth, fifth, and sixth in another, and then those rooms were upstairs to the right, in the old school building, then downstairs, the seventh, eighth, ninth; and we thought we were really big shots when we went down to the seventh grade. Then we had what we called an eighth grade graduation, there at Harrington, and we had a little ceremony, at night. Then we, we would change classes; we had a home ec and a, well, there were three rooms, there was an upstairs with a library, at one end of this one room, where usually we had history and English classes. Downstairs was the science and the other one was the Latin–home ec room, and we changed classes during the day, after we got down to the seventh grade. . . . First school teacher that I can remember is Mrs. O'Grady, she taught the first three grades at Harrington.

R: What do you remember about her?

Anne: Well, she wasn't a very neat lady in her dress, and, uh, she just wasn't very clean. She would have some of the kids, we would have to take lunch boxes, sacks, to eat, we didn't have a cafeteria back in those days, and she would have different kids in the family bring her lunch, and she would pay to have—I 'member that.

R: Was it a good thing when you had to bring her lunch, or was it bad?

Anne: Well, I never brought her lunch, we never packed her lunch, it was a family by the name of Dresden, I remember, did that.

R: I wonder if they thought that was an honor or a chore.

Anne: I *think* they probably thought it was an honor to do it. She didn't seem to be a very capable person. [Begins to chuckle.]

R: What was the incident you remembered about her?

Anne: Just part of her, she just, uh, even in her dress she wasn't very neat, and she [laughing] lost her underwear one day!

R [laughing]: You mean it just, walking along, fell off?

Anne [laughing hard]: It dropped off!! [More laughing.] I was in the first, second, or third grade, and probably the third to have remembered it. But it did happen. We were huntin' everywhere to find a safety pin!

R: Was she embarrassed?

Anne: Oh, I think so, yes. I should think so. I think as I remember, though, she was—I learned to read and write from her—she was a good teacher that way, but she was just very, just wasn't very neat. [II, 1]

Denny, three years younger than Anne, had a near disaster when he was vey small, she recalled. Sally had driven "the kids" to Harrington in their old car, but as often happened in the early days of driving (and she had just acquired her license), the car would not start. All the children heaved to, pushing on the back bumper, and when the car lurched forward, five-year-old Denny forgot to let go, and was dragged and skinned up badly till screams and shouts stopped the horrified driver. Another time Denny was the object of a frantic lost-child search in the countryside. Late in the afternoon he crawled out from under the summer kitchen, where he had enjoyed a long summer's

The Years of Change

nap, oblivious to the serious concern of a family who lived on the edge of deep woods and high cliffs [II, k].[5]

The two youngest children were girls, born when the oldest child was in high school. Anne still marvels that Helen is so outspoken: "I don't know where she gets that!" Even as a youngster she was independent and assertive. To everyone's shock, when their father was greasing her all over for a case of the "itch" they had all caught at school, she "got mad and hauled off and cracked him!" [II, k].

Paula, as the youngest of seven, was no doubt everyone's pet. Once when queried as to how she managed to get a treat out of her mother on a trip to town, she saucily announced to her envious siblings: "Why I just cry and cry and cry, and then I get what I want!" [II, k]. Both Paula and Helen were (and are) vivacious, beautiful, and extremely active. Again according to Anne, one was "more a daddy's girl, and one was more a mom's girl," whereas Anne felt close to both parents;

> Anne: I was close to both. But in different ways. We soon learned which one we could work, which one you could get what off of. One for one thing, one for something else. I think dad, well, he kinda raised himself. The neighbors were good to him, the Kellys, the Dresdens, the Foxes. His aunt wasn't too good to him. She liked Frank [his younger brother].... If anyone was frivolous it was probably dad. He was the one that bought candy and the nuts and the oranges. I remember one time he bought me a dress! I remember goin' mushroom hunting with him. He'd race us and things like that. One time he brought home a new car, after he had gone to town for groceries! [II, l]

Thus we have our only hint of Robert the man. He remains a shadowy figure, for Sarah's references to him have been almost all indirect, except for describing his employment (chap. 5, above) and for a comment on the father's role:

> R: Did your husband work with your girls the same way your father did with you?
>
> Oh, I always felt free to go to him if I had a problem. I always felt that he had good advice, and then when he

would, you know, correct them 'n everything, it would have more effect. Yes, they always feared their father, you know, just as we're supposed to fear Jehovah today; you know the Bible says that we must fear Jehovah, and do, you know, what's right, and whenever, even today, I think that they pay a lot of attention to him. [Use of present tense is puzzling here: he had been dead for thirteen years; presumably she meant they remembered and honored his values.] I think he wanted what was right for them. [4]

(A younger daughter, Helen, was intrigued by my use of the tape recorder to gather her family's history, and attempted to collect her own information from her mother. But she too was frustrated by the omissions. Apparently baffled, she wondered aloud, "I can't find out *anything* about dad!")

The Penfield children grew, and one by one they left home to marry and start homes of their own. Sarah taught school one year when the two youngest were in high school.

Death brought the most drastic change. First Sarah's sister-in-law and close friend, Evvie, was killed in an automobile accident. Five months later Sarah's oldest son, Robbie, died from the stomach disease he developed in the Korean war, and in four more months, Robert died of cancer.

Finally the youngest—and last child at home—married. Paula and her husband lived with Sarah for two years while they both worked in Blufton, till their first child was born and they moved to town. After a lifetime of being surrounded by family, Sarah was alone.

The strenuous daily routine continued, however. No matter that the table was set for one instead of nine. The huge garden was still planted and tended, the fruit cellar still loaded with the bounty of Nature and her partner Sarah. After all, children and granchildren needed to eat. Amenities softened the stark house, as James installed the first bathroom, Dennis, kitchen carpet, and Adolph, a kitchen countertop. A freezer supplemented the still-loaded shelves of the cellar, improving the flavor of those foods that she deemed were better frozen: raspberries, cherries, strawberries, apples, peaches, broccoli, cauliflower, corn, lima beans, peas, onions (if they were spoiling or sprouting), and, of course, all the meats.

Two jobs interrupted the normal routine briefly. While baby-sitting for her youngest daughter in Blufton, she was approached by the local priest, and agreed to teach in the Catholic school there for one year.

> Teachers were really scarce [1965], and I said I would. They needed teachers real bad. Then they went back to the Catholic teachers the next year. They want sisters if they can get 'em. They don't allow you to teach religion. It was nice to work with them, though, I just loved them. [7]

The "right" party was in again, and, because her daughter worked for the county judge, Sarah was made postmistress of nearby Harrington:

> Didn't you know that the road workers and all, that they change with politics? It's a political job. I just substituted for, I don't know, maybe five, six months till they took the post office away. . . . They had talked for years of taking it away, you know. To tell the truth there was only one family that weren't reached on the, uh, that they, the man didn't reach on the route. [9]

The old store, next to her birthplace at Hillview, was reopened, but its proprietor was soon dissatisfied. Her son Jim approached her with the idea of running it, but she preferred not to be so involved;

> The lady that owns the place, she said she'd rather work out, and well, Jim talked about taking it over and I told him it wasn't worth it. He wanted me to get interested in it, and I told him, no, I didn't want to be tied down to anything like that, so she just sold everthing out and closed it up, and she's worked at Sears last I heard. But yes, it was a pretty nice little grocery. [7]

Later Sarah expressed some regret that she had made the choice to stay at home.

> I believe this, that after my husband passed away I didn't realize that I could've went ahead and done something, you

know, special maybe for a few years, and uh if I started out then and got away—I would have had to get away from the country, but uh I just didn't make that move and uh I didn't want to go very far from the children. I just thought I couldn't leave them so I just didn't do anything much—only what I'm at. I was here if they needed me you know. I have never mixed in their affairs or anything even if it bothered me—then I was here if they were sick.

R: What do you think you might have done? Did you have anything that you might have liked to do?

Oh, I don't know. If I had been close to Children's Hospital I would have loved to have gone into the hospital and did some work with the children, things like that—there's been a lot of things I think I would—but it'd been too far away you know. [20]

With the children all married, the advent of grandchildren in each family was Sarah's great joy. They were her one impetus to travel, though fortunately most lived close by. Only the eldest, Sally, lived far—sixty miles north, in Columbus. All moved—either immediately or as soon after marriage as economics made possible—to places "out" from town, on acreage at the extreme edge of the city or town, or on an actual farm. Sally lived on several acres of exurban land; Robbie's widow stayed outside Blufton with the four children; Jim soon took up residence in a trailer on the corner of the family land, moving ultimately to his own farm a few miles east; Anne moved from Columbus to Cloverdale (eight miles east), then to land once owned by Penfields, adjoining her mother's; Dennis bought a large farm near Cloverdale; Helen made a series of moves, each to larger, more rural property; and Paula moved to a large farm near Blufton. With most of them close by, children or grandchildren constituted a steady stream of coffee-drinkers and cookie-eaters, helpers and helped, with canning, freezing, shelling, sewing, quilting, and cooking.

Sarah's relating an encounter with one unexpected visitor provided great hilarity for all of us. An old student of hers from one-room-school teaching days (before her marriage) came to

The Years of Change

call. She felt obliged to be hospitable to this student she had had as a "baby," and he stayed for a long time chatting. He revealed his memory of her birthdate, how old she was, what she liked; as Anne giggled, "He must have had quite a crush on her, she was probably only a few years older than him anyhow." Sarah related the ending with glee: when he asked if he could kiss her, she felt she couldn't "refuse this old student," so she let him. Then he asked if he could kiss her again. "Here I was just in out of the garden, not cleaned up, all sweaty, *MY!*" At that point she apparently began to suspect he was not her little "baby" student paying tribute but was looking for a bit more—a home. (She did not reveal if he did in fact kiss her the second time; but he was indeed looking for a home: he is now married to a former widow on the other side of Harrington.) [f] Apparently no one had appeal for Sarah, for in telling of her brother-in-law's teasings that it was "time for her to marry again," she brought vehement closure to his conversation—and to ours—with just one word: "*Never!*" [d].

Yet loneliness, shaded with fear, became an overriding problem. After living alone for approximately eleven years, Sarah ameliorated the problem by asking her sister Martha, bedridden in a Florida nursing home, to live with her.

In an impressive mixture of family devotion and unselfishness, Sarah invited a sister she had not seen for more than thirty years to share her home. They had only age (both were in their seventies) and the same mother and father in common. Martha left the home farm as early as possible, at nineteen, and retained no sentimental nostalgia whatsoever for those days of isolation and hard physical labor. She lived in small cities, and always worked outside the home—in a department store, a bank dining room, and in an abortive attempt to run a hardware store. She had no children, though she was close to her second husband's son and daughter-in-law.

Since the two women lived such different kinds of lives, their attitudes and values were, expectedly, dissimilar. Certainly it is not easy for one woman to adjust to having another in her home, particularly one whose habits and attitudes and values are so very different. Martha smoked; Sarah hates the habit—

the principle, the cost, and the smell. Martha took over most of the cooking, in an effort to contribute to the household operation; Sarah had always considered this *her* domain, prided herself on the quantity and quality of her culinary output, and counted on the enticements of heaped-full cookie jars and always-ready fruit pies for children and grandchildren. Martha had had a (seemingly) carefree life, never had children (why not, Sarah must have wondered), and chose divorce and a lifestyle never countenanced by her traditional siblings. Sarah had seven children, so divorce was never an option, either practically or philosophically. Neither woman in her seventies considered herself "old." Yet Martha's emphasis was on physical appearance; though there were few daily visitors, she carefully followed a daily toilette, with a complete selection of cosmetic preparations—much to Sarah's disgust! Martha confided that she had even "kept" her red hair until she was seventy. Sarah's emphasis is, conversely, on physical accomplishment; though her work load could be easily a mere fraction of what it is now, she carefully adheres to a rigid schedule of arduous labor, deriving an enormous sense of satisfaction from doing so.

They both enjoyed company thoroughly, and their common nieces and nephews, as well as Sarah's own large family, included Martha in all family activities—mainly back-and-forth visiting. With Sarah's care and the whole family's attention, Martha's health improved enormously after her move from Florida. She even made an impressive recovery after each of three major operations following that move here.

SUMMARY

Though agriculture continued to be Ohio's single largest industry, the problem of industrial obsolescence increased after World War II. Appalachian Ohio's coal industry was revitalized in the 1970s, and its recreation features were developed. Projections for the 1980s show a stabilizing trend for population figures, which had dropped in the 1960s.

Little could be recovered concerning the latter stages of Sarah's marriage and widowhood, either because nothing noteworthy could be recalled or because it was a too traumatic

The Years of Change

time. Certainly it was one of extreme change, with all seven children marrying and leaving home, her oldest son and her husband dying. As a widow, Sarah had brief encounters with public life—a teaching job and a government job. She apparently preferred private life, and has pursued no other potential employment situation, continuing to work long and hard on the homestead. Loneliness and fear became a definite problem after she was left alone, assuaged in part by inviting her ailing sister to live with her eight years ago.

    1. Roseboom and Weisenburger (1976:387–88) and Richardson (1977:34).
    2. Knepper (1976:260) and Roseboom and Weisenburger (1976:388); World Book Encyclopedia (1980:532-32a).
    3. Knepper (1976:261, 266–70).
    4. OCDD (1974).
    5. A summer kitchen is typically a separate farmstead building, attached to, or located in close proximity to, the kitchen of the main house. It was designed, of course, to keep the intense heat of seasonal canning and baking from the main house. The Penfields' no longer stands, but it was approximately fifteen feet east of the house (fig. 5). Anne can "smell pickles" when the name is mentioned [II, k].

7. Sarah Today

Today Sarah's community is changed. Farm population continues to drop, and farmers increasingly seek supplementary employment, working more and more days off the farm. Wives and daughters are joining the work force increasingly (well over twice as many women from the area were employed in 1970 as in 1940). Commuting has become a way of life; and with better highways—along with a television set in every home—isolation is no more. The landscape itself has changed: trailer-home sites proliferate, as farmers sell off untillable land and former city dwellers respond to exurbia's call. Still, a cultural entity remains.[1]

Community, school, but especially church activities continue to dominate the social scene, with a variety of money-making activities or get-together events. There are fish fries at the Grange, square dances at the school-community center, ham dinners, school homecomings. Churches also have suppers, a special program once a month for Family Night, and boys' and girls' baseball teams. Churchwomen prepare meals for different events, such as auctions, to make money.

A vocational and technical high school and college are drawing an increasing number of students, male and female, with career-oriented training. Girls speak more often of preparing for jobs, not simply of graduating from high school and getting married.

At seventy-nine years (and twenty years after her husband's death), Sarah herself continues to retain the habits, patterns, and values originating, and cemented, in that happily remembered childhood. She persists in working long, strenuous hours, no matter what the season or the job, on a nearly endless routine of chores both inside the house and out.[2]

Spring housecleaning (in a house that looks spotless!) continues to be a major ritual and involves scrubbing every drawer and cupboard, every stick of furniture, every pair of curtains, every screen and window, every rug and carpet, every wall and ceiling. Applying fresh wallpaper and paint to one or more rooms is often an onerous addition to the schedule. This year's attack on a bedroom ceiling precipitated a small disaster: as Sarah ripped off the old paper, a large portion of ceiling accompanied it. But her son Dennis responded to the calls for help and installed a new tile ceiling. Sarah herself painted the *out*side of the two-story house again last summer, relenting enough that time to allow her son to paint the third story eaves, and a hired boy, part of the upstairs.

Sarah has an abiding interest in the farm, its operation carried on skillfully by her son James.[3] After he plows for her, she plants an immense garden, still weeding it with the cultivator, still canning and freezing prodigious amounts of the always bounteous harvest. James gives her meat for her freezer, and she gathers berries and nuts. She does not, however, keep chickens for eggs now.

Life still revolves around home and family:

> Your children are you. They're your life. And your future. [12]

All the children are married and live close by, or relatively so. Sarah has twenty-three grandchildren (her mother had twenty-one) of whom she is inordinately proud. Few are the conversations that do not refer to them. Her constant cooking, preserving, and baking are primarily, of course, for the children and grandhildren, and her relationship with them all is very positive.[4] Most of the children visit her often; all are concerned for her welfare. Sarah is independent, nonetheless, and instead of asking her children for assistance, she is always helping them, from picking peas and canning tomatoes to wallpapering and mending blue jeans.

> I know whenever there's anything I can do, I always go and help 'em. [12]

She tries especially to lighten the burden of her youngest daughter, eager to take one or more of her six children for a day or two. Perhaps Sarah identifies more with this daughter than with any of the others, since Paula has the largest family (Sarah's other six children average only 2.4 offspring). No doubt the model was Sarah's mother, who gave special help to Sarah, *her* only daughter who raised a relatively large family.

> Do you know that Paula, it cost her a hundred and sixty dollars for the paper for her living room, and I and Anne went and helped her paper it, and it's perfect! A paperhanger couldn't, we, well we spent plenty a time. And it is a gorgeous room! She has real delicate blue, um, panels, and then she has a kind of a, well, it's a yellowish, between a yellowish and I don't know what, and her drapes are. And she's got the prettiest living room.
> R: You are an expert wallpaperer, there's no question.
> And then she did Billy's room in two colors, you know, and I went down to help her. Oh, that paper's something else. When she put her living room paper on, the people that she bought said they weren't going to, and he's a paperhanger, and he said he just wasn't going to handle no more of it. That he wasn't going to hang it.
> R: If he'd a seen what you did on my kitchen ceiling he'd a died.
> That'd be a sight, wouldn't it? Those tiny little checks could run off so easy. Little tiny checks. Oh dear! [9]
>
> I'm going to paper, Susan [daughter-in-law], I'm going to help her paper her house. They'll have a nice home when they get through with it. Jim's been working on it a lot this summer. Really three or four rooms. The kitchen I papered a long time ago, all I have to do is just kind of go over it. The paper's really nice, only a few places, and she's got enough to fix that. I did Shelley's room. It's nice. I helped Susan pick out the order for that paper. [11]
>
> I was there [at her youngest daughter's] at daylight picking peas, and they didn't know it.... Pretty soon here come little Penny out to the patch, and she stayed with me. And

> Paula—her bedroom is on the side next to the garden, and she says when she gets up she always looks out there 'cause the cattle pasture's out there too. And she saw I and little Penny. And she said to George, "What do you believe, my mother's out here stealing my peas!" ... So I had them all picked before they got up. And she had little errands she had to run, so I hulled them. [11]

She babysits for the younger grandchildren and is a "buddy" to the older ones. Just as one daughter remembered, "Mom always had a little egg money if we needed something special," so, now, does grandma manage to help each of the grandchildren with "something special," such as buying a bathing suit for a tot or quilting a comforter for a teen. She always smiles broadly and becomes even more animated than usual when discussing any of the grandchildren.

Though it was beyond the scope of this life history to include interviews with all of Sarah's other children and grandchildren, this interview with her granddaughter Debbie is included in part, revealing a very positive image of her grandmother. Debbie graduated from high school seven years ago and tried urban living, but has since chosen to work in Madison and commute to the country;

> R: Debbie, what comes to your mind when you think of your grandmother? I have purposely made the question vague, so just tell me what you think of right away.
>
> Debbie: Well, I think of *work*! I'm so amazed at the work she does! It's constant. It never stops. It makes me feel like I do *nothing* [this is the same sentiment Sarah's daughter, Anne, has voiced many times, and the one I too have echoed vehemently].
>
> I love to hear about her life. She grew up in a time that I can only dream about. It is hard for me to believe that my own grandmother lived in those times.
>
> [I marvel at] her food, though she puts too much sugar in everything, especially when she knows she's not supposed to have it.

Sarah Today

Raising seven kids. I couldn't do it. I don't want to do it. I have no desire to do it *whatsoever*.

R: Do you want any children?

Debbie: I'm not sure. If I do, two at the very most. Too much responsibility, too time-consuming. I like children. I like to have them visit. But when I'm tired of them then I like to give them back, say "Here!" to their mom. You can't do that if they're yours! Paula was here the other night with all five of her girls, and they were all at her at once, all talking at once, it's like being in a madhouse!

The main thing: over the years she's learned to do a lot with very little, or so it seems to me. Like milking cows, gardening, washing on a scrub board, it's hard for me to imagine! Seeing so much change. She actually lived when they had a horse and buggy, when they walked to school! You read about it, but don't really think about it as happening to your own grandparents.

I can't remember when grandpa and Robbie died, but she can talk about it and it seems like someone close to me died. Seems like she's accepted it really very well. Maybe just in time you do adjust, I'm not sure.

It always fascinates me, if you mention someone, she can recite their history. I probably don't know one one-hundredth about the people around here, though I've lived around here all my life [she was twenty at the time]. That's probably the biggest thing—her knowledge of everything around here.

She's always been there. She's babysat with us so much 'n everything. When I was little I liked to go there an awful lot and spend time. She's completely different from Grandma Hoffman. She doesn't complain, she never cries about anything, she doesn't feel sorry for herself.

I think she's amazing. A lot of times when I'm walking along and see old people, I feel so sorry for them. They look so lost and sad. Grandma never gives you that feeling. I think when I see old people, I never want to be like that. But grandma doesn't give you that feeling.

> I would've liked to know her when she was younger. I want to see some pictures of her. Her sister-in-law told me she had had eight graduation pictures taken, and no one has one now. I'd sure like to find one. [IV, a]

In an informal conversation, Sarah volunteered that she hoped Anne's girls would move to the city, as that was the only place they would be able to get good jobs. This completely surprised me, both since that is a nontraditional female role and since she is always touting country life over city. She was anxious that a grandson take accounting or some potential white-collar kind of study course, rather than the welding he planned. I do not know how overt she was in recommending these avenues to the grandchildren themselves, since she seemed to feel their parents would handle it;

> R: Is there anything special you would like to see your grandchildren do?
> I think their parents will push them and whatever you know. Now I think that Barbara and Dennis, whatever their children want to be they'll give them a chance to go, 'cause Denny makes awful good money and Barbara too. [She just began teaching, after finishing four years of college.] She'll be a good teacher; so Nancy is graduating this year, and by the time she is through—Nancy makes awfully good grades—I don't know whether Robbie's decided what she wants to be yet or not. She first thought she wanted to be a veterinary even, because she loves horses. You know there was eight girl veterinaries that graduated the other day at Ohio State! [21]

Like their mother, each of the daughters takes pride in a well-kept home.

> Helen is a beautiful housekeeper. So's Sally. So's Paula. And so's Anne. Did you ever go to Paula's? I was gonna say, her house is always just spic 'n span, with all those little kiddies. She makes them get around and help, too, she's teaching them to work. You'd be surprised what little Sarah can do. Really, it's wonderful, she's teaching them to work. They

Sarah Today

have their own beds to make, 'n she goes in and inspects them. Even that baby! even Penny makes her own bed. She does. [11]

Again, like mother, each daughter sews as well:

Anne, did you ever notice what a beautiful sewer she is? And Heidi [Anne's daughter] is just as good or better. Sally is good, and Paula is good, and Helen is marvelous! And so is Ginny, my brother's daughter. She's making so many pretty garments for the girls now, Anne is. What Anne does, she is so particular. She gets that, I think if I get tired, I go mebbe a little faster, but my husband was always, you know, precise.... They learned in school. Anne did lots herself, never got any help. Sally can sew too. Helen is a beautiful sewer. She makes Bud's suits. You should see them! She tailors 'em. She makes all their clothes, coats. [11]

Each maintains a garden, varying in size from large to huge. Each daughter, and daughter-in-law, cans and freezes extraordinary amounts of the resultant produce to assure her family a well-laid table throughout the coming year. Each bakes as a matter of course. In addition, all but one has worked at either a part-time or a full-time job at different periods in her married life. This is a difficult proposition for Sarah. She firmly believes *woman's place is in the home*. Nonetheless, she also attempts to understand the financial necessity behind their working. No other reason, such as a need for expansion of horizons, or desire for a career, or relief from monotony, would be tolerated so long as children remain at home—as they still do in each daughter's case.

Visiting the children offers the only real pleasure away from home, though it is difficult for her to leave "all the work."

Yes, I go to Sally's [in Columbus, sixty miles distant] every so often. About three weeks after Martha went to the hospital, she called me one morning. I had just torn the stove apart and was cleaning the stove and was going to clean the refrigerator, and it was eight o'clock in the morning, she called me, and she was bound that I was going to Columbus.

A Woman's Place

> She was bound that I'd come right then. "Get ready and come." So I began to say "no," and I'll just surprise you, and I said "Yes, I'm coming." I said, "You look for me, but I know that I'll be there." I just dropped everything and away I went. Came back in the evening, had a long day, so we went around to the different trading, she just takes me to all the trading posts, where you can find knick-knacks. You know, sometimes you will find something real nice if you really want and she does that. There's one by the church there; it's just a community organization, and they have people bring this in, then they get a percentage for selling it. If you buy anything you can't take it back, you know, nothing is exchanged anything. And the ladies of the church in the congregation run it, and Sally she knows about Fostoria now and good china and things, and so she slips in there sometimes and she picks up, she's really got a gold mine, and it's stuff she might have picked up. [21]

But travel continues to hold no fascination for Sarah.[5] "I don't like it," is her simple and definitive statement. Trips to the doctor and an occasional shopping trip constitute far more time-consuming trouble than she would prefer;

> We don't get the least bit lonesome. And going to town for us, and running around, makes us more tired than if I stayed here and worked outside all day. Of course we go to Madison to the doctor. [9]

> Oh, the old folks in Blufton, they have so much, Blufton has so much for their senior citizens, you know. I don't know, maybe we'd enjoy some of them if we were in there.... Well, I pieced one quilt and quilted it this winter, and then I pieced another one, and, uh, things like that, and I'm not much for—unless I can just mix up the cards and—I won't play cards. To me it's a waste, see. I want something I can have. [10]

When further explaining her dislike of travel, Sarah made a play on her own words (though I have never heard her tell a traditional type of joke; see Appendix E for a traditional classification of Sarah's few "verbal genres").

I don't like to go too much, 'cause I like to quilt in the winter and sew. And I'll tell you what. We go to bed with the chickens. We would, we'd have to stay up a little bit later to shut our chickens away. [Laughter] If we happened to have any chickens we'd have to stay up. [9]

Martha read novels constantly, borrowing books from the library under a new system that sends them through the mail. Sarah has little time to read, so magazines, primarily the *Readers' Digest*, fill her needs. She would like to study the Bible, as one of her daughters does, but instead reads the church magazine:

Oh, I think they could have all been pretty good students if they wanted to be, but Helen's learning more now than she ever did in school because of this [church work]. . . . Bud and Helen do lots of studying when they're, but he can become a minister, and he does, he goes to lots of different towns now. Every two or three weeks he gives a talk. There isn't much—they really know the Bible when they come around; if you want to ask them anything, 'cause they really spend the hours on it. I wish I was more studious than I am.
R: Do you study the Bible?
It's such an interesting thing. Its such a interesting thing.
R: Do you spend a lot of time studying?
No, but I study all the *Watchtowers*. See, they come twice a month. The *Watchtower* and *Awake*, and it comes twice a month, and things like that, I don't leave them pass by. I study every one of those. So I pick up quite a bit. Not like I should. [21]

Though Sarah decries television for its effect on family life and neighbor relationships, she has a new set, and she watches it fairly regularly. "Grand Old Opry" is a favorite, and she becomes personally involved with its participants;

Sarah: We don't watch it much. We're really not television fans. But I really like to have it, and the picture went bad in my other one, and I just decided, well, I had fixed it so many times, I thought, well when the picture tube—that was over a hundred dollars—it'd just be something else, so I went and bought this portable.... What's her name down there, oh, what, she's so famous, she got a citation last night, she's been on there for about forty years. You know who I mean, she's s' silly, and always s' homely. But she was dressed so nice last night.... And they came in in real old-fashioned cars. All the cars were alike, and they brought them all down, you know, and it was really a sight to see, the parade was. Sally's been there several times, and she said she'd go ever' Saturday night if she could, she loves it. [So does her son James.] She says those old men'll come down there from the mountains and then they'll take their shoes off and come in barefooted. And she likes to see those—*MINNIE PEARL*'s who I was tryin' to think of! You know, she's been wonderful in her way. She's one of the old-timers.... Oh, she had a big family and she didn't know how to take care of them, and she started in this in order to try to provide for her family. I've read her life story.

Martha: She's supposed to be in her eighties.

Sarah: Oh for lands sake! She doesn't look it, does she? I was gonna say, I believe they said she'd been on there for forty years, and she's raised a big family. Well, anyway, she sure looked good in that last night. She was fixed up so nice. And she is terribly homely! when you see her. Sometimes she *wants* to look that way.... Ernie Ford was there, and was one of the ones on the platform, and he is, he was dressed so marvelous last night. And I think he's got a voice out of this world, especially a religious voice. And he was there. It was really wonderful. [6a]

Predictably, as with all older people, health is a predominant concern. Stories of friends' illnesses dot the conversation, and the rising cost of sickness is a constant threat. Life in an old-age home is a grim specter, especially since Martha had such negative firsthand experience. Resentment runs deep for those who seemingly get rich from others' misfortune.

Sarah: These old age homes, d'you know those people, even the ones that's doing it for the wage that the county and the state gives 'em, it's a wonderful income, and still they won't

take 'em. And you go in those homes and they say that there's the awful, AWFUL the way they are treatin' those old people. I don't think *any* of those homes'll take them for less than $300, around $350, and why you know those old people don't eat more'n ten dollars worth of food a month. They're bound to make big money. But oh, I guess some of those homes they say are really *terrible*! They find 'em chained to beds, and chained to—find them in any kind of position. Now down here at Northfield, they say they're really, down at that little home they fed them really good 'n everything. But you know they took it away from him, because they said he had to put in a sprinkling system and he wouldn't put it in. I guess it must be pretty expensive, isn't it? He just shut that place up and they took the people away.... But my oh my, most of them refuse to take 'em, state patients, you know, and why they could, that's a good pay. I can't see why they feel they have to have such a terrible amount. Well, for instance, the one that you were in [to Martha], wasn't it $700 a month? And really, to tell the truth, it was just a name, that she was in a good one, she didn't get anything. She said that she could eat her breakfast, but the rest of the food, the rest of the day she couldn't eat food. And, uh, it was very little care Martha can tell you, it was very little care she—just the name she was in— probably a good nursing home. It wasn't! She said doctors come in and look at ya and say "How are you feeling today?" and walk out, and what was the bill?
Martha: Ten dollars each time.
Sarah: And he'd hardly come in the door. It's all fixed. You'da thought your med—your doctor wouldn't come on these trips, that all those things couldn't been included.... If you couldn't soon get rich taking a few patients at that, there'd be something wrong with ya, wouldn't ya? And you could feed 'em good, too, couldn't ya? The *doctors* are doing it, the doctors are owning these places. The doctors, the lawyers, and the undertaker. Include anyone else? The undertaker finished out. People don't have anything to look forward to. If you don't have a lot of

insurance and you get sick, it don't matter if you were rich, you're not going to have anything in a few days. Seven hundred dollars a month! You're not going to have anything very long!

Martha: The hospital is even more.

Sarah: Oh my gracious yes! The hospital now, the cheapest is $119 a day.... Unbelievable! They're gonna have more state cases than anything else. The state'll have to pay the biggest part. [4]

In a discussion of funerals, her daughter stated that one does not have to be embalmed, though that would preclude having the casket open. Sarah replied:

No! Elmer wasn't. Elmer wasn't embalmed, my brother. How long's he been dead, about five or six years? five or six years, has he? Elmer, my brother. He wasn't embalmed, see, but they didn't open the casket. He didn't want to be embalmed.... Oh, I've heard a lot of people that say they don't want to be. See Martha [her sister] has her arrangements all made, she's going to be cremated. But I'm not having anything to do with it. I'm not having anything to do with it, though, I'm just going t' wait till it happens, and if I'm in here, if we're alone, I'm just gonna call Ellen [another sister]. Or else her stepson. She doesn't want to be brought back, either. She's, that's her desire, she wants to do it. Her husband was—cremated.... Oh, did you know that they claim they burn that casket, but I don't believe a word of it. I bet they slip it out. You pay for that casket and they slip it out. They never burn that casket! Oh, they say it's the biggest—racket in the world, nothing they can do about it. [12]

Needless to point out, Sarah maintains strong opinions. She is indignant about many aspects of life today, for example, local, national, and international politics, education, food prices.

Sarah: Well, those trustees [township] get about $600 a month. Well, at least, now you take like Sam Robins [paid to maintain roads], he's on the roads every day. He sees when

Sarah Today

he is out in that truck where these muck holes and things are, he sees where the work should be, and everything. Well, why not give that truck driver extra money for gravel and stuff, of course I don't live on the back roads, but that [trustees' salaries] could go for gravel and stuff and you're not getting anything on them.
Martha: They say they—
Sarah: —Oh, you go over towards Jim's and that road is just one deep hole after another. They've not even give any for two years, or even give a little oil. There surely is a little fund coming into them, so where's it going?
Martha: Well, where's it come from?
Sarah: Well, your oil and gas. They're supposed to get a good thing from the oil and gas, gasoline taxes and things, the trustees are. Where's it going? They are getting their salary. They don't fail to get their check.
Ellen: Well, it's all the whole—what can you say and what can you do about it, the whole situation? For instance, our schools down here, you can't tell me that there isn't a whole lot of that money being misspent, misused when they would have plenty of money for their schools. Seventy-five per cent of your taxes go for your schools and then they don't have enough.
Sarah: The same way with a trustee. I would think if you had a good man on the job, why he sees us every day. These other people don't get out only to go get their check more or less, to tell the truth. [17]

Sarah: What do you think of the Canal Zone? Don't you think it's terrible? I don't think the United States should ever come away, do you? I was afraid it was a Communist thing, and this man last night, this colored man, they explained the whole thing, and there is a lot of Communism behind it.
R: What did he say?
Sarah: The ruler, for instance, is a Communist, and I just can't remember all now, but he named different ones in

back of it. Of course I know Castro has wanted it, he's worked for it, he wants it.... It's a political thing, I think. [13]

Sarah: You take this old country, Shah, what country is that is in so much trouble now? [Iran] They said kids up at Ohio State the other day was out with their big plaques and everything, they think America will go right in and lift them out of anything. All they need is ask for money, isn't it? And surely doesn't have it all the time.

Martha: Well, it's been the history since how many years now—

Sarah: —now that's what they were parading around for the other day was to get America disturbed on that. Well that old man [the shah] has been in that many years, I think he'd better step out and let a younger person in there, maybe they know more about it.

Martha: He's something else.

Sarah: Well, I think it is time to leave. I just wonder if he is capable.

Ellen: He's got himself surrounded with bodyguards and so forth.

Sarah: Oh, it's going to be a big turmoil before it's over.... I said those kids were parading the streets thinking America is going over there and lift them right out of there.

Martha: They probably will.

Sarah: I said, when is America going to have enough of it? Can you always do it?

Martha: We are protecting ourselves and protecting other countries.

Sarah: I say if Carter don't slip over there himself he'll be sending Vance, no doubt.

Ellen: That's Ms. Carter's—Carter's mother is over there right now.... Send that old senile lady over there that, really, actually I wonder how much education the woman really has?

> Sarah: If you would listen to her, she didn't use any wonderful, fancy words. . . .
>
> Ellen: As smart a country as we have and so forth, it doesn't seem as though we have any intelligent people.
>
> Sarah: I don't believe she is intelligent. Now they are playing it up, just for publicity. I don't believe it.
>
> Martha: What about that Billy?
>
> Ellen: Oh, you mean that Billy Carter? He is just as silly as could be. Well, he's just smart enough that people, he's making thousands.
>
> Sarah: My husband would have a fit if I said that, and he's a Democrat [note present tense] but I don't believe in politics. [17]

The sisters felt tax money going to the schools was also being misused, for "foolish kinds of things" like special reading teachers or sex education personnel, for example.

> Sarah: Now Carter is talking about doing away with the subsidy for the free lunches. Oh, I'm not for that! There's so many babies and they can't help it, that goes to school that would sit all day, and they cannot, and they said that was twenty-five per cent of their grades right there, where children went to school all day some didn't have a good meal.
>
> Ellen: I agree with you; now our Columbus schools, they have to furnish breakfast.
>
> Sarah: Oh yes, feed the babies, my goodness.
>
> Ellen: Aren't we upholding the lazy people, not wanting to get up and get breakfast for kids?
>
> Sarah: Babies can't help that though, so you've got to take care of the babies. . . . You can't help those old lazy people if they are going to lay in bed.
>
> Ellen: But you know what? You know what? We have such a demand for people that want to adopt children, people who can't feed their kids can—
>
> Sarah: —absolutely, and let somebody else have them.

> Ellen: And let somebody else have them. They talk about it on TV, reporting a child is being mistreated and abused, and what good does it do when the judges turn around and give the children back?
> Sarah: It's been where children, where they have had warm lunches and that their grades will go up as much as twenty-five percent. . . . The child don't do any good on a hungry stomach. [17]
> Martha: There will be a lot more changes in the next generation [concerning the openness of sex discussions and actions].
> Ellen: Oh, wouldn't you like to know what's going to happen?
> Sarah: It's going to be so bad that people won't use their breath on it. They will think it's all right.
> Martha: Sarah, it's not going to be any worse.
> Sarah: Maybe it will be more out in the open, let's say.
> Martha: That's what it is now. It's never been changed.
> Sarah: There will be more publicity. They will have more fun publicizing it. [18]

Resentments run high, too, when discussing change in their lives, change Sarah did not ask for, change she neither wants nor enjoys, yet change she feels powerless to control. Because there is no one person or event obviously responsible, the ubiquitous "they" receives most of the blame. As we discussed aspects of past and present socializing, Anne stated emphatically:

> Anne: See, time has taken care of all this. There's no more thrashin', people aren't together any more for this kind of stuff. Funerals, everyone goes to the funeral home. You just take it down, really, till there's no reason for people to get together any more. . . . They took the school away, they took the school away, that did away with the—
> Sarah: —yeah, it took, that took away your community, when they take your children away, it takes your interests 'n

everythin'. And the people fought about it terrible. And they—
Anne: —just one thing right after the other.
Sarah: They took our children away, and to tell you the truth, we had *awfully* smart children up here. They could go to college or *any*thing, they really were prepared up here. They had two or three good—
Anne: —they were prepared to go right out and get a job, than they are graduating now from the bigger schools—
Sarah: —they had two or three good teachers that really worked hard with the children, and they came out on top. And they took away the school, and when you take the school away you've taken *everything* away. [12]
Sarah: We used to walk now for four and five and six miles to church at night, you know. And maybe forty and fifty in a group. Now that was lots of fun. Yeah, it was really lots of fun.
Anne: People didn't have television back then.
Sarah: No, and they had lots of fun going and coming.... Really the country people did have a wonderful time. They had hardships, but they had lots of fun....
Anne: The modern equipment took care of all of it [e.g., threshing, bean hullings, barn raisings].
Sarah: And people have got more greedy, I think. I think that years ago, I don't think the dollar meant much [emotionally].
Anne: Funeral parlors took care of the wakes.
Sarah: I don't think the money meant so much to people. I think they got more money—
Anne: —consolidating the schools did away with community gatherings. [12]

Modern equipment has in fact made each farmer more self-sufficient, less reliant on neighbors. Sarah's two sons and one of her sons-in-law all farm, trading labor and equipment regularly within the family. Yet their machines handle crops so quickly, with so few laborers, that the traditional big dinners for harvesters are no longer an institution. A lack of neighborliness is blamed also on so much commuting to city jobs, and on watching television:

> Well, the husband's taken away for the day, he goes to town and works, maybe drives fifty miles. He comes home, he has to have his rest 'n everything, I think it's a time when they don't have time for much pleasure. We have nice neighbors, it isn't that, it's just . . . [9]
>
> But as I say, when radio come, or when television came along, I think people'd just rather stay at home. Watch things like that. Now I wouldn't myself, but I do think that's, that there are a lot of people who don't care to do anything but watch television. [9]
>
> We had more time to visit and there *was* more social life. But today neighbors never go, it seems, back and forth.[6] It isn't because they're not friendly, but it just seems—don't you think television and things like that are takin' over, not for me, but I think they have their television programs laid out, and don't want to miss 'em for anything. But I wouldn't mind to miss television, it doesn't bother me at all. So I think a family is more, uh, withdrawn today than what they used to be. I know that we as neighbors used to gather in and have, well, mebbe ten or twelve of the ladies would gather in and we'd quilt or something, you know, and have a big dinner 'n things, which we don't do any more. . . . Yes, uh huh, even when the children were little. Um hum. Um hum, everything like that. And it seems as though today, no, they don't neighbor at all back and forth. [11]

Since everyone has a car or cars, no one stays home, which precludes neighborhood visiting.

> Sarah: They can live right next door to ya; you take this little Wilson girl, she's raised within a mile of me, I met her out not very long ago, and I didn't even know who she was. Just recently that I know her when I see her. Same way with the boys, I'd have to ask them who they were if I met them

out someplace—right here within a mile. People don't do that any more. They don't just—it's not that they aren't friendly—I would do anything for them when they first came there. . . .

Martha: A lot of times you go, we go, and you wouldn't find anybody home, too. It isn't like it used to be, when they had to stay home.[7]

Sarah: They have their plan made and everything, and maybe—it's just different, that's all there is to it. [10]

Often it is outside influences that are to blame for unhappy change:

This is a nice community. The people here, I said, well, you'll say, well, bad things are happening in our community, but you'll find it isn't our people that's always lived here, it's people that, like the Wheelers, and people like that that goes and comes. [12]

One of the most compelling areas in which she sees change is that of women's roles, their status, and their opportunities. When Sarah was young, there was almost no opportunity for women to work outside the home, unless they taught school:

Sarah: Back in those days if you didn't teach—about the only thing we had, wasn't it?

Martha: It was all you could do. Wasn't nothing else to do. [5]

Martha: When Sarah and I were young ladies, if you couldn't teach, there was nothing else in the world you could do, and teachers couldn't live a normal life. They weren't permitted to do this, they weren't permitted to do that. If they were seen drinking a can of beer, they wouldn't be able to teach! And of course smoking a cigarette would be definitely out. [4]

Sarah: There were no jobs.

Martha: When we were growing up and when we were in our teens, there was nothing for a woman to work at. If she couldn't teach, the only thing in the world she could do was go out and work a day's work in the house.... Housework! And then if you got two dollars a week you were getting a big salary![8] [4]

And not even teachers had much chance to save any money:

She [a retired teacher] told me, "It won't be money I'll leave...." No, see, teachers didn't have much chance to save, much chance in the early years. [5]

But during the depression, men had no jobs either, which further affected women's job opportunities.

Martha: There was a time when they would absolutely find out. Is your husband, did your husband have work? The woman wouldn't get a job then. Because there weren't that many, and they shared them, see.[9] [4]

Martha: Well, they made a ruling. Up until that time a lot of the families were involved. In other words, they'd have whole families in the store [Montgomery Ward], and people in a small town resented that somewhat, because they felt that the people in town should have a chance, a chance for the job. So they made a ruling that no relative, no two relatives could work at the same store. So naturally I was the one who left. [5]

Gradually jobs in other fields opened up, though they were not usually high-status types.

We have several [fire] towers here, but they don't pay nothing for it. No, it's not a good, not a decent wage. It's usually men that are old; that can't do anything else, that does it here. No, they, most anyone can get the job, 'cause no one seems to want them [it].... Women have done it. Some women have. But I don't think they stay very long. It's a lonesome place out there all day long. [4]

But today there is definite change; women have moved into the public sector:

Now right here in our own little community, you know, this little girl right over here she run for trustee, and I don't suppose she ever shoveled a, one shovel of dirt in her

Sarah Today

life. . . . But they wouldn't have thought of voting for her, oh I'll say mebbe ten years ago even, wouldn't have thought of going to, like that. No, things are changing fast. Oh no, we've changed a lot in the last ten years! [4]

We had the clerk was a woman, but she turned it down, so one of the teachers took the job. I think that they [a woman] would get it if they asked for a job. I think they'd get it just as well as a man. [4]

Today, where you take the lawyers, like, and all the businessmen, their wives are teaching. Back when times were scarce, when jobs were scarce, they wouldn't of done that, if one in the family had a job. [4]

Martha: A few years back they thought that the teller in a bank had to be a man, and very few tellers are men anymore. They're nearly all ladies.
Sarah: Very, very few. I don't believe there's one at Blufton, in the bank there.
Martha: And the bookkeeping problem was the same thing, and I don't think you have any men in the bookkeeping department. . . .
Sarah: And the vice-president of the Blufton Bank is a woman, and she's been there a long time, and she has the vice-presidency now, she's a redhead. [4]

Harrington has a woman preacher now. You know the Bible says that a woman should not get up in the church and speak, so it is just something, don't you notice how the women are working for now priests and things, in the priesthood, they're coming into the priesthood, and a lot of the Catholic people are fighting it terrible, but they're coming. Things are changing. I think that this lady, she's, well, she's a retired schoolteacher, she was a science teacher all her life, she's a retired teacher; she seems like a nice person. . . . So she's been in the church up here quite awhile, and she's had both congregations now, see they have a little, it's a country, more or less, congregation. [9]

Sarah: But this fighting for priesthood the Catholic people

> don't like it. They are ordained. . . . Well, just look how the Catholics [nuns] have changed, in the last three or four years, even in dress, their dress, how they've changed.
>
> Martha: Well, times have changed, so they have to have a change. We can't live in the same old—when times change, you have to change along with it.
>
> Sarah: Many rites have never changed. They still raise, wear their little caps. [9]

Sarah's own church (Jehovah's Witnesses) is one that has not changed:

> Oh no, a woman doesn't get to get up on the rostrum and talk at all. They go pretty much to the Bible. They send you out in missionary work and things like that, but no, they never become preachers. [10]

The changes Sarah has observed over the century's progress have been enormous in scope, far-reaching in effect. But they are not, she feels, necessarily all for the better. She regrets the poor quality of service in stores. Whereas only the rich had private transportation when Sarah was young, now everyone expects it. Women *have* to pay for the "two, three beautiful cars" per family, the "beautiful homes."

> Sarah: Oh, I think there's a roundabout change today, really I do. Sometimes I think the mothers just *push* their daughters out. You know they seem to want them to get married s' young. I think that's the one reason for the divorces today . . . too early marriages. They're not prepared.
>
> Martha: Well, I think times have changed so that in the average household a man cannot provide for his household any more. The woman is almost forced out into the public. And actually two people have to work to keep a family of any size.
>
> Sarah: You know, if you've traveled back in the country . . . they've built these beautiful homes, well, it isn't a thing to see two, three beautiful cars sitting outside. Well, look what those people have to, what they have to, you have to

Sarah Today

have insurances on 'em, or you're going to drive the wrong one. And just look what they're going through today. It's no wonder that the wife has to be out making the money.... And they don't mind plunging themselves head over heels *in* debt, and then that's where the trouble starts.... And they plunge themselves so highly in debt, and then, just start in fussing.... Yes, uh huh, then they start fussing. Do you know that when I was a young girl that it was only the rich families, in what we call the better class, you know, that had a horse and buggy. Most everybody walked, or drove their horses and wagon to town—ten or twelve miles to get a few groceries.... Very few that had a horse and buggy. [4]

Women live different lives today.

Oh my gracious, I should say they do, they go to town and get their hair fixed, they have all, yes, they have all, um, most of them all, nearly everybody have all the conveniences, they have their washers and their dryers, and things that the old ladies, we didn't even have anything like it. Yes, I think they're living pretty modern. I don't think there's a home in the country that doesn't have a bathroom. [4]

Yet Sarah, for whatever reasons, reveres the past of her childhood;

It wasn't like it is today.

They're doing everything the easy way now.

There was more of a sociable life then ... your happiest period.[10]

Nonetheless she recognized some good in the present:

[It's] a wonderful period in some way. Because there's work and there's money for people to make. Where we've lived through the depression when you didn't know whether you could buy the second loaf of bread or not. So in a way it's a wonderful time and in a way it's a terrible time. [7]

This ambivalence is particularly marked in her attitudes toward the changes in woman's role. Change for her, as for nearly everyone, is unsettling. Some changes are expected, such as the changes of life. Though these have usurped her youthful vitality, her nuclear family, and, in fact, much of the reason for existing, they are still "in the picture of life." They can be—and are—met with courage, with stoic pride:

> It [neighboring farm] could be made a beautiful place. You go back there, walk back there to that woods. It is gorgeous! And it's only a step from that woods down to where my mother was raised, you know, that all opens up down there. And that is a good farm. If somebody wanted cattle, start a cattle ranch, or something, put a farm, a fence around it and just buy your hay and things and keep a good herd of cattle, be nice, wouldn't it? Oh, sometimes I wish I was young again! [4]
>
> My father used to say, "When you get ready to live, you die." And you know, sometimes that is true. [2]
>
> He [a neighbor], every time he would see my son, he'd say, "Dennis, if I could have my youth back, I'd give all my money away," and he said, "Just give me a thousand dollars and I'd start all over. I could make the money," he'd say. . . . He sure wanted his youth back.
> R: Do you?
> No, I don't. Huh uh. No. Huh uh. No, it isn't in the picture of life. . . . Uh, no, I—it's all in the picture of life, and God has it all fixed up for you, you know. [9]

But some changes are not "in the picture of life," and they are worse than unsettling. In Sarah's case they are manifested by widely equivocal attitudes, many of which she herself seems unaware. Nowhere is this ambivalence more marked than in her attitudes toward woman's role. A whole dichotomy of values evolved in her conversations, none quite juxtaposed in her speech or, apparently, in her thoughts. A full awareness of the striking changes in women's status and opportunities elicits, on the one hand, her positive image of women.[11]

> Sarah: We find that some of our great minds come from, you know, females. And why would the males be so smart if

Sarah Today

they didn't have a smart mother? *Sure* they're as important!
Martha: Well, I think the mother is with the children more. Usually they spend a lot more time with the mother than the father does, and she has a lot more influence.
Sarah: Sure, you know there's an old saying that the "hand that rocks the cradle is the hand that rules the earth." And they get to—we know some fathers that're awful close, but not as usual, we know that, and so the mother does [?] [unclear tape], but sometimes the father has to take them. And they've done a wonderful job. But really, the child needs the mother. [4]

Yes, I think they are commencing to go back and study history and find out a woman's role. Why should they be a slave to a man? They were really intended, God said, bone of, or Adam said, bone of my bone, flesh of my flesh. All right, why wasn't she equal then to him? Yeah, I think it's a fifty-fifty. If one goes beyond that then, why it's all right.
R: You both seem to have a strong image of a woman being equal.
Oh, I really do! I really think that it's a fifty-fifty. Why shouldn't it be? [4]

I do too, think that they do [some people think women are inferior], I mean it is very, very wrong. [4]

I don't care what you say, nine times—at least five times out of ten—the woman has more brains than the man! [9]

There isn't anything younger than a man! No, there isn't anything younger than a man! [agreeing with her daughter] Why are men running the world when women are much more capable, thoughtful, and stable? [f]

Sarah has strong feelings about the injustices women have borne, possibly recalling the inequities in her own childhood, when the girls worked in the fields, but the boys *never* worked in the house.

They had the silly idea that the boy could do the same thing, be guilty of the same thing as the girl, but it didn't hurt him like it did the girl. And people would forget that! But they wouldn't forget it if the girl did it. Yet I think that still holds today. I think they still forget an illegitimate child, they soon forget who the father is, but they never forget the mother, 'n she carried it. [4]

And I think if a woman stands up and works in a factory beside her husband, when her paycheck comes, it should be just as much as his, if she does the same thing equal. All right, then when she comes to wash her dishes, then he's got just as good a right to get a dishrag and wipe 'em as *she* has to. And he'll take off someplace and go to a club, mebbe, and leave her do all of it. Well then, that's wrong! Yes, I think that they should share and share alike. They'll be lots happier that way. [4]

[During discussion of a television program on wife-beating:] I don't think there's anything worse! Why, I have always said, "That is just like animals, that is stooping to animal level! No man better ever hit me, or me him.[12] Why no, I wouldn't have it! I'll bet they didn't get anything figured out on that progam either. No, you should talk it out. [Her vehement protest may indicate, as others have intimated, a problem she, or someone in her family, actually had had.] [i]

I think that's *rotten*. When a woman can go someplace and she doesn't have a penny to reach down in her pocket. No, I never had it like that. I should say not. It's a terrible thing! Yes, that does happen. You're right, it really does happen, and it happens too often. And she doesn't even have a few cents! Just they don't give her nothing! [4]

Oh, as long as they keep the price down and the girl doesn't get as much money for the same work, naturally they'll get the jobs, won't they.... If you can hire a girl, she will work more steady than a man will, and if you can hire a girl cheaper, you're going to hire her, aren't ya? And she'll be more concerned, no doubt, in general, than the boy will at the job. [4]

No, I really don't think it was right [lower pay, fewer job

Sarah Today

> opportunities], especially if some women had to support themselves. . . . You know they can go out and do the same as a man, why not get paid the same as a man? [5]

> We found that the doctors have their nurses, and the dentists . . . it really isn't fair because women do a lot of work men get the big money for. [5]

This very positive image could be attributable to her mother's having been a strong character, and the ultimate role model for Sarah.[13]

> Mother was the ruling member of our family. There's no doubt about that. Not that she was the domineering type, but she just looked forward. We probably made her more domineering. [?] [unclear tape] There was never any differences of opinion there. . . . I think mother was the dominating one in the family. I don't think he [her father] ever made any decisions without going to her and asking her about it. I don't think he ever made any big decisions without asking mother. I don't think they were ever unfair with each other, but what I mean is, I think he always said, "What do you think about so and so?" I'm that way too. I always went to my mother, I know I always asked her advice, even after I was married. [5]

Ambivalently, her other conception of woman, as "the second sex," also emerges:

> Eve destroyed man in the Garden of Eden, and women have always destroyed men. Not all women, I don't mean, but women have—one woman can destroy the health, for instance, of dozens of men. [3]

> Even in court, when they want to really stress something and make people really believe it, they always go to the Bible, Chapter 31. Here. [She then indicated passages such as, "Do not give your vital energy to women," and, "A capable wife who can find? In her the heart of her owner has put trust" (Proverbs 31:3, 10–11)].[14] [4]

> Sarah [concerning a local woman who was made a township

199

A Woman's Place

trustee]: I don't suppose she ever shoveled a, one shovel of dirt in her life. She didn't know, I don't imagine, anything more about digging a ditch than anything in the world. Never saw her out in her garden. And I think people went and voted for her for the fun of it. They thought, "That's funny." And mebbe she's a good trustee, I don't know [very doubtful tone].

Martha: Women have always wanted the parks to look beautiful. They've wanted the roadsides to be clean.

Sarah: Yes, but *they're* not doing anything with them, are they? *Is* the roadsides any better? [4]

When jobs were scarce, if one in the family had a job [the woman could not work]. Which was a good thing, don't you think? [4]

You know the Bible says that a woman should not get up in church and speak. . . . No, oh no, a woman doesn't get up on the rostrum and talk at all. They go pretty much to the Bible. I can show you exactly where [in the Bible] it says a woman shouldn't speak in public. It says to ask her husband. The things that she does not know, to go to her husband for advice. [9]

Men have more strength. . . . And then I think that they can make decisions and be stronger, don't you? When it comes to a tight, serious question, I think that—yes, like the president of the United States I think will always be a man. . . . Woman are, I think they're weaker. They are more sympathetic and everything, and I think that a man is stronger in that way in making decisions. [9]

The phrase "women's libbers" is always spoken with pejorative overtones. For one thing, Sarah holds them responsible for the fact that "men no longer rise when a woman enters the room, nor do they give her a seat on the streetcar." This image apparently has captured many minds and hearts. It is exactly the same example used by a woman geographically far removed from Sarah, in Scotland. When I interviewed her in 1978, Mrs. Donaldson spoke disgustedly of "women's libbers," who have "put away good manners. Now no men will give up their seat on the bus, even if a woman were tottering on one leg. They won't open a door for her!" (Mrs. Donaldson's life has had quite amazing parallels to Sarah Penfield's, including many of her views on life today.) Jeannie Simpson, nearly halfway around the world in Wyoming, shares the Scots woman's sentiments. In her thirties in 1977, she believed that "women's libbers are asking for too much, and have set women back. I *want* to be domineered, to have someone hold the door for me."[15]

And not all women's "advancements" in job opportunities are favorably viewed by Sarah.

> They said that no, that whenever they were equal to a man let them act like a man. That's what they say about their jobs. Out in jobs today, when women are wanting to be policemen, the men are *totally* disgusted about it [as is her tone of voice]. [4]
>
> They say that now, they're wanting to be in the fire department, you know, go out on the fire wagons, which a woman doesn't belong at night out on the fire wagon, and climbing on the ladder. The, they're asking to be embarrassed, and the men'll embarrass them! The men'll go all the way. That's what I'm afraid. They're just teetotally—they're just not nice women to begin with or they wouldn't put themselves there. That's the way I feel about it. When it comes to climbing ladders and going up in the fire—and all those things—they're wanting to be *everything*! Policemen! Now mebbe, mebbe some policewomen in some cases, you know, with child abuse, there maybe would be some place for women on a police force, in some cases; maybe they could handle that good, I don't know [doubtful tone]. [4]

Such changes strike at the core of Sarah's value system: her whole pattern of living has been founded on a belief in home and family as the nucleus of the universe, with the mother at the center. Woman's place is in the home, and nowhere else. Her job is to raise children:[16]

I really think it's a mother's place—*a woman's place is in the home*[17] and early life of her children, and I, I don't think it is wrong for a woman to want to get out and do something—it can get awfully monotonous, but I think we have different periods though. You are needed more, you know, especially with children, if you start a family. [5]

If the lady stays single [then woman's role is as important as the man's], but as long as—if she becomes a mother, then her children, you know, at the early stages, they come first, surely. But then if she wants to go out after that and make a life of her own, for herself, why not? After the children have, you know. But just to go out and neglect her children, I wouldn't think of—I wouldn't believe in that, would you? In their early life, they need you—so much. After that why shouldn't she have a few years of her own? [4]

So the home's falling apart, and they ask why, well, that's it [women are working].... And when she comes home she's so tired, that probably she don't see much of the children, don't know much about what they're doing, too tired to ask 'em what they've done today or where you've been, so that's the way it goes. [11]

Ellen saw the pipeline crew on her way home, with [horrified tone here] a *woman* on the surveying crew!! What is the world coming to, *what is our world coming to* when there those young girls are out with the men. They're going to get what's coming to them. Now just look what that Judy has done, working with Allen on a truck and now breaking up his home! It's *terrible*!! [11]

Yes, I think to be a good wife and to be a loving wife that you have to have a good meal on the table, your house clean, your children clean and nice and respectable to their father and everything, and that then is the big thing in a home. [10]

[This was an acid comment after Martha had mentioned the Phil Donahue show (a daytime television program).] They probably didn't get anything figured out. And I'll bet their husbands don't get a decent dinner tonight! The same ones hang around that show every day. Will, Sally's husband, you know, is a butcher, and he says those doctors' wives sit around and play cards all day long, and then they come in there and buy a piece of meat and ask him how to fix it [voice filled with disdain]! Can you *imagine*! And Will, he'd never fixed a meal in his life, but he tries to act just like he knows and tells 'em what t' do. [1]

Yet the knowledge that her daughters have worked—or are working—is reflected by qualifying statements on public roles for women:

Well, the thing today is that two working can't dress and clothe their children. [However, this was immediately followed by "Each one has to have a *car*. They can't share the same car. Where it used to be we could share the same road because we'd *walk*. We're living a different life. We're living in a different age."] [4]

I don't think it is wrong for a woman to go as far as she can today. Because I think even in politics she's gonna be more honest. A woman in the White House would *never* have done what those people have done. [4]

But let 'em go as far as they can. I think they have rights. Like even a woman, if she is smart enough to be president, why not let her try? She *couldn't* do any more than they've been doing. No indeed. And do you know [chuckling somewhat ironically], I think we'll have one. I think that some of these times that we'll have. [4]

But it really takes two checks today to live, doesn't it? So we have problems, don't we? Who's gonna solve them? [11]

Another aspect of Sarah's ambivalence was introduced earlier in chapter two: the dichotomy between optimistic bearing and pessimistic outlook. Her actions are so brisk and positive, her general attitude jovial and optimistic. But one cannot escape the doomsayer proclivities laced through nearly every conversation.

You know, it's an awfully dangerous thing to leave your children go today. Did you know there's a social disease the doctors can't do a thing for? It's got them baffled, and there was one in Vietnam that they told the people back here that their sons were dead, and they're on an island, and I did know the name of the island—they just rot, but this is a viral, well, it's in the *Reader's Digest*[18] this month and I think every mother that has children should know it, and there is no cure for it. And a woman it comes back on them quick. More often than a man, and the children they say as they give birth that one out of four will be absolutely mental, very, very mental, and one out of four will die, at least one out of four will die. You know the rest wouldn't be well, would they? It's a very serious thing. The doctors haven't been able to find anything at all for it and it's called a virus, virus, so just look what you are sending your children, you know, little young boys, the pipelines means rough people—oh, they're awful, they drink and they carouse around at night, and it, and the best of them weaken sometimes, you know. [2]

In California they say they do, the public schools in California use tranquilizers on those children! They're just too emotional, they haven't been on drugs, but they're just too naturally—today children are that way, they just can't get them settled, and they have been giving them tranquilizers in some of the schools. You knew that, didn't ya? Yeah, they can't do anything with them, they're so irrational. They're not mentally off or anything, but they're just so jittery. They say that come from the Second World War, the children that was born after these soldiers came back just, uh, and I believe it really is the truth, they're more emotional. . . . And what do you believe the children they have [children who have been on drugs] will be like? You know doggoned well our generation is going to the dogs, isn't it? With what their children, their generation is going to be. Tch, tch. [4]

We should think of the love thing that you can do for each other. It's all wrong. But how are we gonna correct it? It's in the last days. You see, the Bible says that the families, the families will really turn against each other. Which is happening. All those things are coming to pass. They're coming fast. Lookit—something horrible, the murdering and everything, isn't it horrible? [6b]

I think it's a terrible time to bring—I think it's so hard on the babies and parents both. Well I think it's a terrible time to bring the little things into the world. There's just nothing but suffering ahead for us. . . . What kind of future have they got? [8]

Sarah: Isn't the whole world in a terrible—that old ruler of Uganda, isn't it Uganda? He's killed so many, how many did this man say had defected from there? Fifty thousand he's killed of his own people!

Martha: That's what he said.

Sarah: But you know the *Time* magazine said that, he's married, he's got more than one wife, but he had a couple of young men from this one wife, and he took them and showed his wife's body where he'd cut her arms and put one on each—he'd changed 'em and sewed 'em back, he'd murdered her. Haven't you been reading this whole thing? *Crazy!* Oh, he's a great big horrible looking thing, and *Time* magazine has all that stuff.

Martha: He's in the hospital.

Sarah: He is? Well they surely will keep him there. He must be crazy the way he murdered his people. So it is just like that, I mean, well, the end of the Bible says, nation shall rise against nation, and they surely have their—just no peace it seems anyplace. It's terrible, isn't it! [13]

Ambivalence is thus evidenced by pessimistic proclamations juxtaposed with optimistic life-style, by real versus ideal ambiguities, by thesis balanced by antithesis. Change is threatening the foundations of the world as she views it, and conflict seemingly becomes a hallmark of living. Sarah has been forced to handle not only a physically onerous existence, but one emotionally demanding as well. She has steadfastly and courageously fulfilled the personal and societal expectations defined by her spatial and temporal reality, but the cost has been high.

Still, Sarah speaks of her life in a positive way. Even though heart trouble, arthritis, and diabetes plague her now, she philosophizes:

> Well, arthritis is the same as rheumatism—it's associated with each other; my feet are so numb sometimes they have no feeling. Sometimes I'll take a hot water bottle, and try to get some feeling in.
>
> R: How can you walk?
>
> Well, the more I use them the better they feel.
>
> R: You mean when you are sitting around or lying down they get—
>
> —Oh yes, but for my age and most people don't even live that long and raise seven children. I told the doctor when he says I'm pretty good, I said "Well, I don't have anything to kick"—I said, "why I'm living and so many people my age aren't even living." I don't have anything to kick about. I'm just afraid of, you know, if anything happens to me why I'm ready for it. I don't baby myself, you know, but I do try to take decent care of myself 'cause I just hate to have a cold when your throat is so raspy and everything. I think these pills are helping alot—I took them real carefully like he told me and they're driving it out. I'm sure I caught it from Martha. . . . I know Martha brought this to me because she came back with it from Columbus [after visiting Ellen].
>
> R: What was that you said a little while ago, you said, "I'm all paid for." I love that expression.
>
> I've lived a pretty good life. So many people don't live to be that age. I mean I, I never expected to live longer than my husband, and my sister in Columbus was never sick and she died at sixty-eight. She never got out and worked in the fields and everything like I have.
>
> R: Maybe that's what made you healthy.
>
> Might have been. She had only one child, you know, and she didn't have children to get—when I was up home and, see, I was much older than the little ones and I carried babies and took care of them and then I had mine and took care of my

grandchildren an awfully lot and I feel, you know, it's been a pretty good life.

R: What do you think is a good life for a woman? What would you look for—

—Well, maybe we couldn't have what we hoped for. So I think it's just better, be satisfied with—the best thing is to be satisfied. You can always be searching for something you know.

R: If you had it to do all over again, would you—

—Well, we all say that, "Now if I just had my life to live over again." Don't you think you'd follow that same pattern and not realize it? You know we are not going to live it over again. So we just have to go on from where we're at. Make a new beginning I guess. [20]

And every day Sarah does make a new beginning, burnishing and polishing furniture, memories, habits, beliefs.

Sadly, yet another change touched Sarah's life. Martha did not survive her fourth operation, and died in 1981. The day-to-day irritations, the deeper value-laden differences are gone. But loneliness returned full force. The problems of age multiply, for with the loneliness comes fear—fear for physical safety, for financial security against illness, and of illness itself. These are difficult times, these latter days.

Almost in epilogue form, one last-minute development has occurred in the saga of the Penfield farm. In past years Sarah often expressed a desire to see the entire acreage broken up and sold, so she can look out and "see lights at night," and so she can "see the children enjoy the money they get." Unfortunately, she had no legal power to accomplish that: Sarah was not a joint owner of the property when her husband was alive, and he did not will her the property. This was true despite the fact that, judging from the county deed books, most women there—including both the preceding generations of Penfields and her own generation (Robert's brother's wife)—were listed as joint property-owners with their husbands. In his will Robert had left the farm to their seven children, and he left a smaller, undeveloped farm nearby to Sarah. (It was literally true then that she has lived all her life in just two houses—her father's and her husband's.)

Though Sarah made her wishes to sell the farm clear to the children, they were not able to agree on conditions for a sale.[19] Suddenly, Sarah took matters into her own hands, hammered a handmade cardboard "4 sale" sign in the field opposite the house, and negotiated with the resultant prospective buyers. The children, somewhat in shock, met and reluctantly acquiesced to her decision and arrangements. The house, garden, and several buffer acres were retained for Sarah, but will be sold and the proceeds distributed to the children when she either elects to leave or dies. Sarah was not at all naïve about the farm's value: she asked for—and received—the highest dollar yet paid for large parcels in the area.[20]

SUMMARY

Today Sarah Penfield lives in the house to which she came as a bride more than fifty years ago. She maintains not only the energetic pace but also the patterns and values characteristic of her whole life, modeled upon her mother's life. Family remains the central core of her existence, and most of her activities are centered around the needs and desires of her seven children and twenty-three grandchildren. She has witnessed great change in social climate and conditions in her seventy-nine years. She cites consolidation of the schools, increased mobility, and television as the most cogent factors in the breakdown of family and community cohesiveness. One of the greatest areas of change she sees is in that of opportunities for, and status of, women.

Some of the rapid changes of this century have been expected and "in the picture of life" for Sarah; others have been worse than disturbing. Although she has a strong, positive image of woman, her abilities and her rights, Sarah is concerned that the new freedoms are undermining woman's ordained place: in the home. Divergent conceptions of the female sex—she is equal/she is inferior—undermine her views of herself and her children, of a healthy, positive future for her grandchildren. Inner conflict sharpens the reality of daily existence, and the optimism she evidences in her physical, motor activities is contradicted by the pessimism overt in her cognitive, verbal expressions.

1. See also Hicks (1976:vii). Figures for women in the work force come from the U.S. Census, 1972; Ohio Bureau of Unemployment Compensation, 1942.
2. For similar activity in older women, see also Lurie (1961:xv), Kelley (1978:123), Underhill (1936:86), White (1975), and Donaldson (1978).
3. See also Hagood (1939:77).
4. See also White (1975) and Hicks (1976:44).
5. Or for Donaldson (1978).
6. See also Hagood (1936:171).
7. See also Hicks (1976:34).
8. See also Filler (1980) on an Ohio teacher; see Hoffman (1981) on teachers 1830–1920. See Stratton (1981) on Kansas frontier teaching—and manuscripts from woman pioneers. See Treiman and Hartmann (1981) on continuance of the problem.
9. See Scharf (1976:21–25) for documentation.
10. See also White (1975).
11. Ibid.
12. Cf. Gallagher (1976:137). Pagelow (1981) quoted estimates that more than half the married women in America had been victims of wife-beating one or more times. She also analyzed why they continued to stay with the batterer. See also Gilbert and Webster (1982) and Roy (1982).
13. See Chodorow (1974:58).
14. See also Gallagher (1976:80) for similar sentiments about "God's plan."
15. See Walum (1974) for views on the door-opening "ceremony." See Jordan (1982:xxix) for "cowgirls" negative views of "women's lib stuff."
16. See Welter (1966) for literature of the nineteenth century that promotes this ideology. See Scharf (1976) for literature from 1920 to 1940.
17. The same words used so ubiquitously in nineteenth- and twentieth-century literature and oral tradition. See Gallagher (1976:80) for an example of the same words being used by an older woman.
18. Reuben (1974).
19. See Chiñas (1973:89) for the same kind of situation in a Mexican family. See Hicks (1976:58–59) on children's nostalgic feelings for—even of moral obligation to—keeping the "old homeplace."
20. See Hicks (1976:50) for the new significance of rural, marginal land as financial investment.

8. Conclusion: Sarah, the Capable Wife, and Other Women

Much like her favorite Flower Garden quilt, stitched with bright scraps of cloth, Sarah's life story is pieced with vivid fragments of memory. A myriad of textures and themes unfolds, some unique to Sarah, some shared by other women as well. In several ways the story is *not* similar to Sarah's perfect quilts, since there are missing pieces, broken threads, in the pattern of her story. But no one person's life can ever be presented in whole cloth. How then is it possible to piece this patchwork together? That is, how can we make sense of this mass of material, the anecdotes, the details, the contexts, the contradictions?

I have divided this concluding chapter into three sections. First I have summarized Sarah's biography by an analysis of her life patterns as *dimensions, turnings,* and *adaptations*. Then I have outlined the contribution of life histories in general, and this one in particular, to scholarly research. Third, I have used Sarah's life history as a paradigm with which to assess its potential similarities to other women's lives.

Sarah's story brings us glimpses of life as it has actually progressed for a rural midwestern woman, neither as one of the "noble pioneers" we have romanticized beyond recognition nor yet as a stolid drudge. As Lange described them, these women of the soil are a hardy stock, "not our well-advertised women of beauty and fashion, but of themselves a very great American style."[1]

Sarah's "style" is that of a woman steeped in tradition—traditional life and lore, attitudes, and values. She is physically and emotionally a strong woman. Yet the rapid changes in this century have created both ambivalence and conflict for Sarah, as they have for women who have led similarly traditional lives.

SARAH PENFIELD, THE CAPABLE WIFE

Making sense of the mass of material in a life history has long plagued researchers. Criticisms of life histories have, since 1935, consistently decried the absence of analysis and interpretation, yet few critics or writers have proposed a model with such analytical and interpretive features. Mandelbaum, in 1973, was one of the first to do so, and his model remains one of the best.[2] His method divides a life story into three elements: *dimensions, turnings,* and *adaptations. Dimensions* are the biological, cultural, social, and psychosocial elements; *turnings* are the major transitions in a life; and *adaptations* are the continuities maintained, and the changes effected, throughout a life course. The framework goes beyond chronology, outlining the set of equipment available to an individual, the specific life developments he or she must face, and the way each uses his or her unique equipment to manage those developments.

I have used this model to summarize and analyze the Penfield data, since I consider it not only the best of the few frameworks devised but excellent for my purposes. Further, a new model from every eager life historian would only preclude the establishment of the standards so crucial for improving life history analysis.[3]

Dimensions: Biological, Cultural, Social, and Psychosocial

Sarah is a woman. The biological dimension of being genetically constituted female necessarily involved Sarah in that set of cultural, social, and psychosocial dimensions common to the sex. It also influenced her adaptations (or lack of them) to later turnings. It is important to remember that social and psychological relationships—a combination of values and attitudes and beliefs and potentials—are also entailed in the biological fact of sex.[4] Certainly the potential for motherhood is a key example of that element of the dimension.

Sarah used (and later termed it *abused*) her body by working in the fields as a young woman and later as a married one. It is to this, rather than to bearing seven children, that she has attributed her extensive "female problems." Consequently her daughters were not allowed to do similar heavy work, though Sarah never fully discussed the reasons with them. Bodies and biology are too personal (see chap. 5, n. 1). Thus we know little more than surface facts. But it is fairly obvious that Sarah came equipped with far better than ordinary motor energy, enabling her to accomplish prodigious amounts of physical labor. This, in circular fashion, had a cogent effect on her own, her family's, and her community's perceptions of her as strong, able, vital, and hardworking.[5] Today that image (her own and others') continues to prevail as Sarah Penfield channels her incredible energy into achieving tremendous quantities of work—all this in spite of heart trouble, arthritis, and diabetes.

Sarah has lived on, and participated in, the development and maintenance of a subsistence farm/patriarchal household typical of her area. A behavioral guide to social interrelationships in such a setting, the cultural dimension includes the mutual expectations, the understandings, and the behavior patterns of the people among whom an individual grows up and in whose society he or she becomes a participant.[6] Since the nineteenth century, a number of those dimensions have been maintained in Sarah's rural midwestern society. Males worked only outside the domestic sphere; females, as girls and later as women, worked at both outside farming and inside domestic jobs. Males were the head of the household, but females were expected to contribute to the household both physically and financially. However, women were seldom considered "in charge" of family finances, even when they were actually the chief conservators and administrators of house and farm. Males, even as youths, were free to go when and where they wished; females kept physically close to the farmstead—house, garden, and fields for care of domestic animals or crops. Politics were a male concern only. Males were also in charge of social and educational activities; females were in charge of cooking and serving meals in both work and recreational get-togethers. Socializing within the community was limited, though neighbors helped each other with heavy work or during emergencies. Family and extended kin groups were the dominant base of both social and work groups. Travel outside the community was rare and almost always family-oriented. Males were farmers, usually on a family farm or one in the near vicinity; females (except for the few who taught) married and raised families. Though marriages were not arranged, the bride and groom generally were raised in the same area, and often had attended the same school. Schools were an integral part of the community, as were churches, which had a social as well as a religious component. Religion was a strong moral and philosophic influence in nearly all the families.

This general outline held true during the lives of Sarah's grandparents, her parents, and Sarah herself. It changed in small degree for her children, then more still for her grandchildren, with the changes revolving primarily around employment. As southeastern Ohio farming became less and less competitive and as mobility increased, men began to commute to jobs in nearby towns and cities, especially during and after World War II. Women joined them in increasing numbers in the late 1960s. Now boys often train for urban-type jobs in vocational, rather than regular, high schools; girls, frequently graduates of consolidated or technical high schools, expect to work in town or city at least one or more years before marriage (though marriage still remains the most important goal). Schools, but still more the local churches, remain important social forces. Family and extended kin groups continue to be the primary organizing element. Travel, only somewhat less rare, is still usually family-oriented.

Sarah's individual choices followed cultural dimensions almost implicitly. Those individual conflicts, choices, decisions, and solutions are the social dimension within—or without—a particular cultural framework, often overlapping the cultural dimension.[7] In Sarah's case, her only culturally uncharacteristic choice was to pursue her education, not only through high school but two years of teacher's training as well. This was nonetheless within the dimensions of the family itself, and was no doubt a result of her mother's exhortations. We do not know why she chose to marry Robert, though this decision too was well within cultural parameters. He was a local boy, a friend of her brother's. And her goal, like her mother's and grandmother's had been, was to start a home of her own and raise a large family. As she once told me, "I think everybody, I think everybody themselves looks forward to having their own [home], don't you think? I think that's the normal thing. . . . I don't think people ever accumulate anything that amounts to anything until they get responsibilities. . . . Yes, and have something to live for, that's something you really live for 'cause they know their parents aren't always going to live and be around and they need roots" [20]. Sarah was twenty-four. No doubt the phrase "old-maid schoolteacher" was at least as haunting—and as humiliating—in the 1920s as it had been earlier. The social dimension also includes rewards and penalties: the rewards are choices—e.g., marital or professional or economic—that are ultimately happy ones; the penalties are choices that are subsequently unhappy ones. (In practice, however, most people in every society recognize penalties only after the fact.) Sarah chose to marry a local man, as her mother and grandmother had done, with the inherent reward being her society's approval for maintaining the culture's behavior patterns. The penalties involved never have been stated overtly by Sarah (there have been only oblique statements, such as "Well, maybe we couldn't have what we hoped for").

Sarah had many models for her concepts of her culture's patterns and ideals: secular literature, religious literature, and her parents' and grandparents' revered examples. The literature of the day (Sarah was an avid reader) offered many illustrations of the ideal woman. Nineteenth-century romantic literature was pervaded by the concept of True Womanhood. The four cardinal virtues by which a woman judged herself (and was judged) were: piety, purity, submissiveness, and domesticity. Piety, religion, was the core of woman's virtue and the source of her strength. Purity was also essential, and young women of every generation in the rural community were, it was hoped, sheltered more than adequately—physically, mentally, and emotionally. Submission was taught by both the written and the unwritten word. Certainly the church was one of the more powerful of those teachers: did not the marriage vows themselves command the new wife to love, honor, and *obey*? Domesticity signified true woman's place as *in the home*, a comforter, nurse, mediator with God, housewife, mistress of every variety of needlework, and gardener. Even educated women were charged with exercising domestic virtues, but in the proper state of marriage, "that sphere for which woman was originally intended." The corollary to marriage was motherhood, the "noble, sublime task."[8]

In addition to the compelling exhortations of nineteenth-century romantic literature, the whole genre of western novels also had broad appeal. Sarah often expresses admiration for the pioneers. "Their life wasn't too much different from our early life," she once empathized. The frontier woman had risen above the "gentle lady" image to combine economy and industry as a strong, capable, institutional, comrade woman[9]—an apt description of Sarah herself.

The church and the Bible were pervasive influences. Both figure in Sarah's memory, descriptions, and daily conversation. In fact, she still retains both awe of, and respect for, the description of woman's role that she had me read from her Bible, describing how "God really thought" of it: biblically she is "a capable wife," whose owner trusts her; she is—to paraphrase—food procurer, nurse, farmer, vintner, trader, spinner, dyer, seamstress, quilter, lawyer, mother of sons and daughters; one who is strong, pure, righteous, beneficent, watchful, and never lazy.[10]

Besides the influences of secular and religious literature, Sarah was steeped in admiration of her parents' and her grandparents' traditional modes of life. Her mother's behavioral model was undoubtedly the primary shaper of her personality and her activity. Thus she believes implicitly in the family as the base of all society, with the woman as its center, in her place *in the home*, a mediator with God the Father. Her skillful narrative revolves repeatedly, consistently, around the values of motherhood, family, and religion; this is true whether she is relating personal anecdote (e.g., her glorified childhood life with her mother at its center, her daughters' homemaking skills, or knowledge of the Bible), whether moving beyond to the community (her identification of neighbors in terms of kinship status, or the churches as social and religious centers), or whether referring to the "outside" world (Minnie Pearl in television for her family's sake, Ernie Ford for religion; women's working destroying their own or others' homes).

All these models—secular and religious literature, her parents' and grandparents' examples—of the ideal woman in the social dimension provided Sarah incredibly demanding goals to achieve. Ultimately, she threw herself into the role of farm wife and mother with all the strength and determination possible—certainly a considerable force.[11]

Obviously Sarah has strong convictions about the centrality of motherhood and family, about the importance of religion. This psychosocial dimension focuses on the individual's subjective worlds of feelings and attitudes. These feelings and attitudes are still likely to be similar in considerable part to those of others' in their culture and society, since all are drawing upon, and operating from, the same cultural matrix.[12] In addition to those convictions, Sarah has a seemingly strong image of both herself and her family and their roles in the community (private ones for her daughters, public ones for her sons). Certainly her attitude toward the value of work is overwhelmingly positive ("I trained myself properly")! In addition, she resents the decentralization of education, the misuse of political power, the specter of inflation, and most social change. She is outraged by those who take advantage of the underdog—children, the sick, the infirm, or the aged.

Beyond those overt views we are told little. But then, never exposed to the world of Freud, Sarah was not practiced in identifying unconscious feelings and attitudes, much less in verbalizing or analyzing them. Therefore, we must draw conclusions based (1) on Sarah's conflicting testimonies, (2) on what she did *not* say, and (3) on my participant observational deductions.

Her conflicting testimonies uncovered a depth of ambivalence toward woman, her role, and her place. We are left wondering whether she welcomes enlarged job opportunities for women or abhors them; whether she understands why more than half of the married women in the country are working or castigates them for it; whether she thinks woman's place is always in the home or whether under extenuating circumstances some combination of work and home is possible; whether she believes that woman is equal to man or that she is the second sex.

As to what she did *not* say: some information may have been lost to me because I came from another subculture with a different world view. Some may have been blocked by Sarah's unconscious level, actually preventing her from making a "real" assessment of the societal "ideal" of woman's place in the center of a happy home. And some may have been omitted deliberately by Sarah for obvious personal reasons.[13] One result of these omissions may be that Sarah does not sound "real" or "vulnerable." It was suggested that I should have tried "probing the areas of omission" by more interviews with Sarah alone. But even if she *had* poured forth personal materials, my distress over the invasion of her privacy, of the ethics of the situation, would have compounded mathematically. Actually, we have had a multitude of informal visits alone over the years, visits too numerous to list in, or having taken place since, the interview schedule (Appendix A). Nonetheless, Sarah has continued to keep up that guard, to project the ideal either deliberately or unconsciously, I do not know which. To make inferences as a participant observer, then, one must leave the confines of tangible evidence (e.g., the taped and transcribed interviews of Sarah and her family). Such inferences are necessarily tentative and conservative.

We can surmise that there are problems in Sarah's family life, in spite of her projections of it as ideal.[14] Such problems are simply a part of being alive and human. No doubt a profile of the "average" rural family (if there were such an entity) would correspond to Sarah's. Every family, rural or urban, has its share of alcoholism, divorce, ne'er-do-wells, religious differences, and strained marital relationships. And every family would be equally careful not to discuss these with outsiders (especially ones with tape recorders in the background).

Perhaps Sarah's continued idealizations disguise her concern, even anger, at the chauvinistic behavior of some of the male in-laws of the family. Her marriage relationship is a large question mark, especially since the time period covering it is the one about which Sarah says so little—to anyone. As an oral historian reminded us, "Freud told us long ago, our memories suppress the unpleasant—unfortunately for oral history."[15] Sarah cannot remember how she met her husband. There is no detail of their courtship, their wedding, their early life, or, in fact, any aspect of their personal relationship. Robert remains a shadow, a ghostly nonpresence. Sarah vehemently decried her sister Martha's divorce. But then, divorce was not an option for a woman with seven children, no land, no personal income (despite the fact that she was the primary custodian and conservator of the farm), and certainly no cultural or social or familial sanction. Does she protest too much? Sarah did not encourage her daughters to marry, according to Anne, but neither did she discourage them: it would have been an unconscionable break with tradition and with her own idealized image of woman as wife and mother. She did emphasize the value of education—"you can never have too much"—and hopes her granddaughters will stay in town to work and continue theirs.

Evidently she did not live "happily ever after." The strain of excelling in the cultural proscription of woman-in-the-home, as she was taught to do and did, must have produced and underscored deep ambivalence and conflict. That conflict emerges through Sarah's contradictory statements. She constantly idealizes and romanticizes her early years, even though they are the same ones that Martha strove to escape. Woman's role, however limited, was comfortably circumscribed then, following the paradigm she knew so well. And the role was modeled by an adored mother, sheltered by a beloved, loving father.

Almost a rhetorical ideal, she decries unequal treatment of women, possibly because she always champions the underdog. At the same time, she cannot realistically approve the mores that accompany change in women's status. They attack the matrix of her whole conception of woman: as wife, mother, and partner of God from her earthly throne, the home. Ideally, she hopes her daughters and granddaughters will follow her in the conception. Realistically, she sees the personal denigration in being subservient to a patriarchal husband as well as the economic necessity for working outside the home.[16] Mirroring these conflicts in a strange mixture, her buoyant optimistic lifestyle is almost negated by gloom-and-doom moralizing.

Turnings

Turnings (more popularly called "turning points") are the major transitions of a person's life. A turning combines new roles, new interactions, and new self-conceptions, and thus involves cultural, social, and psychosocial dimensions.[17] No single events that triggered major decisions or changes of outlook or situation stand out in Sarah's mind. Her major turnings were the culturally common rites of passage—marriage, motherhood, and widowhood.

However, the first turning, that of electing to attend high school, was less conventional. Still, education was greatly valued and advocated in her own family. Sarah's mother vehemently encouraged her eleven children to learn ("My mother was especially education-minded.... She used to read all night"). Sarah's aunt and later her older sister made high school possible by inviting her to live in town with them during the school week. High school was rather uncommon for women in that time and place, but Sarah's decision to attend college was even more unusual in the community.[18] It was, nevertheless, a move strongly supported by her family. After all, her oldest sister had preceded her at Ohio University several years before.

The second turning followed more accustomed patterns, returning home to live, teaching in one-room country schools ("If you couldn't teach, there was nothing else in the world you could do, and teachers couldn't live a normal life"). Marriage was the next turning, completely within the cultural matrix ("The whole family was married.... [The pattern was] to marry someone from around here. I think maybe it still is.... They kinda come back"). The new roles and interactions and self-conceptions created by marriage and then motherhood were comfortable ones, ones for which Sarah had prepared (and had been prepared for) all her growing years.

No major turnings were revealed then until the period in

which her husband died and the youngest children left home: Sarah was widowed and alone. The dimensions changed as Sarah was deprived of her accustomed roles as wife and mother. The new role was a difficult one, except for the fact that it was within expected cultural parameters. The next turning involved her decision to share her home and her life again, this time with an invalid sister. Again it was consistent with her fixed values on family and on nurturing.

And the last turning so far came with her resolution to sell the family farm, a move atypical for Sarah, since it involved initiative and assertiveness not characteristic of her usual role of traditional subservience to a husband. Still, it was consistent with community, and especially family, mores: her sisters had all worked in the public domain. In fact, Ellen, though a practicing nurse still, has long been an avid real estate trader, alledgedly with consistent and impressive financial success.

Adaptations

As a life develops over time, it includes continuous adjustment and periodic adaptations to cope with the new conditions of turnings. In each life history, the question arises: How did that person, given his or her opportunities, adapt—or fail to adapt? What changes were made, what elements were maintained?[19]

In the overall picture, Sarah's major adaptive behavior seems to have been a continuously forceful reliance on traditional concepts—of self, of family, of community, of the value of work—all implanted by family and community in her formative years.[20] She threw her considerable strength and determination into establishing a new home and family, later into continuing it. If she did this in spite of a difficult marriage, Sarah must have experienced a broad spectrum of disappointments, frustrations, and conflicts, none, of course, revealed in her idealized retellings.

Disappointments and conflicts are certainly a part of everyone's life. Therefore, they must be adapted to, managed, to reduce their inroads on the effectiveness of daily life. It is important to remember that adaptations are not necessarily a resolution of conflicts, but often an accommodation to them. Did Sarah, in addition to her overall reliance on traditional modes of behavior, employ other adaptations or conflict management methods? I observed several.

(1) She behaved as if a situation still existed. The one obviously traumatic turning in Sarah's life came when her own nuclear family had dissolved and she was left painfully alone. The explicit loss was compounded by an implicit one, deprivation of role: she was no longer needed, as wife or mother or nurse or cook or gardener or quilter or mediator. It was a devastating stage for Sarah, as it is for women worldwide, a stage that can (and does) transcend any barriers—city or country, rich or poor, black or white.[21] But it is an especially difficult stage for those who, like Sarah, have been a strong personal and cultural influence through their traditional roles in the home. Subordinate though they may be to husband and even children, they still gain a sense of extensive personal power through these duties (albeit sometimes a power perceived rather than real). The traditional mores and values that Sarah had embraced early in life were clung to all the more tightly in later years. She continued her daily life *as if* her roles of wife and mother had not changed drastically, thus alleviating the sorrow and devastation from loss of those demanding roles.[22] She did this by pursuing her appointed rounds of gardening, preserving, and cooking *as if* for many eaters; by cleaning *as if* for many dirt-trackers; by making up beds *as if* for many sleepers; by sewing *as if* for many wearers. In spite of being offered opportunities outside the home, she remained more comfortable inside it, still available as mother, nurse, comforter ("I was here if they needed me, you know").

(2) She changed the situation itself. Sarah used a replacement figure for the loss of family by inviting her sister Martha to live with her, thus placing Sarah again in the role of motherly nurturer with a sense of purpose.[23] It was undoubtedly difficult: their thirty years of silence grew out of Martha's complete divergence from the accepted "paths of righteousness," i.e., from traditional woman's role. She had not only left the farm but had wanted no children, had worked outside the home, and

had divorced a husband the family all liked, a man from their own community. It was an unusually major responsibility for an older person to assume. Yet the invitation not only eased Sarah's loneliness but also cast her again in the role of nurturer and nurse. She thus changed the situation to one where she was needed (especially by someone dependent), responding—characteristically—with an active, physical approach.

(3) She changed the perceptions of a situation. Sarah reduced the level of dissonance in her perceptions of a negatively changing world by joining a markedly conservative church.[24] It reflected her concept of woman's submissive and pious role ("A woman should not get up in church and speak. . . . A woman shouldn't speak in public. . . . The things she does not know, go to her husband for advice") as well as her own pessimism about the state of the world in general ("You know doggoned well our generation is going to the dogs, isn't it? . . . It's a terrible time to bring the little things [babies] into the world. There's nothing but suffering ahead for us. What kind of future have they got?"). This alliance also meant continued emphasis on traditional concepts of a patriarchal family and a patriarchal religion. However, it also added new conflicts: with several of her immediate family members, who objected—some violently—to a number of her new church's rulings, for example the prohibition of patriotic displays or attendance at the rites of other churches, such as weddings and funerals.

(4) She ignored a situation, or at least one aspect of it, that is, one set of values and demands. By the very act of being contradictory in speech and in action, Sarah is apparently able to use a *compartmentalizing* technique: she can identify with one set of values, beliefs, and corresponding actions at one moment, then with a contradictory set at another, by placing each in a separate "compartment."[25] Thus she is able to speak of woman as inferior to man ("The president of the United States, I think will always be a man. . . . Women are, I think, they're weaker"), and later of woman as equal ("If a woman is smart enough to be president, why not let her try?"). She has extremely strong feelings that "woman's place is in the home," yet she is able to compartmentalize this while admitting that "today two working

can't clothe and feed their children." The majority of the time she has acted out the traditional subservient wife role; she denied or undervalued her own contributions to, and her control of, the family and family finances, subsuming them in those of her husband, the patriarch. But at one point she compartmentalized those actions and values when she departed from tradition by insisting upon actively negotiating sale of the farm. She thus assumed a dominant role and countermanded her husband's actions (represented by his will). Certainly it was a significant break. We can only guess at the conflicting emotions that might have engendered such a drastic move. Her expressed desire to see the children enjoy the proceeds? A wish to have, for the first time, a small amount of extra money for herself? A need to experience finally a measure of control over the farm she had worked her whole adult life to upgrade and maintain? It may have been a desire to express tangibly the other side of the coin: that, as a woman who had administered and managed and improved that farm through the years, she was equal, as well as any man, to making such a managerial decision. Or it may have been a combination of all of these. Sarah does not tell.

It is not surprising that Sarah adhered so closely to tradition, raised as she was with such strong elements of cultural conditioning in a setting that offered few choices. The surprise is that she departed from it at all. But even if she had overtly questioned her role, mechanisms for dealing with such ambivalence and conflict were not easily available to rural women. Consciousness-raising groups did not emerge until the late 1960s, and these assisted younger urban women primarily. Sarah faced the conflict between tradition and modernity alone. Shared emotions do not seem to be an alternative in her culture. Her adaptations do indicate, however, her skills in continuing to grow as a person. Sarah is perhaps prototypical of those many women who have fought daily battles and gained small victories in the "long burdened marches across time and space."[26] Sarah has lived a long, fruitful life, modest by economic standards, but rich by the familial and spiritual ones she values. She has persisted and persisted, with tenacity and determination, in achieving her culture's highest standards for woman's role. She has become—at whatever personal cost—the biblical "capable wife" whose "works praise her."

SARAH PENFIELD'S LIFE STORY AS A STUDY

The story of Sarah, the capable wife, illustrates both a singular life and a representative life. Sarah is uniquely herself. She is also one among many. There is value in a word portrait of one woman: the individual is not obscured by graphs and statistics, but remains an artistic, holistic entity. Moreover, since theoretical research—especially in its early stages—is more a matter of finding the right categories than of measuring within them statistically, it is particularly fitting to use this kind of qualitative data for researching women's roles.

There is also importance in the story as a larger study, a set of data that can be an elegant combination of art and science, stemming in part from the humanities, in part from the social sciences—a true interdisciplinary study. It should be utilized, and utilized more often, as an end of scholarly interest rather than simply as a "tool," that is, a means of data-gathering incidental to more ambitious goals.[27]

This type of life history may serve as a personal document available to several disciplines—anthropology, folkloristics, sociology, rural sociology, women's studies, linguistics. For the life history provides a way to span the sometimes artificial limits of individual disciplines. It offers alternative ways of approaching contemporary problems so that we might achieve each discipline's ultimate goal: further understanding of the human condition.

I had intended at first to list neatly the results gained from my data as they applied to each of these separate disciplines. Now I see this as a disservice: Sarah, her family, and her area's history are not discrete pieces of biological, cultural, psychosocial elements but a sum of many parts, and deserve to be treated holistically rather than atomistically; in addition, if the life history can offer a valuable common denominator for scholars, *all* the results are important and have integral value for *each* discipline.

We see some of the benefits to be derived from the life history of a rural Ohio grandmother. It has brought the abstractions necessary in a community ethnography into sharper focus by detailing the real life of an individual in her society. It has thrown light on that society and its functioning: Sarah's narrative illuminates speech patterns, local attitudes and values, subsistence modes, socialization of children, the importance of kinship structures, sex roles, and social, educational, and religious institutions of her society. Most life history studies have concentrated on how the individual was shaped by culture. In this history we see some of the other side: how the individual shapes and perpetuates the culture.[28] For example, as an active, productive, forceful person, Sarah played the dominant role in the family, and was a strong model for her children, even though her husband was—as the culture dictated—nominal head of their household.

Further, this life history adds yet another basis for comparative study by describing an ecological niche in our civilization not previously studied. This is especially important in view of the general sweep of change that is causing so many customs and beliefs to pass unrecorded in formerly isolated areas (which southeastern Ohio was).[29]

There are still other valuable aspects of the life history. Its importance as a new oral genre is underscored; the strength tradition has in a person's life is again illustrated, perhaps even beyond our expectations. These qualitative materials provide ample linguistic data and demonstrate the significance of verbal behavior in communication. As H. L. Mencken reminded us (in dramatic but, unfortunately, gender-specific terms), "A man's language is his very soul. It is his thoughts and almost all his consciousness."[30]

The expansion of our perceptions of rural society is also valuable. Though it may be an overstatement to speak of an "archaic American hatred of the cities,"[31] a suspiciousness of city life emerges in Sarah's narrative. We need to learn more of the differences among the attitudes, beliefs, and values of rural and urban citizens. Country people are not, as their city cousins so often believe, either too phlegmatic or too unintelligent to move to the city. Most of them choose their rural life-style, even though commuting is often expensive in both time and money. (In a lovely reverse twist of the city boy's opinion of the country, Sarah's grandson wondered, "Why would anyone want to move to the city? There's nothing to *do* there!") Fuller recognition of city and country differences becomes even more important if large numbers of rural residents are nevertheless forced to migrate to the city again, adding to the cultural nonmix.

The data help us understand not only diachronic patterns of culture in a rural midwestern society (the traditions historically passed down from generation to generation) but also synchronic ones in the specific time frames treated (the effect of those traditions on the dispersed members of the current generation). In building upon the life of a "common person," as opposed to a famous one, we accomplish two things: we see history in phenomenological terms, as Everyman—and Everywoman—saw it. Individuals become their own historians, with history "the memory of things said or done" (what the crops were, what mother taught us, or how the hay was made, rather than what the great issues and who the famous presidents were in the past). The data repeatedly show how situations and events are perceived and interpreted by individuals, so we can begin to understand their values and objectives (e.g., World War I was momentous to the Flynns only in its disruption of their heavy emphasis on family ties and on living in the locus of the rural family domain). And, with a common-person biography, we move toward alleviating the "poisonous snobbery of great man/ significant event history." In directing research toward the common person, emphasis is focused on better communication and understanding between the scientific community and the public.[32]

It is almost a truism to speak now of the need to study the lives of the other half of our population as well as those of men, and to study them from a female's vantage rather than from only a male's reportage.[33] Strides in both the academic and the nonacademic literature have been giant ones in the past ten years, especially the past five. But many years of catching up remain. Thus the life story of one woman adds another small piece to this incomplete mosaic.

SARAH PENFIELD AND OTHER WOMEN

Sarah's story is one small piece, then, in a larger mosaic, a mosaic that reminds us of our own place, too, in its patterns. We are always contending with "that tension—that particularity of our selves as against the attributes we have with others who live much as we do."[34] Can the contradictory Sarah, then, offer a pattern, or a paradigm, for ambivalence in other women? But can one person *ever* be described as a paradigm for her age or sex or region or class, as "typical"? Sarah, of course, does not stand for all women, or all women of a certain age, class, or region. In that sense she is not a "type." Yet like the ubiquitous Flower Garden quilt, her life may be a version of a pattern so widely known it can be recognized as a type. Biographers know that one person's story can shed light on the stories of others too. The goal is "to move from the particular person to the broader arc of humanity" without distorting the truth.[35] Can Sarah's story illuminate the lives of other women who have a "split personality" image of themselves (inferior to man/equal to man) and their role (woman must work in the home/woman has a work choice)? Along with its methodological and historical perspective, this book addresses that theoretical question as well.

The theme of ambivalence surfaces in many feminist novels and nonfiction works. However, theoretical literature concerning women's lives has been introduced only recently. Therefore, the extent to which conflicting attitudes and behaviors trouble women in various geographic areas and age brackets is still speculative. There were signs of conflict in the early to mid-1970s. An extensive study of women of all ages, all over the United States, revealed a decided counterreaction to the idea of liberalizing woman's positions, as well as an insistence by white- and blue-collar women upon holding the traditional "position" of their own sex. Marabel Morgan's "Total Woman" concept scored heavy popularity as she urged wives to concentrate on being submissive to their husband's leadership. A considerable share of female audience members demonstrated growing animosity toward women speaking for equal rights. And Phyllis Schlafly built a large and supportive following after she founded STOP ERA.[36]

Certainly the accelerating spread of hostility toward the Equal Rights Amendment was a telling indicator of female (along with male) disagreement over appropriate attitudes and behaviors for women. It was also an indicator of skillful political opposition and of ambiguous legislative wording: the very simplicity of the amendment offered, according to its opponents, unending legal loopholes detrimental to women.[37]

Many women feared that the ERA was antithetical to home and family, and would somehow mean that all women *must* work outside the home. Many housewives believed that equal rights *excluded* them, since they were not "working women" in the classic sense (another divisive semantic). Older housewives (the group from which the anti-ERA forces drew most of their support), being financially dependent on spouses, assumed that they would be hurt by the ERA. Still others anticipated loss of the status and power inherent in the wife and mother role. The fears multiplied mathematically: of physical reprisals; of fighting in a war's front lines; of unisex toilets; of moral decay (for example, "We were told in our church that ERA meant the end of marriage, that school books would show pictures of people having sex with animals, and we've got to protect our children").[38] The values of the women who upheld the concept of True Womanhood in the nineteenth century—piety, purity, submissiveness or deference to males, domesticity—were thus recast by women in the twentieth century who remained (consciously or unconsciously) bound by traditional ideologies. And the ERA was stopped.

Whether or not these fears were warranted, they obviously were popular and widespread. Underlying the hostility of these tradition-bound women to legal equality was a contradictory perception of themselves as equal to, and yet unequal to, males. Although this is not a new hypothesis, especially among feminists, the power of this basic pattern has been underestimated,

A Woman's Place

so much so that we need to retrace our steps and attend to these "obvious" paradigms. A model illustrating this mixture of attitudes is shown below, using Sarah's ambivalent perceptions as an example: part of the time she sees woman as equal, part as inferior (to man); ideally she believes woman's only place is in the home, yet realistically she sees the need for many women to work outside it. Although this model uses Sarah's ambivalences as an example, it is applicable, too, for examining the values and attitudes concerning gender for other American women as well—women in different age brackets, in different ethnic groups, in different geographic locations.[39]

As we have seen, Sarah is a physically and emotionally dynamic person with a strong self-image. How much more difficult it would be to assess oneself in positive terms without the kind of forceful and supportive background Sarah had. How much more formidable to conquer ambivalence and conflict without the firm childhood conditioning and powerful role

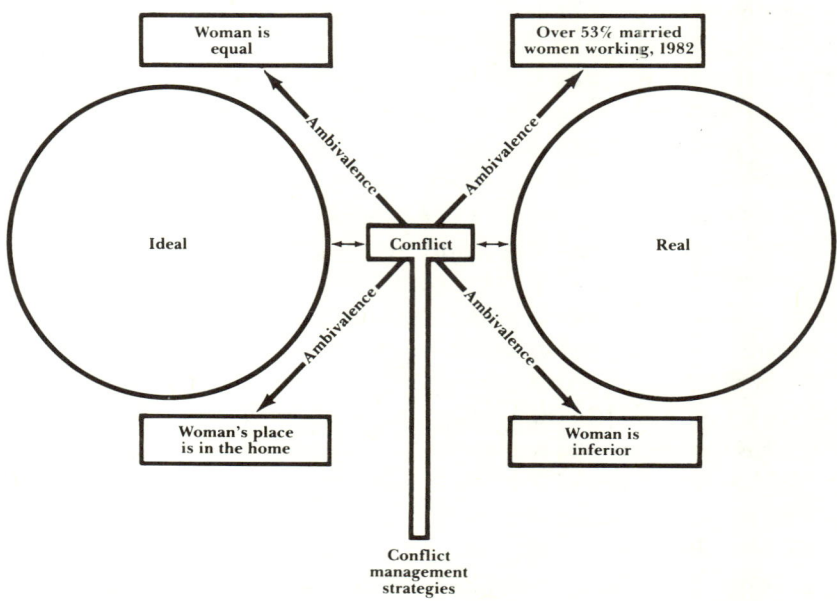

Ambivalence and Conflict in Tradition-bound Women

230

models Sarah had. Yet in a society that gives its males public and private sanction and encouragement, it has been difficult for even this strong, capable woman to maintain a positive image of the female, self and other. As the study of women's lives continues, we will undoubtedly find more and more evidence of conflict generated by traditional upbringing. One such study collected biographies in the 1960s and 1970s from women of different ages and races across the United States and reported on unusually strong, interesting, achieving women. A number of these examples underscore ambivalence and conflict in their attitudes. Reporting the emphasis on male superiority during their childhoods, a New England woman recalled: "I was brought up to defer to a man completely. My father always had the last word in our. . . . He became such a god in our home."[40] Similarly, another urban worker related: "My poor mother was always trying to fix herself up: for him, for his approval. . . . She turned and told me that a woman has to hold her husband, even if she is married to him. . . . I wanted to ask my mother, right then and there, why, why—what's the point of holding on to someone like that? She was becoming a nothing, and I could see it. . . . I didn't like the way she bowed and scraped before him."[41] A New Mexico Pueblo woman, from another culture, another region, echoed: "I didn't like the way I was brought up to think of men—the ones who gave life to women, as the sun does to the earth. But I didn't want to be against my people—and I knew the Anglos spoke worse words about their women."[42]

Not only were they taught that men were the most important, but also that boys were too. Career options for girls were thus different ones: "I remember once in the sixth or seventh grade, hearing my mother say to my father that if I was a boy, she'd really push me in my schoolwork, but a girl, it's different."[43] To the young woman who aspired to being a doctor, grandmother enjoined: "Medicine is not a good profession for women; it's too tough and women aren't strong enough. . . . Women weren't 'made' to be doctors or lawyers, but were 'made' to be wives and mothers."[44] Still another wanted to be a doctor, and her classmates jeered, especially a girl who wanted to be a secretary:

"She kept razzing me: who did I think *I* was—not wanting to do what 'everyone else' was quite pleased to be thinking of doing!"[45]

In spite of their strengths and their achievements, the strands of ambivalence and conflict are a running theme even with these women. One, a woman with astute introspections, was always qualifying herself with a disclaimer or a renunciation: "Who am I, after all? I'm just a housewife, an American woman with a husband and three kids, so why should Jesus Christ Almighty stop in His shoes and listen to my whys, and my bellyaching?" Later: "There I was, the one who was pregnant, thinking I'd done something wrong, and would be criticized by my husband, the one who had everything in the world to do with getting me pregnant!" She is a nurse in a large hospital, a career she struggled against enormous odds to achieve. "I must be a mixed-up person: some mornings I leave the house and I almost want to stay, and just sit there and enjoy what Tim and I have built up for ourselves. Other mornings, on my day off, I get restless, and I miss the hospital routine." She is the same one who, more political later, demurred to answer any questions at first: "We're [in this suburb] just average housewives on this street. I don't think we have any opinions one way or the other. . . . If you want to know what we think here, you'll have to come on the weekend, when my husband is around."[46]

Still another aspect of conflict for these women arose from the clash of values in the workplace. The continuing ambivalence and conflict between any kind of feminist ideals and the reality of living and working with particular men are familiar ones, even to—perhaps especially to—poor women. As Laura, the New England woman, pondered her early problems of getting ahead in the working world, her friend told her that "every woman who has a serious interest in a career has to come to terms with men . . . [who] really have the ultimate authority: they are the principals or the superintendents, or they run the hospitals, the wards; they even supervise the education of the students. . . . I've been propositioned so many times, I honestly lost count. . . . You can say no, but use the man's interest to help your career along." Laura protested that such an attitude was "cheap and calculating." Her friend replied, "I'm not trying to tell you what ought to be in some heaven. I'm trying to tell you what *is*—what goes on every single day. . . . If you want to live in this world, then you've got to keep your eyes and ears open, and know what the score is!"[47]

Similarly, the bank teller realized in high school: "A woman who wants to get ahead in this world of ours won't get far if she seems too independent. She has to look as if she's a little helpless, or in trouble." And, "If she tries to push into a man's world, she'll be on their ground, and she'll lose—even if she does all right, she'll lose. . . . A lot of women won't admit to themselves there is that connection [between work and sex] even though in the back of their minds they know better."[48]

Another study of married persons recorded a clear discrepancy between both husbands' and wives' values and their behaviors in the marriage. It was projected that there would be obvious conflict between men and women with such differing values. There would also be conflict for those who came to realize the discrepancies between their *own* values and behaviors.[49]

One might expect more unconventional concepts and values to be implanted by education, in direct ratio to years of attendance: that is, the higher the level of schooling, the less traditional the attitude. However, studies of even college women showed that their systems of belief are based on concepts of *appropriate* female behavior, and that, consequently, they still aim for traditional—that is, "appropriate"—jobs.[50] The New England woman quoted earlier, a college graduate and an executive, recalled that during her career "I was fighting some notion I'd inherited from my family that a woman who marries should spend her time fixing up a home—and waiting: for her husband to come home, for a child to arrive. . . . I didn't want to give up my career but I was afraid to pursue it too hard, now that I was married. I had to find a way of keeping going, but shifting gears enough to appease my sense of what I 'should' do—become a good wife."[51] Later she worried, "If I become a 'feminist,' I'll end up counting incidents, surveying attitudes, conscious and unconscious, finding fault endlessly, and soon I'll be without a job. Then I'll be even more bitter, and some life it'll be!"[52] In Chicago a young career woman and new mother shared her concerns: "It was dismaying how quickly the traditional assumptions surfaced when we found ourselves so pressed: I felt guilty about leaving [my baby] Sarah to go to work, and Curt felt guilty about leaving work to take care of Sarah."[53] Even my own concepts of "appropriate female behavior" are ambivalent on occasion. A number of times I have caught myself wondering why a young mother in my class was not "home where she belonged, taking care of her children like she should!"

How accentuated such reactions must be for women who are even more inclusively tradition-bound. Certainly we have observed this in both Sarah and her daughters: though either circumstances or choice dictated their entering the labor market, they nonetheless have continuing strong traditional behaviors, attitudes, and values concerning woman's role, woman's "place."

Whatever ambivalence women express, sex roles are changing, and changing dramatically. Even Sarah—an older, rural, heretofore isolated, traditional woman—is beginning to recognize that. Her daughters and her granddaughters are experiencing it. Statistics show that a startling transition has already taken place. Women's longevity has increased enormously. Women are marrying either later or less often. They are divorcing more often, remarrying less frequently. Nonfamily households have increased; and one-parent households have doubled, with the vast majority maintained by the mother. Despite the sharp drops in unemployment, women are entering the labor force in increasingly greater numbers and proportions even during childbearing and child-raising years.[54] Sarah's daughters provide examples of many of these changes. One salient fact emerges from these statistics: the projections for the next two decades promise a very different nuclear family makeup than is now thought to be standard. There will be new family structures, new housing patterns, even more fragmentation of traditional roles.[55]

Sarah, the Capable Wife, and Other Women

If ideologies do indeed shape women's lives, and if many women today have been exposed to traditional upbringing, then talk of equality between the sexes achieved through enlarged public roles is premature. Until women are able to obtain and maintain perceptions of themselves as equal to men, as having role choices as diverse and as viable as men's, it will matter far less what statistics reveal concerning the rising percentage of female workers or the larger number of female heads-of-household. It will matter far less what strides are made by *individual* women in the arts or commerce or athletics, in any one of a myriad of potential careers. A true status of equality must be accompanied by the sustained belief of women generally in themselves as equal, as "inheritors of the fruits of the earth" *and* of their own labors.

Granted, this conclusion poses another chicken-and-egg problem. How can women preserve a strong self-image while they are yet exposed to prejudice and exploitation? How can they have the strength and determination to overcome prejudice and exploitation without consistently strong self-images? And how can men develop complementary images of women as strong and equal if they do not see strong and equal behavior?

No one study or group of studies can be conclusive. By studying Sarah's daughters, her granddaughters, their country cousins and their city cousins, however, we can begin to resolve the conflict of these ambivalences, perhaps by the very approach Sarah uses so effectively: tenacity and determination.

From available statistics and projections it seems certain then that both girls and women will attempt to, or be forced to, break out of the traditional wife/mother role. There is a potential of serious disorder in our society unless this physical change in female living patterns is accompanied by attitudinal changes in both women and men toward females' appropriate behavior. Consequently, there is profound need for broader understanding of conflict in women and a recognition of the inhibiting power of ambivalence. For it is vital that our country obtain the twin capacities of Sarah's sons *and* her daughters. By resolving these conflicts, a woman's place—the literal and the figurative—

can become far more significant both to herself and to her society: the "great American style" of both rural and urban women can offer even broader strengths and more meaningful contributions.

    1. Lange (1967:13).
    2. Mandelbaum (1973:180). See chap. 1, above, note 8, for references to other life history criticisms since 1935.
    3. Langness and Frank, while reiterating the historical calls for analysis, posited Mandelbaum's framework as "probably the most important scheme available for gathering and interpreting the lives of others" (1981:72). Frazier (1978:139) made a strong plea for setting up standards for life histories. See Kelley (1978: esp. 31) for another type of framework. Langness and Frank devoted a whole chapter to discussing analysis and detailing extant analyses (1981:63–86).
    4. See Richardson (1981). See also Rohrbaugh (1979: Part 1, 13–77), Bernard (1981), and Lott (1981). Komarovsky pointed out that "to be born a woman means to inhabit, from early infancy to the last day of life, a psychological world which differs from the world of man," quoted in Bernard (1981:v).
    5. See Rusek (1978), Bermosk and Porter (1979), and Goldwag (1979) concerning holistic relationships and the interdependence of mind, body, and spirit. "Our sense of our bodies . . . is the basis upon which we build our self image" (Richardson [1981:140]; see also chapter 8). Richardson also reminded that, using the biocultural view, social and cultural life is explainable by social and cultural factors; it cannot and should not be reduced to the biological level (1981:175). See also MacCormack and Strathern (1980) and Ortner and Whitehead (1981:1) who posited that what gender is reflects more than biological givens; gender, sexuality, and reproduction are . . . "symbols, invested with meaning by the society in question."
    6. Mandelbaum (1973:180).
    7. Ibid.
    8. Welter (1966) reviewed the concepts of "True Womanhood" in nineteenth-century literature. The quotations are Burnap, in Welter (1966:170).
    9. Stoeltje (1975:41). See Luchetti and Olwell (1982) and Jordan (1982) for differing treatments of women of the west.
    10. See pp. 3–4 for Sarah's quotation of her favorite biblical passage.
    11. Nor was Sarah the only one to do so: see Baxter (1978:45–46).
    12. Mandelbaum (1973:180).
    13. Kluckhohn (1945:146) made an important statement concerning these omissions: "What the informant does *not* say, when and how he says what he does, may have for the subtleties of both cultural and psychological analysis an importance equal to that of the explicit content. Surprisingly enough, anthropologists have been somewhat insensitive even to the cultural control and

patterning of emotional manifestations. They would do well to reflect upon these statements by Dr. Whitehorn, a psychiatrist: 'Sometimes such conventionalized patterns of behavior and the corresponding verbalizations are used with the deliberate intention of deceiving others, but this is not the phenomenon of which I now speak. . . . My own observations would lead me to believe that in ordinary living these modes of behavior commonly called "the emotions" are the modes of reaction by which one *resolves*, and in effect, *escapes from* the essential emotionality of the experience. That is to say, the emotions . . . are the expression of sentiments in whose development there has been a large measure of cultural or conventional training.'"

14. See also Chiñas (1973:92).

15. Fry (1977:85) discussed Freud. Swain (1965:68) commented on our "extraordinary facility for forgetting unpleasant things."

16. This is not a simple subject, of course. Working-class women look at marriage as an economic necessity rather than as an option, according to some (Ferree, in Richardson [1981:221]). But there are also cultural implications: "Working-class men and women may be unhappy with their lives or their current interpersonal relationships, but may find it difficult or impossible to identify with 'solutions' that require a man to give up part of his 'macho' image or a woman to identify with life roles other than those of wife and mother" (in Schaffer [1981:308–9]).

17. Mandelbaum (1973:181). However, the word *turning* implies change or movement (for example, "turning a corner"), and is not so applicable for a woman in a traditional society: her potential for changes are limited and few.

18. Figures for the number of rural women who attended college in Ohio are not available; no records have been kept or statistics collected that would be applicable.

19. Mandelbaum (1973:181–82).

20. See also Hagood (1939:76); see Abrahams (1971:67) on the use of traditional expression in the face of threat. See Hicks (1976:49) for the dysfunctional aspects of tradition in the face of change.

21. This is a subject in itself, of course, and one that has generated extensive comment in the literature, e.g., Sheehy (1974, 1981), Stevenson (1977). André (1981) discussed the programs in the public and private sectors aimed specifically at "displaced homemakers," and the variety of related services.

22. Parkes (1972:63, chaps. 4, 5) discussed mourners acting "as if" life were still the same, not acknowledging the dead person as gone from the environment, e.g., leaving the furniture in the place that person wanted it.

23. This is similar to the concept of "replacement child" in Lavigne (1980:40). Sheehy (1981) found a "sense of purpose" was the guiding principle that carried a large number of individuals over difficult passages in their lives (she termed them "pathfinders").

24. This is an adaptive process in which finding others to agree with one's own cognitions seems the best way to eliminate dissonance (Festinger 1968:200, and esp. chap. 10).

25. See Goode (1960:486) and Poloma (1972:esp. 190–93).

26. Coles and Coles (1978:273). See Stevenson (1977:esp. 121–22, 184) with reference to continuing growth as persons; she shows growth *can* continue until death, especially if society will expect and allow adaptations.

27. Langness (1965:1,53); Dégh (1975:x–xi).

28. Langness and Frank (1981:73).

29. See Bourguignon (1980) for an excellent comparison of Joyce's chapter (1980) on Sarah Penfield with the eleven other chapters included on women in societies around the world. (One of Bourguignon's students wrote, "Sarah Penfield's life history let me know we aren't really that much more advanced on women's issues than are other countries around the world.") Bohannan (1978:1) called for the study of econiches. Kardiner (1945:37) advocated detailing the individual's life, as did Bourguignon (1979:172).

30. (1937:44). See also Hall (1959, 1966) for discussions of "body language," the "silent language" of space and time concepts. Angell (1945: 178) discussed using data to help us understand individuals' objectives.

31. Schlesinger (1975).

32. DuBos (1965) called for academics to return to the "original human basis of their work . . . with a greater emphasis on human values." Becker (1932) wrote of Everyman, and Ives (1976:251) of "great man/significant event" history.

33. See, e.g., Rosaldo and Lamphere (1974:vi), Ardener (1975:viii), Jordan (1975:199), Friedl (1975:v), and Reiter (1975:12).

34. Coles and Coles (1980:7).

35. Ibid., p. 3. See Aberle (1967:130) on application of life history analysis, in a critique of Simmons's *Sun Chief* (1942): "Only by seeing the individual in the social network, only by understanding the range of individual reactions, can we advance to an encompassing view of [Hopi] society in operation."

36. The study was Coles and Coles (1980:6); Morgan (1973); Felsenthal (1981:242). See Richardson (1981:251–57) and Snyder (1979:13–38) for a history of the women's movement, or feminist social movement.

37. Felsenthal (1981) is a biography of Schlafly. The Equal Rights Amendment's short wording is:

Section I: Equality of rights under the law shall not be denied or abridged by the United States or by any State on account of sex.

Section II: The Congress shall have the power to enforce, by appropriate legislation, the provisions of this article.

Section III: This amendment shall take effect two years after the date of ratification.

See Becker (1981) on the origins of the ERA, and Greenberg (1976) for a bibliographic study of it.

38. Felsenthal (1981:chaps. 15–20); the comment of a Mississippi woman (279) was noted by an AP reporter. See Fitzgerald (1981) for an excellent review of Felsenthal.

39. See Seward (1945), Potter (1964), and Gross, McEachern, and Ward

(1966) for earlier works recognizing this kind of conflict, or at least potential for conflict, in women. See Dowling (1981) for a treatise on women's fear of independence. See McNall (1981) for the recurrent theme—the young women's ambivalence—reflected in two centuries of women's fiction in America.

40. The project was reported in Coles and Coles (1978 and 1980). The quote is from Coles and Coles (1980:26).

41. Ibid., p. 66.

42. Ibid., p. 185.

43. Ibid., p. 84. Fox (1977:805) notes that the form of control over the social behavior of women most prevalent in Western tradition is that of "normative restriction." As a value construct, the term "nice girl" connotes "chaste, gentle, gracious, ingenious, good, clean, kind, virtuous, noncontroversial, and above suspicion and reproach." There is continual pressure, transmitted at first by peers and parents and later by the girl herself to act like and thereby become a "nice girl" (Maccoby in Fox [1977:809]).

44. Coles and Coles (1980:21).

45. Ibid., p. 204.

46. Ibid., pp. 198–99; 222; 236; 6. Thomas, interviewing 56 women across rural America, heard the same thing from those farm women: "'I don't know why you want to talk to me,' nearly everyone said. 'I have nothing to say,' (1981:xv) and, 'There's nothing important about me.'" (xviii). Strasser, yet another interviewer, found that the women discounted their experiences, and after a lifetime of hard work would ask, "Why did I want to record 'this junk'?" She also noted that "humility finds daily reinforcement in a society that measures value in money and holds the work of those who earn no money to be without value" (1982:4).

47. Ibid., pp. 35–36.

48. Ibid., pp. 71, 74–75; see Richardson (1981:223): egalitarian marriages "will remain mythic ideals until women have the same access to the distribution of valued goods."

49. André (1981:129–31) reported on Araji's study and her own projections. Noting another societal cause of conflict in women, Ferguson (1973:2) discussed the baffling pairs of opposing adjectives used by sociologists to describe real women, as well as those used also by literary critics to describe those real women's reflections in literature. Examples were passive-aggressive, possessive–self-sacrificing, frigid-lustful. The only common factor was that their standard was the same: men's characteristics were the norm, women's the abnormal. Bardwick and Douvan (1971) offered a Freudian-based theory on the social pressures that exaggerate initial biological differences and create stress and ambivalence; reviewed in Rohrbaugh (1979:168–72). Bernard (1971:151), in a review of the extensive literature on marital satisfaction and mental health, concluded that (1) conforming to feminine sex-role stereotypes—dependent, cautious, indecisive—enhances a woman's chances of viewing her marriage as happy. However, she suggested that women who conform to societal expectations and norms for marriage judge themselves "happy"—confusing it with "adjusted"—at great cost to themselves, often the

serious psychological disability and depression reflected in statistics on women.

50. Cerra (1980); Lipman-Blumen (1972:34–42).
51. Coles and Coles (1980:41).
52. Ibid., p. 57.
53. Curley et al (1981:40).
54. Statistics on women illustrate sharply changing sociological patterns. Longevity increased form 48.3 years life expectancy in 1900 to 77.8 years in 1979 for the total female population, 78.3 for the white female population (U.S., Department of Commerce 1981a:69). The median age of females at first marriage rose from 20.3 in 1950 to 22.1 in 1980 (U.S., Department of Commerce 1981b:1). The percentage of women who have never married has increased. The divorce rate in 1980 had more than doubled since 1970, but had nearly tripled since 1960 (U.S., Department of Commerce 1981b:2). Women are remarrying less frequently. In fact, the number of unmarried couples tripled between 1970 and 1980 (U.S., Department of Commerce 1981b:1–2). More than one of every four households in 1981 was a nonfamily household, that is, maintained by a person or persons not sharing the quarters with any relatives; this is an increase of 85% since 1970 (U.S., Department of Commerce 1982:2). The falling birthrate and this disproportionate growth in nonfamily households contributed to a decline in the average household size from 3.14 persons in 1970 to 2.73 in 1981 (U.S., Department of Commerce 1982:1). Even the Census Bureau recognized these changes and was moving from the traditional practice of using "head of household" as the central reference person to the new term, "householder," "because of its hierarchical implications" (U.S., Department of Commerce 1981b:4).

The one-parent household total had doubled since 1970; those maintained by men increased 95% and by women, 97% (U.S., Department of Commerce 1982:1). These one-parent families accounted for 21% of the families with children in 1981 (1 out of 5, compared with 1 out of 10 in 1970). The number of families maintained by a never-married parent has increased by 349% since 1970. *The vast majority (90%) of one-parent families are maintained by the mother* (my emphasis; U.S., Department of Commerce 1982:5). One out of every five children lived with only one parent in 1980 (U.S., Department of Commerce 1981b:1).

Even though unemployment figures continued to climb at the end of 1982, and the overall employment ratio was at its lowest level in at least thirty-five years, the participation rate for adult women rose a full percentage point in the labor force in one year, to 53.2%, while participation for adult men and teenagers declined (U.S., Department of Labor 1982:7–9). Fullerton (1980:11) projected that "women will account for ⅔ of the growth in the labor force by 1995; most of that growth will occur in the prime working age group."

55. Smith (1979), Bohen and Viveros-Long (1981), and Lipman-Blumen (1976:67–79) discuss fragmentation of traditional roles. Wekerle, Peterson, and Morley (1980), and Freidan (1981:esp. 237–342) forecast new structures and patterns. Compare with historical material on working women; see, for example, Tax (1981), Walshok (1981), Cardinale (1982), Kessler-Harris (1982), and Katzman and Tuttle (1982).

Appendix A. Identification of Numbered or Lettered Interviews as Sources of Quotations

	Date	Place	Present*	No. of Typescript pages
	I. Sarah Penfield (taped interviews)			
1.	24 October 1972	Penfield residence	Anne (daughter)	35
2.	10 November 1974	Penfield residence	Mr. Joyce (researcher's husband); grandson (briefly)	56
3.	27 April 1975	Penfield residence	Martha (sister)	45
4.	13 October 1975	Penfield residence	Martha	43
5.	14 October 1975	Penfield residence	Martha	17
6.	14 October 1975(a)	Penfield residence	Two granddaughters, Martha	11
	13 December 1975(b)	Penfield residence	Martha	6
7.	13 December 1975	Penfield residence	Martha; neighbor's girl	10
8.	14 June 1977	Penfield residence	Martha	16
9.	14 June 1977	Penfield residence	Martha	58
10.	14 June 1977	Penfield residence	Martha	24
11.	18 July 1977	Joyce residence	Anne	24
12.	18 July 1977	Joyce residence	Anne	26
13.	13 September 1977	Penfield residence	Martha	27
14.	13 September 1977	Penfield residence	Martha	54
15.	13 September 1977	Penfield residence	Martha	21

Appendixes

Appendix A (Continued)

	Date	Place	Present*	No. of Typescript pages
16.	7 September 1978	Joyce residence		2
17.	10 December 1978	Penfield residence	Martha and Ellen (another sister)	52
18.	10 December 1978	Penfield residence	Martha and Ellen	35
19.	18 December 1978	Penfield residence		28
20.	18 December 1978	Penfield residence		51
21.	18 December 1978	Penfield residence		21
	I. Sarah Penfield (field notes and postinterview notes)			
a.	13 October 1975	Penfield residence	Martha	3
b.	14 October 1975	Penfield residence	Martha	1
c.	24 November 1975	Automobile	Martha, Anne	4
d.	13 December 1975	Penfield residence	Martha	8
e.	14 June 1977	Penfield residence	Martha	6
f.	18 July 1977	Joyce residence	Anne	3
g.	13 September 1977	Penfield residence	Martha	4
h.	10 February 1978	Penfield residence	Martha	1
i.	20 February 1978	Penfield residence	Martha	2
j.	4 October 1978	Penfield residence	Martha	3
k.	18 December 1978	Penfield residence		3
l.	18 February 1979	Penfield residence	Martha, Mr. Joyce, Ms. Joyce	1
m.	7 May 1979	Penfield residence	Martha	2
n.	20 June 1979	Automobile	Anne	4
o.	19 July 1979	Penfield residence	Martha, Mr. Joyce	1
	II. Anne Penfield Hoffman (taped interviews)			
1.	11 September 1978	Joyce residence		10
	II. Anne Penfield Hoffman (field notes and postinterview notes)			
a.	October 1975	Hoffman residence	Mr. Hoffman, 3 grandchildren, Mr. Joyce	1
b.	24 November 1975	Joyce residence		7
c.	May 1977	Telephone		1
d.	14 June 1977	Hoffman residence	Debbie (Anne's daughter)	3
e.	10 July 1977	Joyce residence		1

Appendix A (Continued)

	Date	Place	Present*	No. of Typescript pages
[f.	18 July 1977: see I. f, above]			
g.	19 June 1978	Joyce residence		1
h.	29 April 1979	Hoffman residence		1
i.	1 May 1979	Automobile		1
k.	17 May 1979	Joyce residence		1
l.	20 July 1979	Joyce residence		4
m.	4 April 1982	Joyce residence		2
	III. James Penfield (field notes and postinterview notes)			
a.	18 August 1976	Joyce residence	Susan (James's wife)	5
b.	23 April 1979	Joyce residence	Joyce family, James's neighbor	4
	IV. Debbie Hoffman (field notes and postinterview notes)			
a.	4 September 1977	Automobile		2

*In addition to subject and researcher

Appendix B. Transcription of "Autobiography" Recording, Interview 16

My name is Sarah Penfield, Sarah Flynn Penfield. And I was born in the year of nineteen o three in the township of Bay, Ohio. I have lived in this community all of my life, I am now seventy-four years old. During my lifetime I attended a little country school, we had all eight grades in this little schoolhouse, we experienced many happy times, uh, we had social gatherings, and, uh, in the school we learned many of the different things that helped us throughout life, uh, we especially studied arithmetic, spelling, reading, and writing, till we became pretty good in that, later in life then we had our little high school, which was a great help to us. [Cleared throat.] We learned all the different household chores, our mother was very efficient in teaching us cooking, sewing, we helped with many of the outside chores with our father, we learned how to milk cows, we learned how to raise vegetables and can them [low laugh, pause]. Along with our many days of labor and things, we had our good times, uh, at this little school, we many times, many times in the evenings we would have spelling bees, we would often have pie socials, we would have, uh, box socials, and, uh, many different social gatherings, which we enjoyed very much. The neighbors were very friendly at this time, we always helped each other in case of emergencies or sickness, and things of that sort, and, uh, oh dear, I'm stuck.

R [from kitchen]: How about when you were, before you went to school, when you were real little, can you remember anything, any stories that your mother told about when you were a baby? Or do you remember anything from when you were real young?

We, uh, when we were small, we liked nature very much. We spent many hours, there was a woods near our house and rocks and we spent many hours as children, especially we liked to cut grapevines and we liked to make swings, and we liked to climb up the sides of the hills, which were pretty high. We played games around the rocks, many hours were spent that way. [pause] Give me some more suggestions.

R: Do you remember any specific incidents, did your mother ever say any stories about—?

We were, uh, interested in stories our mother in the evenings would tell us stories, we would set by the fireside and toast onions in the ashes of the stove, and our mother would read to us, many interesting stories, and we loved to go to Sunday School, we, uh, went to church of an evening, and sometimes we'd walk three and four miles in a group to get to these gatherings. Now.

R: Okay, were there any things that you remember about, stories about your brothers and sisters?

In my family, we had a very large family, we had, there were six girls and then five boys. [long pause]

R: Do you remember anything particular about it?

Well, there were social gatherings, which we attended, and we liked to visit the rocks, and take hikes through the fields, and through the woods. [pause] And of course, being children that were raised in the community, we raised about everything that we needed for our livelihood, we raised large patches of cane, which we made into cane syrup. We also raised fields of buckwheat, which was ground and made into *delicious* buckwheat cakes, we raised all our own pork, we had our own cows, we had our own milk and butter, we enjoyed doing, taking care of them, we had our horses, we loved to ride horseback. Many times we would go out in the fields and help our father with the hay season when he needed help, we enjoyed all these sort of things that go along with farm life. [pause] Now. [She tiptoed into the kitchen where I was and whispered to me, so as not to be recorded, presumably.] I won't talk loud, or I'll probably talk into it, I'll spoil it. I'll quit for today, and mebbe I can take some notes, we can take some notes and then I'll have something new [to tell into the recorder].

R: Okay.

Wouldn't that be better?

R: That's fine.

Appendix C. Sarah

5 GENERATION

○ FEMALE   △ MALE   ⌀ DECEASED

JOHN FLYNN — ? HEILBRONN

FLYNN

— EDWARD — — — — — — HAROLD

MARTIN — HANNAH   MARTHA   SARAH FLYNN PENFIELD — ROBERT PENFIELD   CHARLIE

PENFIELD

SALLY — WILL   ROBERT — JEAN   JAMES — SUSAN   ANNE — ADOLF   DENNY — BARBARA

SHELLEY   DEBBIE   HEIDI   FRANK

nealogy Chart
GENEALOGY 1830–1981

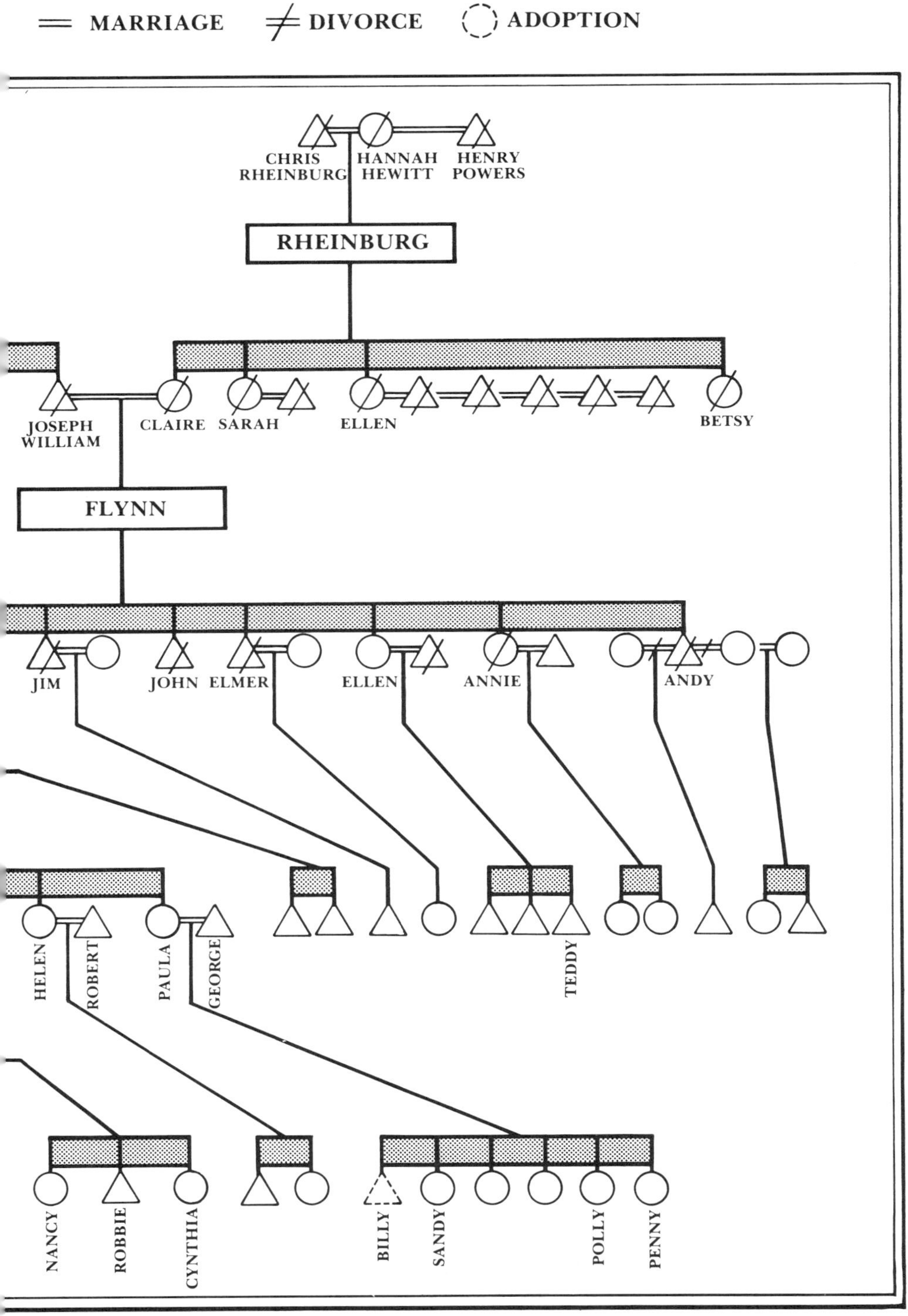

= MARRIAGE ≠ DIVORCE ◯ ADOPTION

Appendix D
Other Versions of Personal Experience Story

Below are other versions of the personal experience story, Chapter 5, p. 138.

I know one time, Frank, Robert's brother, he was always trying to torment somebody, and, uh, and his brother-in-law was sitting out and he had put him to cleaning the pig ears, and he told him he had to clean 'em till he couldn't find a hair, which would be an awful job! And, I went to the barn to milk, and, uh, Percy looked at me, he asked if he had to do it, and I said "No, we always threw those away," and he said, "Well, I'll fix him." So he got a raw kidney and got him a slice of bread and he fixed Frank a sandwich. They just goof around like that. And they would stay all night and have a really good time. [9]

We had company, you know, like my husband's brother would come on Sunday and we'd spend the day together, or some of my family, and little things like that. . . . Like when we butchered now, Martha was telling you about it. It was awfully cold, and maybe my husband would butcher a pork for his brother and we'd get together and have a lot of fun those days. And I can remember when Percy, my sister-in-law's brother, came along, and, uh, Frank, Robert's brother, was always acting the fool, and he told him he had to clean the hair off the ears, and he didn't dare leave the hair on, and it was so cold and I went to the barn to milk and, uh, he was sitting down there and he asked if he had to do that; he was just about frozen and I said, "No, Frank's just guyin' you." So he went and got a kidney and a couple of slices of bread, and took a raw kidney and made Frank a sandwich. Just goofing around, things like that, you know, and we all stayed together. I think we slept three double in a bed, and we all stayed, you know, at night, then all night and stayed together. We had good times. [14]

Appendix E
Sarah's Verbal Genres

Earlier I suggested that the life history be treated as a genre in itself, with any "subgenres" a part of the pattern of this one person's life. For although a life history can be separated folkloristically into sections of discrete genres, there is always the danger of losing either the context of the original situation or, worse, the sense of the performer as an entity. However, Sarah has already been presented in context throughout the book, so in order to add comparative material, her few verbal genres are presented here.

Although Sarah is an extraordinary bearer of tradition (as well as a skillful narrator), she is not one in the classic generic sense: standard verbal categories are barely represented in her dialogue.

Sarah tells no myths or legends or tales. She referred to only three songs. She delivers no jokes, and only a few proverbs are scattered through her accountings. (Unfortunately, folk names and their etymologies cannot be included; since all names have been fictionalized, this category is automatically eliminated.) A few belief items are threaded into her conversation. The closest she comes to standard oral presentation is with the personal, or local, legend—presented elsewhere (Joyce 1982). Material culture genres, obviously more easily discernible, have been referred to throughout the biography; for example, butchering procedures, making soap, apple butter, and molasses. Several were conspicuous with Sarah: quilting, crocheting, gardening, and foodways in its broadest spectrum, including preserving.

Appendixes

The songs, and mention of dancing, were elicited by my own guitar-playing and singing, and by my literally striking a chord of recognition with "Skip to M' Lou":

Sarah: Oh yes, you go according to what the words are, the words. [to granddaughter] Do you want to hear that one, honey? "Fly in the Sugar Bowl"? Okay, we're gonna hear it.
[Martha and Sarah sing along with R, to "Skip to M' Lou."]
Sarah: And they'd always swing, you know, they'd *skip* to m' Lou, skip to m' Lou.
Martha: Had to keep time with it.
R: Then what?
Martha: You'd skip around the circle, and twine—twine's not the right word, circle in other words.
Sarah: "Skip, skip, skip to m' Lou" is when you go round—
Martha: —your partner'd swing ya, and then skip—
Sarah: You would skip when you say "Skip, skip"—
Martha: —instead of waltzing, you'd skip.
R: Yeah. What are some more words?
Martha: I don't remember the rest of them, really [laughs].
Sarah: Do you know "The Little Brown Jug"? My father always loved that.

> The little brown jug, don't I love thee?
> Set her down by the roots of a tree.
> Ummm—

Martha: "Little brown jug, don't I love thee?" That was a liquor jug, of course [laughing].
Sarah: Oh yes, well, uh, that was "Johnny, Fill up the Jug," that was a different one:

> Johnny, fill up the jug,
> I'll never get drunk any more.

Martha: Yeah.
Sarah: Maybe that'd come to me if I put 'em down just a little bit. Let's see [sings]

> Fill up the jug, I'll never get drunk any more.
> Little brown jug, don't I love thee,
> Set her down by the roots of a tree,
> Little brown jug, don't I love thee.

Appendixes

Now come on, Martha, you—

Martha: It's a song to repeat over and over again, really. All those are.

Sarah: Yes, but you know they're written down someplace, we could get them, I'm sure.

[Tape problem; sequence broken.]

Sarah: "Swing the ladies around and around." And, of course, that's when they swing, you know.

R: How does that tune go [fingering the tune of "Old Dan Tucker"].

Martha: "It's too late to get his supper"—

Sarah:

> Supper's over, dishes washed,
> Nothing left but the neck of a squorsh.
> So Old Dan Tucker [chuckling]
> Swing them around and around and around.

R: [Sings tune.]

Sarah: Yeah, that's right! [Sings along for a verse.] Oh, there's more to it than that. Do you know sometimes when I'm asleep I'll wake up and it'll come to me. That's a good one, that's fast. They really step that one! [R singing; Sarah fills in the "squash" verse.] Now why, if somebody like that could play the banjo, and someone sing along with ya, and then they'd dance, you know that'd be nice for a change, wouldn't it?

R: [Singing] "Oh, my Lord, how the ashes flew!"

Sarah: That's it!

> Supper's over, dishes washed,
> Nothin' left but the neck of a squorsh.

Little Polly's [granddaughter] enjoying it, Polly's enjoying it!

R: Can you think of another one?

Sarah: Huh uh. [Chuckles] I'm gonna see if I can't get—I'm gonna see if I can remember the rest of it.

Martha: It's been years and years and years since I've heard them.

Sarah: Do you know something, if you'd write even down to the Grand Ole Opry, you know, something like that. [6a]

The one children's game was recalled by Martha as part of a reminiscence of childhood pastimes:

> Martha: And of course you didn't have an electric ice-cream maker, so you made it by hand. We had that pretty often at home, because we had cream, 'n usually fruit and plenty of eggs. But that was about the only—actually as children I think we spent more time under the rocks than anything else for entertainment. Of course we didn't catch any fish, but we'd go fishing at the lake and our uncle, I can remember we had a sand bag, and I think I can still find that with rocks inside, and you know, I can remember well, going there in that sand and saying
>
> Wooly, wooly, wooly worm, where have you been?
>
> or something like that, and that wooly worm comes right up out of the sand. [14]

The closest Sarah came to telling an actual joke was in her paraphrasing of a "Dear Abby" column, brought to mind by the fact that earlier she had advised her grandson he was too young to get married and start a family:

> I heard the cutest thing the other day, and I believe it was in "Dear Abby." Anyway, this boy wrote in about his mother and she lived in an apartment, and she rented a—oh! she could do—I think she was an artist—she was a little bit of everything, and the old gentleman who lived upstairs was awfully intelligent too, but pretty good age and all, and the son said, "Mother, is there something goin' between you?" you know, and I forget what he called him, the name, and she said, "Son, don't you know there's a pill?" It was kinda cute, you know. I don't generally repeat things like that, but I thought that was kinda cute. [2]

Proverbs are, surprisingly, not a consistent feature of Sarah's narration. Only a few were collected, the first one while she was discussing the value of education for girls, as opposed to their marrying young:

> And it maybe prevents 'em from rushing off and getting married, 'n getting into what we were talking to a little bit ago. Too soon. 'Cause you know they say when the wolf comes in at the door, that love goes, uh, how is that? "Poverty comes in the door, loves goes out the window." [7]

In a discussion of how the housewife works, even though she is listed as "unemployed," Sarah exclaimed,

> Hers is never done! They say "Man works from sun to sun, but a

Appendixes

> woman's work is never done," which is right, you know, especially if there's children. You never get away from it. [11]

In an earlier conversation the "free day" being enjoyed by some for Columbus Day elicited comments from both Sarah and Martha that *women* never get free days, that it is certainly true that "women's work is never done." Sarah quoted her eldest daughter as considering woman's work a "thankless task." But Sarah hurriedly added how important it is, that "the hand that rocks the cradle rules the world." [A] And in a discussion of weddings, the negative fact of divorce came up. Sarah pointed to one friend whose two girls got married and both wanted a big wedding.

> The parents said to them, "I'll give you $500 if you have a common wedding, and they wanted more or less a big wedding. That wasn't even much of a big wedding, and neither one of them are living with their husbands. Divorced. I heard a neighbor say one time that "the bigger the wedding, the quicker the divorce." [20]

Belief items are more generally interlaced in daily speech, though still less than one might expect. Their themes are several, all related to the farm and home scene—insects, domestic animals, weather, herbs, medicine, and pregnancy:

> [In a discussion of lumber and its keeping qualities]
> Sarah: I heard termites won't work in pine, haven't you heard that?
> Friend: Oh, they will.
> Sarah: I have heard termites won't. There is so much resin and everything in pine. I have heard people say pine wouldn't. [2]

Martha recalled a childhood belief in which Sarah's own degree of belief was quite low.

> Martha: I told this to someone at the bank a few years ago, about horse hairs out of the tail of a horse turning into a snake. They didn't believe me, but it was the truth, a horse hair will get a head and it will get a tail and it will wiggle. Am I not right?
> Sarah: I'm not saying.
> Martha: Well, you've seen it.
> Sarah: Well, I just saw funny-looking things, but I don't know—
> Martha: I saw it many a time in that drain.

> Sarah: It's like children getting worms. I think that the eggs are on a cat's hair. I think that worm eggs fly around through the air. There are a lot of these things we don't know for sure—we know there's mysteries—I saw something that looked like a horsehair and it did wiggle like it was alive, but I'm not going to say—
> Martha: Well, I certainly have seen it, and there was catnip around there too.
> Sarah: I saw them wiggle—and I don't know where their life came from, but they did act alive.
> Martha: It sounds fantastic, I know that.
> Sarah: Well, I think that there had to be an egg there someplace that hatched out, I don't know. Those things are so small, it would take a microscope to find it. [14]

My dog had come to visit with me, which turned the discussion to dogs' likes and dislikes:

> What's the reason the dog turns around two times before they lay down? Do you know what the old fable is of that?
> R: What?
> They claim that they were, they were raised where the grass is real tall, and they had to break the grass down to make a bed. It became a habit somehow ... And they will. They'll make about three circles. [9]

In a discussion of funeral practices, wakes were referred to as a means of protecting the body from being disturbed by animals.

> It was on account of cats, rats, and vernim, and different things might do something to the body is what I always heard. And I believe it. I believe it. 'Cause my husband said he set up, it was out on the ridge there, an old lady died and they were real poor people, and he said the cats, uh, and they say sometimes the dogs. I don't know why, but if there's a dog, and someone in the family passes away, they say that dog will just carry on so, and it's done it so many times, I mean it isn't just a hearsay. But it happens. Isn't it funny? [12]

Another animal belief referred especially to pastured animals, cows and horses: laurel bushes are supposed to kill them, i.e., if the animals eat them, they will bloat and die. Therefore, careful farmers must go to the woods and dig them up. Wild cherry trees will also kill cows, not when their leaves are green, but when they have wilted, for example,

Appendixes

when a branch is broken off. This poisons the animals, and they die [D]. A belief shared by many of Sarah's neighbors is that the castor bean is a good plant to use in getting rid of pesky moles. She, however, finds a commercial product far more effective.

Though weather concerns are paramount with farming families, only two direct weather beliefs were recorded:

> The sky is just so full of rain. It's not coming down, but we're gonna have a storm, and it'll rain like that and the kiddies'll tramp around on that old fairground [it was county fair time] 'n 'll surely be a mess, won't it?....And the turkey buzzards. Did you ever notice how the turkey buzzards come out before a rain? [13]

> They say when the wind blows over the oat stubble it's gonna get cooler. [This happens in late July, and she believes August is then cooler.] [O]

Sarah referred to several home remedies, though one simple one came from her doctor in Madison: gargle with one teaspoon of salt and one teaspoon of vinegar dissolved in eight ounces of warm water; gargle it as far back in your throat as you can get it: "It cuts that loose. I kept that solution on the pilot light all night and used it through the night." (Subsequently this led to a discussion of cancer, and a neighbor who always preached that using aluminum [pans] is dangerous, as it causes cancer [K]). When her grandson shot a number of squirrels with his new shotgun, he requested a meal of pot pies from Grandma, who of course obliged:

> Sarah: Yes, he brought some awfully nice ones in here to me the other night, and I dressed it. We wondered when he was gonna come up and help eat it, 'cause Martha had made dumplings like he wanted. He wanted pot pies. In the meantime I went up to my brother, my only brother is real poorly, so we went up to stay overnight with him and I cooked squirrel for him. He'll get one, and another one. But I thought he would like real squirrel, my brother, it's so nutritious.
>
> R: It is?
>
> Sarah: Oh yes, if any of our neighbors gets sick, everybody always tries to get 'em a squirrel.
>
> R: I didn't know that.
>
> Sarah: Mutton's another thing. If you have stomach trouble, did you know mutton's s'posed to be healing?
>
> R: No.

Appendixes

> Sarah: Uh huh. But you know they make even cold creams and things—lanolin comes from mutton, you know—in cold creams 'n things.
> R: We've had a family recipe for a salve for infection using mutton tallow.
> Sarah: Of course, because of the lanolin that's in it.
> R: It has a drawing power too.
> Sarah: Yes, it will, it will. Even tallow will. Even fat that—if you've got a boil or something, even a piece of, uh, fat bacon 'n put on it, any kind of infection. Another thing is the lining of an egg. You take the egg, and take that white lining out, you know, and put it down underneath there, another thing that'll draw.
> Martha: Well, milk and bread's another thing that's good.
> Sarah: Wonderful. Of course, I don't think that, uh, real fat bacon can hardly be beat.
> Martha [chuckling]: And a piece of beefsteak for a black eye.
> Sarah: Scrape, take it out of, uh, take it out of an eye right away is beefsteak, scrape the beefsteak and make a poultice. And potato's another thing, grated potato. Potato grated and put on the eye'll take care of it too. Those older people, I think, just you know, took care of themselves pretty well. But I know beefsteak, they used to get bapped in the eye, would always use it. A piece of beefsteak. . . . And the boiled potatoes too. And grate it. You can put it in the chopper, it won't work as well as if you grate it. Get the properties out of it. . . . I'll tell you something, if you've got a corn, and you take a slice of lemon and put on your toe and you won't have it the next morning. It'll do it! [4]

During a conversation revolving around natural remedies, Sarah mentioned that in the autumn people got polecats. When questioned again, she volunteered further information:

> Sarah: They render the fat—render it and use the oil.
> R: Now do you mean a skunk?
> Sarah: Yeah, a polecat.
> R: And they killed them?
> Sarah: Yes, they kill them. They pick the hides and sell them, sell the hides.
> Martha: I bet you had—
> Sarah: You better change the subject; Mrs. Joyce, they wrote to

> Glenda and their letter was returned [at this point Sarah skillfully turned the conversation to a completely different subject, though it was unclear why she felt she needed to].
> R: Anyway, about the polecat, tell me what they did.
> Sarah: Well, they just rendered the, uh, the fat and used it as a poultice or whatever you want to call it, on the chest—poultice, and they gave it to their children too. . . . I know I had a neighbor, Mrs. Sheets—oh, my husband he thought what people thought around here was just it, and yes, he thought the children ought to be greased if they got a cold. He really believed in it.[1]
> R: And how did it smell?
> Martha: It didn't have the skunk odor.
> R: It didn't?
> Martha: Oh no. You know the skunk—
> Sarah: They have a, you know, when you injure them, that's when they shoot—
> R: Yeah, I know.
> Sarah: Yeah, they won't do anything to you unless you frightened them or—
> Martha: —And after they're dead, that's gone, and of course they can take that part out.
> Sarah: If you want them for pets, a vetinary can do it. [14]

When we discussed the relative merits of drying or freezing peppermint leaves for tea, Martha was of the opinion that drying was best, and Sarah agreed:

> Sarah: I believe it would be. I think it would have more strength and be more better—just keep it as long as you want to, keep it for years. For instance, Sally has sassafras her Dad gave her years ago. He's been dead for fifteen years.
> R: How does she have it, in the freezer?
> Sarah: She has it in cans. She dried it and put it in cans. . . . It's lots of work to do.
> R: It is a lot of work. I didn't like it!
> Sarah: Well, maybe you didn't get the right kind. You want to get the red, you don't want to get the white. And you don't want to get it from your locust; if you dig it near the locust it hasn't any taste. You're never suppose to dig it near locust. You want the, you want the pink—there's a white, did you get the white?

R: No, I don't think so. It had a real orangey red color.

Martha: You got the roots, didn't you?

Sarah: Then you scrape them clean and then you cut that about this thick off. Did you get it at the right time, when the sap was up? See there's just certain times to get it [in winter before the sap runs, and is still frozen].[2] [14]

A discussion of childbirth brought forth several pregnancy beliefs:

They say if you hang up clothes, not to reach up and things like that, but I always did all my papering and work and everything. And I believe exercise is the best thing in the world for you. At any time you can overdo it, of course, but I never did at any time.

R: What did they say—that you shouldn't reach and hang up clothes?

Yes, that you're liable to, you know, have a miscarriage and things. They've always told mothers that. [3]

Later Martha volunteered that you were "supposed to think about beautiful things, beautiful thoughts."

Sarah: Oh yes, they say if you want a child to be musical, you want [to play] steady music; now those might be old-fashioned things, you know, but I do believe this: I believe if you are a cheerful person then you will have a cheerful baby. But I think if a person is sick and irritable that they are going to have an irritable baby. I believe that will happen sometimes. That if you feel before your baby is born, I believe, they do say, if you want your child to be a particular thing, to study that and like it yourself—which, I don't know. You know our bodies are very complicated piece—

Martha: —of machinery!

Sarah: Isn't it something!

R: That's interesting. I don't think I, uh, have heard the one about the playing music, but I—

Sarah: —Yes, I've read those things, you know, that if you want your child to be after, to take an interest in something, you really take an interest in it and it may carry out. I do know this, you can watch and you can watch your children and other people's children, then watch their parents, and you can see how much they're alike—they take an awful lot.

R: Like when—

Sarah: —like the things their parents like and do, they inherit an awful lot. They say 95% of our bodies are inherited. I believe it's true on one side or the other, you know. Then they say we—like the fourth generation—well, people that are drunken they claim that will go back; the government claims that will go back four generations. Same way with that syphilis. It pops out every fourth generation, did you know that?

Well, you know years ago they wouldn't allow the mother to put her feet down on the floor for about six weeks. They were very particular. Today they get them. Some doctors wouldn't allow their wives to put their feet down on the floor for several weeks.

R: What about the midwife? Would they say anything like that?

Sarah: Well, the midwives thought the organs went back in place on the ninth day, and you always had to go back to bed. My mother, if she—she had a lot of children and had to—she would get up, but she would always go back and stay in bed all day on the ninth day. I guess there's nothing to that, they claim the organs take their place. But on the ninth day they were more particular that way. Today the mother gets up right away.[3]

Martha: They even get up on the second day.

Sarah: Oh, they do their work and everything! My gracious yes! See, Indian women did the same thing. They said if they were marching, they'd go off and have their babies and come back and go on. I don't know. So it is a lot different. But I would hemorrhage so bad. I would be careful because I would have hemorrhaged.

R: So you didn't get up right away?

Sarah: Oh, no, my mother wouldn't have allowed me. No, I never got up. When Paula was born, and she's my last one, I stayed upstairs at least ten days, never came down atall.

R: So your mother was really the midwife, and she knew what to do.

Sarah: Oh yes; yes, she was, I think she was a good mother. And I know I'd go to her with things that people would tell you, who want to frighten you, you know, and she was always so good. Oh, all kinds of odd things that might happen—you shouldn't do this or do that, that you might mark the baby. If you see something you shouldn't see, you might cause it to to have a birthmark, you know—things like that.

Martha: They don't believe in that anymore.

Sarah: No, if you got frightened you might have a birthmark, and, no, that's what I say, mother didn't believe in them—she would always say, "Just don't pay any attention!"

R: Somebody else told me they weren't supposed to hang clothes on a clothesline because it would wrap the cord around the baby's neck.

Sarah: Yeah, uh huh, or bend over. Bending would too—bending over or wearing a corset or anything too tight, too. [3]

Some of Sarah's word pictures evoke wonderful images. They also add special flavor to her interesting delivery. "To tell the truth" and "Oh gracious yes!" are favorite markers. "Isn't it wonderful?" or "Isn't that awful!" are excellent techniques for drawing the listener into her story.

Many of her comparisons and modes of expression move her into the category of an accomplished speaker, for example:

> Larry O'Brien was so heavy he could carry a sack of flour on each hip!
>
> He just takes a long breath when he thinks of work [about a lazy relative]! He's not a *beaver* like James and Denny.
>
> [Concerning fame] They have their come and they have their go.
>
> [Rather than say a neighbor was stupid] He doesn't know beans!

And, in a poetic vein,

> [Of the man who did not balk at the high price of a farm] He didn't turn words.
>
> My mother never wanted to turn her pages back [live her life over].
>
> I'm all paid for [I've lived longer than I expected to].

1. See also Gallagher (1976:113).
2. See also Haygood (1939:chap. 9).
3. Compare Gallagher (1976:59): the women stayed in bed nine days.

List of Works Consulted

Aberle, David Friend
   1967   The psychosocial analysis of a Hopi life-history. In *Personalities and cultures*, pp. 79–138, ed. Robert Hunt. Garden City, N.Y.: Natural History Press.

Abrahams, Roger
   1970   *Deep down in the jungle: Negro narrative from the streets of Philadelphia.* 2d ed., rev. Chicago: Aldine Publishing Co.
   1971   The Negro stereotype: Negro folklore and the riots. In *The urban experience and folk tradition*, pp. 65–85, ed. Américo Paredes and Ellen Stekert. Austin: University of Texas Press.
   1972   Personal power and social restraint in the definition of folklore. In *Toward new perspectives in folklore*, pp. 16–30, ed. Américo Paredes and Richard Bauman. Austin: University of Texas Press.

Abrahams, Roger, and George Foss, eds.
   1970   *A singer and her songs: Almeda Riddle's book of ballads.* Baton Rouge: Louisiana State University Press.

Allen, Barbara, and W. Lynwood Montell
   1981   *From memory to history: Using oral sources in local historical research.* Nashville: American Association for State and Local History.

Allport, Gordon
   1942   *The use of personal documents in psychological science.* New York: Social Science Research Council.

American Anthropological Association
   1973   *Professional ethics.* Washington, D.C.: American Anthropological Association.

André, Rae
   1981   *Homemakers: The forgotten workers.* Chicago: University of Chicago Press.

List of Works Consulted

Angell, Robert
    1945   A critical review of the development of the personal document method in sociology, 1920–1940. In *The use of personal documents in history, anthropology, and sociology*, pp. 175–232, ed. Louis Gottschalk, Clyde Kluckhohn, and Robert Angell. New York: Social Science Research Council.

Ardener, Shirley, ed.
    1975   *Perceiving women*. New York: Halsted Press.

Arms, Suzanne
    1975   *Immaculate deception: A new look at women and childbirth in America*. Boston: Houghton Mifflin Co.

Arnow, Harriette S.
    1954   *The dollmaker*. New York: Macmillan Co.

Astin, Helen S.
    1975   *Sex roles: A research bibliography*. Washington, D.C.: National Institute of Mental Health.

Atwood, Margaret
    1970   *The journals of Susanna Moodie*. Toronto: Oxford University Press.

Baden, Clifford, comp.
    1981   *Work and family: An annotated bibliography, 1978–1980*. Boston: Wheelock College Center for Parenting Studies.

Bardwick, Judith M., and Elizabeth Douvan
    1971   Ambivalence: The socialization of women. In *Woman in sexist society: Studies in power and powerlessness*, pp. 147–59, ed. Vivian Gornick and Barbara K. Moran. New York: Basic Books.

Barnes, Daniel
    1979   Toward the establishment of principles for the study of folklore and literature. *Southern Folklore Quarterly* 43:5–16.

Barnouw, Victor
    1973   *Culture and personality*. 2d ed., rev. Homewood, Ill.: Dorsey Press.

Barton, Charles
    1982   *Howard Hughes and his flying boat*. Fallbrook, Calif: Aero Publications.

Baskin, John
    1976   *New Burlington*. New York: W. W. Norton & Co.

Basso, Keith
    1976   "Wise Words" of the Western Apache: Metaphor and semantic theory. In *Meaning in anthropology*, ed. Keith Basso and Henry A. Selby. Albuquerque: University of New Mexico Press.

Baum, Willa K.
    1974   *Oral history for the local historical society*. Nashville, Tenn.: American Association for State and Local History.
    1977   *Transcribing and editing oral history*. Nashville, Tenn.: American Association for State and Local History.

List of Works Consulted

Baxter, Annette K.
  1978 *To be a woman in America: 1850–1930.* New York: New York Times Book Co., Times Books.
Bealer, Alex
  1978 *The log cabin: Homes of the North American wilderness.* Barre, Mass.: Barre Publishing Co.
Beard, Mary
  1946 *Woman as force in history.* New York: Macmillan Co.
Becker, Carl
  1932 Everyman his own historian. *American Historical Review* 37 (January): 221–36.
Becker, Howard
  1966 Introduction. In *The jack-roller*, by Clifford R. Shaw. Chicago: University of Chicago Press, Phoenix Books.
Becker, Susan D.
  1981 *The origins of the Equal Rights Amendment: American Feminism between the wars.* Westport, Conn.: Greenwood Press.
Ben-Amos, Dan, ed.
  1976 *Folklore genres.* Austin: University of Texas Press.
Benison, Saul
  1965 Reflections on oral history. *American Archivist* 28 (January): 71–77.
Bermosk, Loretta S., and Sarah E. Porter
  1979 *Women's health and human wholeness.* New York: Appleton-Century-Crofts.
Bernard, Jessie
  1964 *Academic women.* University Park: Pennsylvania State University Press.
  1971 The paradox of the happy marriage. In *Woman in sexist society*, pp. 85–98, ed. Vivian Gornick and Barbara K. Moran. New York: Basic Books.
  1972 *The sex game.* New York: Atheneum.
  1981 *The female world.* New York: Free Press.
Bertaux, Daniel, ed.
  1981 *Biography and society: The life history approach in the social sciences.* Beverly Hills, Calif.: Sage Publications.
Blumberg, Rae Lesser.
  1978 *Stratification: Socioeconomic and sexual inequality.* Dubuque, Iowa: Wm. C. Brown Co.
Bohannan, Paul
  1978 An open letter from the president: E pluribus unum. *Anthropology Newsletter* 19 (December): 1–17.
Bohen, Halcyone H., and Anamaria Viveros-Long
  1981 *Balancing jobs and family life.* Philadelphia: Temple University Press.
Bornat, Joanna
  1977 Women's history and oral history: An outline bibliography. *Oral History* 5 (Autumn): 124–35.

List of Works Consulted

Botkin, Benjamin
    1963   *The American play party song.* New York: Frederick Ungar. First published 1937 in the University Studies of the University of Nebraska.

Botwinick, J.
    1970   Geropsychology. *Annual Review of Psychology* 21:239–72.

Bourguignon, Erika
    1979   *Psychological anthropology: An introduction to human nature and cultural differences.* New York: Holt, Rinehart & Winston.
    1980   *A world of women.* New York: Praeger/J. F. Bergin Publishers.

Brandes, Stanley
    1979   Ethnographic autobiographies in American anthropology. *Central Issues in Anthropology* 1 (2): 1–17.

Brodie, Fawn M.
    1981   *Richard Nixon: The shaping of his character.* New York: W. W. Norton & Co.

Brown, James Seay, Jr.
    1982   *Up before daylight: Life histories from the Alabama Writers' Project, 1938–1939.* University: University of Alabama Press.

Bruce, Dickson D., Jr.
    1974   *And they all sang Hallelujah.* Knoxville: University of Tennessee Press.

Brunvand, Jan Harold
    1971   *A guide for collectors of folklore in Utah.* Salt Lake City: University of Utah Press.
    1976   *Folklore: A study of research guide.* New York: St. Martin's Press.
    1978   *The study of American folklore*, 2d ed. New York: W. W. Norton & Co.

Buvinic, Mayra
    1976   *Women and world development: An annotated bibliogrcphy.* Washington, D.C.: American Association for the Advancement of Science.

Byers, Paul
    1964   Still photography in systematic recording and analysis of behavioral data. *Human Organization* 23 (Spring): 78–84.

Cahill, Susan, ed.
    1975   *Women and fiction: Short stories by and about women.* New York: Mentor Books.

Carawan, Guy, and Candie Carawan
    1975   *Voices from the mountains.* New York: Alfred A. Knopf.

Cardinale, Susan
    1982   *Anthologies by and about women: An analytical index.* Westport, Conn.: Greenwood Press.

Carmack, Robert M.
    1972   Ethnohistory: A review of its development, definitions, methods, and aims. *Annual Review of Anthropology* 1:227–46.

Carpenter, Inta Gale
    1978   Introspective accounts of the field experience: A bibliographic essay. *Folklore Forum* 11 (Winter): 191–219.

List of Works Consulted

Carroll, Berenice
    1976   Introduction. In *Liberating women's history: Theoretical and critical essays*, pp. ix–xiv, ed. Berenice Carroll. Urbana: University of Illinois Press.

Carroll, Berenice, ed.
    1976   *Liberating women's history: Theoretical and critical essays.* Urbana: University of Illinois Press.

Cerra, Frances
    1980   Study finds college women still aim for traditional jobs. *New York Times*, 11 May, p. 46.

Cesara, Manda
    1982   *Reflections of a woman anthropologist.* New York: Academic Press.

Chaddock, Robert
    1908   Ohio before 1850. Ph.D. dissertation, Columbia University.

Chesler, Phyllis
    1972   *Women and madness.* Garden City, N.Y.: Doubleday & Co.
    1978   *About men.* New York: Simon & Schuster.

Chiñas, Beverly
    1973   *The Isthmus Zapotecs: Women's roles in cultural context.* New York: Holt, Rinehart & Winston.

Chmaj, Betty E.
    1972   *Image, myth, and beyond.* Pittsburgh: Know.

Chodorow, Nancy
    1974   Family structure and feminine personality. In *Woman, culture, and society*, pp. 43–66, ed. M. Rosaldo and L. Lamphere. Stanford, Calif.: Stanford University Press.
    1978   *The reproduction of mothering.* Berkeley: University of California Press.

Clarke, S. J.
    1902   *A biographical record of Fairfield County, Ohio.* New York: S. J. Clarke Publishing Co.

Coles, Robert, and Jane Hallowell Coles
    1978   *Women of crisis: Lives of struggle and hope.* New York: Delacorte Press/Seymour Lawrence.
    1980   *Women of Crisis II.* New York: Delacorte Press/Seymour Lawrence.

Collier, John, Jr.
    1967   *Visual anthropology: Photography as a research method.* New York: Holt, Rinehart & Winston.

Cooper, Patricia, and Norma B. Buferd
    1977   *The quilters: Women and domestic art.* New York: Doubleday & Co.

Crane, Julia G., and Michael P. Angrosino
    1974   *Field projects in anthropology.* Morristown, N.J.: General Learning Press.

Curley, Jayme, Sharon Ladar, Linda Matthews, Anna Siegler, and Jane Stevens
    1976   *The balancing act: A career and a baby*, ed. Sydelle Kramer. Chicago: Chicago Review Press/Swallow Press.

List of Works Consulted

    1981   *The balancing act II*. Chicago: Chicago Review Press.
Davis, Kingsley
    1949   *Human society*. New York: Macmillan Co.
DeCrow, Karen
    1974   *Sexist justice*. New York: Random House.
Dégh, Linda
    1969   *Folktales and society: Story-telling in a Hungarian peasant community*. Bloomington: Indiana University Press.
    1972   Folk narrative. In *Folklore and folklife*, pp. 53–83, ed. Richard Dorson. Chicago: University of Chicago Press.
    1975   *People in the tobacco belt: Four lives*. Ottawa: National Museums of Canada.
    1976   Symbiosis of joke and legend: A case of conversational folklore. In *Folklore today*, pp. 101–22, ed. Linda Dégh, Henry Glassie, and Felix Oinas. Bloomington: Indiana University Press.
    1978   Personal interview, Annual Meeting of the American Folklore Society, Salt Lake City, Utah. 10 October.
Deitz, Elizabeth Jane
    1981   As we lived a long time ago. *Goldenseal* 7 (Fall): 9–16.
Denzin, Norman
    1970   *The research act*. Chicago: Aldine Publishing Co.
Diner, Hasia
    1979   *Women and urban society: A guide to information sources*. Detroit: Gale Research Co.
Dollard, John
    1935   *Criteria for the life history*. New Haven, Conn.: Yale University Press.
Donaldson, Elizabeth
    1978   Personal interview, Wick, Scotland. 18 August.
Dorough, C. Dwight
    1962   *Mr. Sam*. New York: Random House.
Dorson, Richard M.
    1964   *Buying the wind*. Chicago: University of Chicago Press.
    1971a *American folklore and the historian*. Chicago: University of Chicago Press.
    1971b Is there a folk in the city? In *The urban experience and folk tradition*, pp. 21–52, ed. Américo Paredes and Ellen Stekert. Austin: University of Texas Press.
    1972a *Folklore: Selected essays*. Bloomington: Indiana University Press.
Dorson, Richard M., ed.
    1972b *Folklore and folklife*. Chicago: University of Chicago Press.
Dowling, Colette
    1981   *The Cinderella complex: Women's hidden fear of independence*. New York: Summit Books.

List of Works Consulted

Dubofsky, Melvyn
    1977   Industrialization in Ohio's Gilded Age. In *Toward an urban Ohio*, pp. 23–28, ed. John Wunder. Columbus: Ohio Historical Society.

DuBos, René
    1965   Science and man's nature. *Daedulus* 94 (Winter): 223–44.

Dundes, Alan
    1965   *The study of folklore.* Englewood Cliffs, N.J.: Prentice-Hall.

Dyk, Walter
    1938   *Son of Old Man Hat: A Navaho autobiography.* Lincoln: University of Nebraska Press.

Dykeman, Wilma
    1962   *The tall woman.* New York: Holt, Rinehart & Winston.
    1966   *The far family.* New York: Holt, Rinehart & Winston.

Eakins, Barbara, and Gene Eakins
    1978   *Sex differences in human communication.* Boston: Houghton Mifflin Co.

Edgerton, Robert B., and L. L. Langness
    1974   *Methods and styles in the study of culture.* San Francisco: Chandler & Sharp Publishers.

Edinger, Lewis
    1964   Political science and political biography: Reflections on the study of leadership. Parts One and Two. *Journal of Politics* 26 (May): 423–39; (August):648–76.

Edwards, Lee R., and Arlyn Diamond, eds.
    1973   *American voices, American women.* New York: Avon Books.

Ehrenreich, Barbara S.
    1972   *Witches, midwives, and nurses: A history of women healers.* Glass Mountain Pamphlet No. 1. Old Westbury, N.Y.: Feminist Press.

Epstein, Cynthia
    1970   *Women's place: Options and limits in professional careers.* Berkeley: University of California Press.

Ergood, Bruce
    1975   *Southeast Ohio personal and social characteristics: A study of twelve townships.* Research Bulletin (January).

Ergood, Bruce, and Bruce Kuhre, eds.
    1976   *Appalachia: Social context past and present.* Dubuque, Iowa: Kendall/Hunt Publishing.

Erikson, Erik H.
    1975   *Life history and the historical moment.* New York: W. W. Norton & Co.

Evans, Estyn
    1957   *Irish folk ways.* London: Routledge & Kegan Paul.

Ewald, William Bragg, Jr.
    1981   *Eisenhower the president: Crucial days, 1951–1960.* Englewood Cliffs, N.J.: Prentice-Hall.

Faber, Inez McAlister
    1982   *Out here on Soap Creek.* Ames: Iowa State University Press.

List of Works Consulted

Falconer, John
    1942   Agricultural changes. In *Ohio in the twentieth century*, pp. 120–34, comp. Harlow Lindley. Vol. 6 of *The history of the state of Ohio*, ed. Carl Wittke. Columbus: Ohio State Archaeological and Historical Society.

Farr, Sidney Saylor
    1981   *Appalachian women: An annotated bibliography*. Lexington: University Press of Kentucky.

Farrer, Claire R.
    1977   Play and inter-ethnic communication: A practical ethnography of the Mescalero Apache. Ph.D. dissertation, University of Texas.

Farrer, Claire R., ed.
    1976   *Women and folklore*. Austin: University of Texas Press. Originally published as *Journal of American Folklore* 88 (March 1975).

Farrer, Claire, and Susan Kalčik
    1974   Women: A selected bibliography from the *Journal of American Folklore*. *Folklore Feminists Communication* 1:12–28.

Felsenthal, Carol
    1981   *The sweetheart of the silent majority: The biography of Phyllis Schlafly*. Garden City, N.Y.: Doubleday & Co.

Ferguson, Mary Ann
    1973   *Images of women in literature*. Boston: Houghton Mifflin.

Fess, Simeon
    1937   *Ohio: A four-volume reference library*. Chicago: Lewis Publishing Co.

Festinger, Leon
    1968   *The theory of cognitive dissonance*. Stanford, Calif.: Stanford University Press.

Festinger, Leon, and Daniel Katz, eds.
    1953   *Research methods in the behavioral sciences*. New York: Dryden Press.

Filler, Louis, ed.
    1980   *An Ohio schoolmistress: The memoirs of Irene Hardy*. Kent, Ohio: Kent State University Press.

Fischer, Christiane, ed.
    1978   *Let them speak for themselves: Women in the American West, 1849–1900*. New York: E. P. Dutton.

Fitzgerald, Frances
    1981   The triumphs of the New Right. *New York Review of Books*, 19 November, pp. 19–26.

Folklore Forum
    1973   Folklore archives: Ethics and the Law. Special issue, 6 (October).

Fontenay, Charles L.
    1980   *Estes Kefauver*. Knoxville: University of Tennessee Press.

Fortmann, Louise
    1981   *Tillers of the soil and keepers of the hearth: A bibliographic guide to women and rural development*. Ithaca, N.Y.: Cornell University, Rural Development Committee.

List of Works Consulted

Fox, Greer Litton
    1977   Nice girl: Social control of women through a value construct. *Signs* 3 (Summer):805–17.

Frank, Gelya
    1979   Finding the common denominator: A phenomenological critique of life history method. *Ethos* 7 (Spring): 68–94.
    1980   Life histories in gerontology: The subjective side to aging. In *New methods for old age research: Anthropological alternatives*, pp. 155–76, ed. Christine L. Fry and Jennie Keith. Chicago: Center for the Study of Urban Policy, Loyola University.

Frary, I. T.
    1942   *Ohio in homespun and calico*. Richmond, Va.: Garrett & Massie.

Frazier, Charles E.
    1978   The use of life-histories in testing theories of criminal behavior: Toward reviving a method. *Qualitative Sociology* 1 (May): 122–41.

Freeman, Jo
    1975   *The politics of women's liberation*. New York: David McKay.

Friedan, Betty
    1974   *The feminine mystique*. New York: W. W. Norton & Co.
    1981   *The second stage*. New York: Summit Books.

Friedl, Ernestine
    1975   *Women and men: An anthropologist's view*. New York: Holt, Rinehart & Winston.

Friedman, Albert B.
    1982   Grounding a superstition: Lactation as contraceptive. *Journal of American Folklore* 95 (April–June): 200–208.

Friedman, Leslie J.
    1977   *Sex role stereotyping in the mass media: An annotated bibliography*. New York: Garland Publishing.

Frontiers: A Journal of Women's Studies
    1977   Women's oral history. Special issue, 2 (Summer)

Fry, Amelia R.
    1977   Suffragist Alice Paul's memoirs: Pros and cons of oral history. *Frontiers* 2 (Summer): 82–86.

Fullerton, Howard N., Jr.
    1980   The 1995 labor force: A first look. *Monthly Labor Review* (December): 11–21.

Gallagher, Dorothy
    1976   *Hannah's daughters*. New York: T. Y. Crowell.

Garber, J. Otis
    1942   Depression activities. In *Ohio in the twentieth century*, pp. 435–74, comp. Harlow Lindley. Vol. 6 of *The history of the state of Ohio*, ed. Carl Wittke. Columbus: Ohio State Archaeological and Historical Society.

Garland, Hamlin
    1899   *Main-travelled roads*. New York: Harper Brothers.

List of Works Consulted

Gaskin, I. M.
    1978 *Spiritual midwifery*, rev. ed. Summertown, Tex.: Book Publishing Company.

Georges, Robert A., and Michael O. Jones.
    1980 *People studying people: The human element in fieldwork*. Berkeley: University of California Press.

Gilbert, Lucy, and Paula Webster
    1982 *Bound by love: The sweet trap of daughterhood*. Boston: Beacon Press.

Gilman, Charlotte Perkins
    1899 *The yellow wallpaper*. Boston: Small, Maynard. Rpt. Old Westbury, N.Y.: Feminist Press, 1973.

Glassie, Henry
    1968a *Pattern in the material folk culture of the eastern United States*. Philadelphia: University of Pennsylvania Press.
    1968b The types of the southern mountain cabin. In *The study of American folklore*, Appendix C, pp. 338–70, by Jan Brunvand. New York: W. W. Norton & Co.

Glassie, Henry, Edward D. Ives, and John F. Szwed
    1971 *Folksongs and their makers*. Bowling Green, Ohio: Popular Press.

Goldstein, Kenneth
    1964 *A guide for field workers in folklore*. Hatboro, Pa.: Folklore Associates.

Goldwag, Elliott M., ed.
    1979 *Inner balance: The power of holistic healing*. Englewood Cliffs, N.J.: Prentice-Hall.

Goode, William J.
    1960 A theory of role strain. *American Sociological Review* 25 (August): 483–96.

Goodenough, Ward
    1970 *Description and comparison in cultural anthropology*. Chicago: Aldine Publishing Co.

Gordon, Francis
    1940 Early history of Hocking County. M.A. thesis, Ohio State University.

Gordon, Linda, and Allen Hunter
    1978 Sex, family, and the New Right: Anti-feminists as a political force. *Radical America* 11–12 (November 1977–February 1978): 9–25.

Gornick, Vivian, and Barbara K. Moran, eds.
    1971 *Woman in sexist society: Studies in power and powerlessness*. New York: Basic Books.

Gottschalk, Louis
    1945 The historian and the historical document. In *The use of personal documents in history, anthropology, and sociology*, pp. 1–75, ed. Louis Gottschalk, Clyde Kluckhohn, and Robert Angell. New York: Social Science Research Council.

Graham, A. A., comp.
    1883 *History of Fairfield and Perry Counties, Ohio: Their past and present*. Chicago: W. H. Beers & Co.

Green, Archie
   1972   *Only a miner.* Urbana: University of Illinois Press.
   1978   Reflexive regionalism. *Adena: A Journal of the History and Culture of the Ohio Valley* 3 (Fall): 3–15.
Greenberg, Hazel, ed. and comp.
   1976   *The Equal Rights Amendment: A bibliographic study.* Westport, Conn.: Greenwood Press.
Greenstein, Fred I.
   1969   *Personality and politics.* Chicago: Markham.
Gross, Neal, Alexander W. McEachern, and Mason Ward
   1966   Role conflict and its resolution. In *Role Theory: Concepts and research.* New York: John Wiley & Sons.
Hadley, Gay B.
   1982   A qualitative study of the developmental conditions in a human service setting. Ph.D. dissertation, Ohio State University.
Hagood, Margaret Jarman
   1939   *Mothers of the South.* Chapel Hill: University of North Carolina Press.
Halas, Celia, and Roberta Matteson
   1978   *I've done so well—Why do I feel so bad?* New York: Macmillan Co.
Hall, Edward T.
   1959   *The silent language.* Garden City, N.Y.: Doubleday & Co.
   1966   *The hidden dimension.* Garden City, N.Y.: Doubleday & Co.
   1976   *Beyond culture.* Garden City, N.Y.: Doubleday & Co., Anchor Press.
Hand, Wayland
   1976   *American folk medicine.* Berkeley: University of California Press.
Harding, Susan
   1981   Family reform movements: Recent feminism and its opposition. *Feminist Studies* 7 (Spring): 57–75.
Harrell, Barbara
   1981   Lactation and menstruation in cultural perspective. *American Anthropologist* 83 (December): 796–823.
Hatcher, Harlan
   1942   Ohio in the literature of the twentieth century. In *Ohio in the twentieth century,* pp. 267–93, comp. Harlow Lindley. Vol. 6 of *The history of the state of Ohio,* ed. Carl Wittke. Columbus: Ohio State Archaeological and Historical Society.
Havighurst, Walter
   1976   *Ohio: A bicentennial history.* New York: W. W. Norton & Co.
Hayes, Ellen
   1920   *Wild turkeys and tallow candles.* Boston: Four Seas Co.
Hicks, George
   1976   *Appalachian Valley.* New York: Holt, Rinehart & Winston.
Hinding, Andrea, ed.
   1980   *Women's history sources: A guide to archives and manuscript collections in the United States.* New York: R. R. Bowker Co.

List of Works Consulted

Hirsch, Jerrold, and Tom E. Terrill, eds.
    1978   *Such as us: Southern voices of the thirties*. Chapel Hill: University of North Carolina Press.

Hirshey, Gerri
    1980   Woman's World. In *The Equal Rights Amendment: Thirty-one editors speak out*. Washington, D.C.: ERAmerica.

History of Hocking Valley, Ohio
    1883   Chicago: Interstate Publishing Co.

Hoffman, Nancy
    1981   *Woman's true profession: Women's lives/women's work*, Vol. 12. New York: Feminist Press.

Honko, Lauri
    1964   Memorates and the study of folk beliefs. *Journal of the Folklore Institute* 1:5–19.

Household Manual, The
    1876   Battle Creek, Mich.: Office of the Health Reformer.

Howard, Jane
    1973   *A different woman*. New York: Avon Books.

Howe, Florence, ed.
    1975   *Women and the power to change*. New York: McGraw-Hill Book Co.

Howe, Henry
    1852   *Historical collections of Ohio*. Cincinnati: Henry Howe.

Hubbart, H. Clyde
    1942   Ohio in the First World War, 1917–1918. In *Ohio in the twentieth century*, pp. 386–434, comp. Harlow Lindley. Vol. 6 of *The history of the state of Ohio*, ed. Carl Wittke. Columbus: Ohio State Archaeological and Historical Society.

Hutslar, Donald
    1972   *The log architecture of Ohio*. Columbus: Ohio Historical Society.
    1981   The Ohio farmstead. *Ohio History* 90 (Summer): 221–37.

Ise, John
    1936   *Sod and stubble*. Lincoln: University of Nebraska Press.

Ives, Edward D.
    1964   *Larry Gorman: The man who made the songs*. Bloomington: Indiana University Press.
    1971   *Lawrence Doyle: The farmer-poet of Prince Edward Island*. Maine Studies No. 92. Orono: University of Maine Press.
    1976   Common-man biography: Some notes by the way. In *Folklore Today*, pp. 251–64, ed. Linda Dégh, Henry Glassie, and Felix Oinas. Bloomington: Indiana University Press.
    1980   *The tape-recorded interview: A manual for field workers in folklore and oral history*. Knoxville: University of Tennessee Press.

Jackson, Jacqueline Johnson
    1970   Aged Negroes: Their cultural departure from statistical stereotypes and rural-urban differences. *Gerontologist* 10 (Summer): 140–45.

List of Works Consulted

Jacobs, Sue-Ellen
    1974   *Women in perspective: A guide for cross-cultural studies.* Urbana: University of Illinois Press.

Janeway, Elizabeth
    1971   *Man's world, woman's place: A study in social mythology.* New York: William Morrow & Co.

Jansen, William Hugh
    1965   The esoteric-exoteric factor in folklore. In *The Study of Folklore*, pp. 43–51, ed. Alan Dundes. Englewood, N.J.: Prentice-Hall.

Jones, David E.
    1972   *Sanapia: Comanche medicine woman.* New York: Holt, Rinehart, & Winston.

Jones, Michael Owen
    1975   *The handmade object and its maker.* Berkeley: University of California Press.

Jones, Rex L., and Shirley Kurz Jones
    1976   *The Himalayan woman.* Palo Alto, Calif.: Mayfield Publishing Co.

Jordan, Philip D.
    1943   Ohio comes of age: 1873–1900. Vol. 5 of *The history of the state of Ohio*, ed. Carl Wittke. Columbus: Ohio State Archaeological and Historical Society.

Jordan, Rosan Augusta
    1975   The folklore and ethnic identity of a Mexican-American woman. Ph.D. dissertation, Indiana University.

Jordan, Teresa
    1982   *Cowgirls: Women of the American west.* New York: Anchor Books.

Jorgensen Twarog, Katherine F.
    1962   The structure and foundation of the kinship system of a Midwestern community. M.A. thesis, Ohio State University.

Joyce, Rosemary O.
    1980   The life history of Sarah Penfield, rural Ohio grandmother: Tradition maintained, tradition threatened. In *A world of women*, pp. 271–303, ed. Erika Bourguignon. New York: Praeger/J. F. Bergin Publishers.

    1982   Toward an analysis of personal narrative: Sarah Penfield's "local legends." In *Papers in Comparative Studies* II, ed. Daniel Barnes, Steven Swann Jones, and Rosemary Joyce. Columbus: Ohio State University, College of the Humanities.

Kahn, Kathy
    1972   *Hillbilly women.* New York: Doubleday & Co.

Kardiner, Abraham
    1945   *The psychological frontiers of society.* New York: Columbia University Press.

Katzman, David M., and William M. Tuttle, Jr.
    1982   *Plain folk: The life stories of undistinguished Americans.* Urbana: University of Illinois Press.

List of Works Consulted

Kelley, Edith Summers
    1972 *Weeds*. First edition, 1923. New York: Popular Library.

Kelley, Jane Holden
    1978 *Yaqui women: Contemporary life histories*. Lincoln: University of Nebraska Press.

Kelly-Gadol, Joan
    1976 The social relation of the sexes: Methodological implications of women's history. *Signs* (Summer): 809–23.

Kessler-Harris, Alice
    1982 *Out to work: A history of wage-earning women in the United States*. New York: Oxford University Press.

Kitzinger, Sheila
    1979 *Birth at home*. Oxford: Oxford University Press.

Klingaman, David C., and Richard K. Vedder, eds.
    1975 *Essays in nineteenth century economic history*. Athens: Ohio University Press.

Kluckhohn, Clyde
    1945 The personal document in anthropological science. In *The use of personal documents in history, anthropology, and sociology*, pp. 77–173, ed. Louis Gottschalk, Clyde Kluckhohn, and Robert Angell. New York: Social Science Research Council.

Knepper, George W.
    1976 *An Ohio portrait*. Columbus: Ohio Historical Society

Lange, Dorothea
    1967 *The American country woman*. Fort Worth, Tex.: Amon Carter Museum.

Langness, L. L.
    1965 *The life history in anthropological science*. New York: Holt, Rinehart & Winston.

Langness, L. L., and Gelya Frank
    1981 *Lives: An anthropological approach to biography*. Novato, Calif.: Chandler & Sharp Publishers.

Lavigne, John V.
    1980 The siblings of childhood cancer patients: Psychosocial aspects. In *The child with cancer: Clinical approaches to psychosocial care research in psychosocial aspects*, pp. 37–47, ed. Jerome L. Schulman and Mary Jo Kupst. Springfield, Ill.: Charles C. Thomas, Publisher.

Leach, Edmund
    1976 *Culture and communication*. Cambridge: At the University Press.

Lee, Alfred E.
    1892 *History of the city of Columbus, capital of Ohio*, Vol. 1. New York: Munsell & Co.

Lee, Rex
    1980 *A lawyer looks at the Equal Rights Amendment*. Provo, Utah: Brigham Young University Press.

List of Works Consulted

Leghorn, Lisa, and Katherine Parker
    1981 *Woman's worth: Sexual economics and the world of women.* Boston: Routledge & Kegan Paul.

Lerner, Gerda
    1969 New approaches to the study of women in American history. *Journal of Social History* 4 (Fall): 333–56.
    1972 *Black women in white America: A documentary history.* New York: Pantheon Books.
    1975 *Bibliography in the history of American women.* Bronxville, N.Y.: Sarah Lawrence College
    1977 *The female experience: An American documentary.* Indianapolis: Bobbs-Merrill.

Lewis, Oscar
    1959 *Five families: Mexican case studies in the culture of poverty.* New York: Basic Books.
    1961 *The children of Sanchez.* New York: Random House.
    1964 *Pedro Martinez.* New York: Random House.
    1965 *La vida: A Puerto Rican family in the culture of poverty, San Juan and New York.* New York: Random House.

Lindley, Harlow
    1942 The Sesquicentennial Celebration. In *Ohio in the twentieth century*, pp. 475–92, comp. Harlow Lindley. Vol. 6 of *The history of the state of Ohio*, ed. Carl Wittke. Columbus: Ohio State Archaeological and Historical Society.

Linton, Sally,
    1971 Woman the gatherer: Male bias in anthropology. In *Women in cross-cultural perspective: A preliminary sourcebook.* Mimeograph, 1971, Department of Urban and Regional Planning, University of Illinois.

Lipman-Blumen, Jean
    1972 How ideology shapes women's lives. *Scientific American*, January, pp. 34–42.
    1976 The implications for family structure of changing sex roles. *Social Casework*, February, pp. 67–79.

Lopata, Helena Z.
    1971 *Occupation: Housewife.* New York: Oxford University Press.

Lott, Bernice
    1981 *Becoming a woman: The socialization of gender.* Springfield, Ill.: Charles C. Thomas, Publisher.

Lougee, Carolyn
    1977 Review essay: Modern European history. *Signs* 2 (Spring): 628–50.

Lozier, Mary
    1973 Interview, Greenup County, Kentucky. 18 July.
    1975 Interviews, Columbus, Ohio. 10 and 15 November.

Luchetti, Cathy Lee, and Carol Olwell
    1982 *Women of the west.* St. George, Utah: Antelope Island Press.

List of Works Consulted

Lurie, Nancy Oestreich
   1961   *Mountain Wolf Woman*. Ann Arbor: University of Michigan Press.

MacCormack, Carol P., and Marilyn Strathern
   1980   *Nature, culture and gender: A critique*. Cambridge: At the University Press.

McMillen, Wheeler
   1974   *Ohio farm*. Columbus: Ohio State University Press.

McNall, Sally Allen
   1981   *Who is in the house?: A psychological study of two centuries of women's fiction in America, 1795 to the present*. New York: Elsevier North-Holland.

Mandelbaum, David
   1973   The study of life history: Ghandi. *Current Anthropology* 14 (June): 177–96.

Marshall, Catherine
   1967   *Christy*. New York: McGraw-Hill Book Co.

Martzolff, Clement L.
   1924   *Fifty stories from Ohio history*. Columbus: Ohio Teacher Publishing Co.

May, Keith
   1981   *Characters of women in narrative literature*. New York: St. Martin's Press.

Mead, Margaret
   1928   *Coming of age in Samoa*. New York: William Morrow.
   1935   *Sex and temperament in three primitive societies*. New York: William Morrow.

Meckler, Alan, and Ruth McMullin, eds.
   1975   *Oral history collections*. New York: R. R. Bowker Co.

Mencken, H. L.
   1937   *The American language*. New York: Alfred A. Knopf.

Miller, Merle
   1974   *Plain speaking: An oral biography of Harry S. Truman*. New York: Berkeley Publishing Co.
   1980   *Lyndon: An oral biography*. New York: Putnam.

Millman, Marcia, and Rosabeth Moss Kanter, eds.
   1975   *Another voice*. Garden City, N.Y.: Anchor Press.

Mintz, Sidney W.
   1979   The anthropological interview and the life history. *Oral History Review* 7: 18–26.

Mitchell, Juliet
   1971   *Woman's estate*. New York: Pantheon.

Montell, William Lynwood
   1970   *The saga of Coe Ridge*. Knoxville: University of Tennessee Press.

Moore, Arthur K.
   1957   *The frontier mind*. Lexington: University of Kentucky Press.

List of Works Consulted

Morgan, Elaine
    1972   *The descent of woman.* New York: Stein & Day.

Morgan, Marabel
    1973   *The total woman.* Old Tappan, N.J.: Fleming H. Revell Co.

Morrisey, Charles T.
    1965   Truman and the presidency: Records and oral collections. *American Archivist* 28 (January): 53–61.
    1982   The imprint of history on life-course research: Oral history and the Berkeley guidance study. *International Journal of Oral History* 3 (February): 51–63.

Moss, William
    1974   *Oral history program manual.* New York: Praeger.

Mullen, Patrick
    1974   Appalachian folk culture in Ohio. Tape-recorded lecture for radio broadcast. Washington, D.C.: National Endowment for the Humanities.

Murphy, Yolanda, and Robert F. Murphy
    1974   *Women of the forest.* New York: Columbia University Press.

National Voter, The
    1982   ERA: Firing up. 31 (Winter 1982): 7–9.

New World Translation of the Holy Scriptures
    1970   Brooklyn: Watchtower Bible and Tract Society of New York, Rev. ed.

Newell, William
    1883   *Games and songs of American children.* New York: Harper Brothers. Rpt. New York: Dover, 1903.

Niethammer, Carolyn
    1977   *Daughters of the earth.* New York: Macmillan Co.

Oakes, Elizabeth, and Kathleen Sheldon
    1978   *Guide to social science resources in women's studies.* Santa Barbara, Calif.: Clio Books.

Oakley, Ann
    1974   *Housewife.* London: Penguin Books.

Ohio Bureau of Unemployment Compensation
    1942   *Labor force and employed workers in Ohio, by county and industrial group, 1940.* Adapted from U.S., Bureau of the Census. Washington, D.C.: Government Printing Office.

Ohio Community Development Division, Department of Economic and Community Development
    1974   *Ohio Appalachian development plan.* Columbus: Department of Economic and Community Development.

Ohio State University Monthly
    1981   Study shows Ohio towns are vanishing. February, p. 43.

Ohio Writers Program, Works Progress Administration
    1940   *The Ohio guide.* New York: Oxford University Press.

List of Works Consulted

Oral History: The Journal of the Oral History Society
   1977   Women's History Issue. 5 (Autumn).

Ortner, Sherry B., and Harriet Whitehead, eds.
   1981   *Sexual meanings: The cultural construction of gender and sexuality.* Cambridge: At the University Press.

Pagelow, Mildred Daley
   1981   *Woman-battering: Victims and their experiences.* Sage Library of Social Research. Beverly Hills, Ca.: Sage Publications.

Paredes, Américo, and Richard Bauman, eds.
   1972   *Toward new perspectives in folklore.* Austin: University of Texas Press.

Parker, Seymour, and Hilda Parker
   1979   The myth of male superiority: Rise and demise. *American Anthropologist* 81 (June): 289–309.

Parkes, Colin Murray
   1972   *Bereavement: Studies of grief in adult life.* New York: Penguin Books.

Paulme, Denise, ed.
   1963   *Women of Tropical Africa.* Berkeley: University of California Press.

Pelto, Pertti J.
   1970   *Anthropological research: The structure of inquiry.* New York: Harper & Row.

Pentikäinen, Juha
   1978   *Oral repertoire and world view: An anthropological study of Marina Takalo's life history.* Folklore Fellows Communication No. 219. Helsinki: Academic Scientiarum Fennica.

Pershing, Benjamin H.
   1942   Religion in the twentieth century. In *Ohio in the twentieth century*, pp. 354–84, comp. Harlow Lindley. Vol. 6 of *The history of the state of Ohio*, ed. Carl Wittke. Columbus: Ohio State Archaeological and Historical Society.

Peters, William E.
   1930   *Ohio lands and their history.* Athens, Ohio: W. E. Peters.

Piercy, Marge
   1976   *Woman on the edge of time.* New York: Alfred A. Knopf.

Poloma, M. M.
   1972   Role conflict and the married professional woman. In *Toward a sociology of women*, pp. 187–98, ed. C. Safilios-Rothschild. Lexington, Mass.: Xerox College Publishing Co.

Potter, David M.
   1964   American women and the American character. In *American character and culture*, pp. 65–84, ed. John A. Hague. Deland, Fla.: Everett Edwards Press.

Preston, Dennis
   1976   Towards a modern definition of folk speech. Paper presented at the Annual Meeting of the American Folklore Society, Philadelphia, Pa., 14 November.

1982 "Ritin' Fowklower Daun 'Rong": Folklorists' Failures in Phonology. *Journal of American Folklore* 95 (July–September): 304–326.

Radin, Paul, ed.
1926 *Crashing Thunder: The autobiography of an American Indian.* New York: D. Appleton & Co.

Randall, Emilius O., and Daniel J. Ryan
1912 *History of Ohio: The rise and progress of an American state*, Vol. 5. New York: Century History Co.

Raphael, Marc Lee
1977 Oral history in a Jewish community: The problems and the promise. *Ohio History* 86 (Autumn): 248–57.
1979 *Jews and Judaism in a Midwestern community: Columbus, Ohio, 1840–1975.* Columbus: Ohio Historical Society.

Rapp, Rayna
1978 Family and class in contemporary America: Notes toward an understanding of ideology. *Science and Society* 42 (Fall): 278–350.

Rawalt, Marguerite
1976 *The Equal Rights Amendment.* Washington, D.C.: Women's Equity Action League.

Reiter, Rayna R., ed.
1975 *Toward an anthropology of women.* New York: Monthly Review Press.

Reuben, David R.
1974 The grim new venereal disease in our midst. *Reader's Digest*, November, pp. 114–17.

Rich, Adrienne
1976 *Of woman born.* New York: W. W. Norton & Co.

Richardson, James
1977 The city in twentieth-century Ohio: Crisis in stability and services. In *Toward an urban Ohio*, pp. 34–44, ed. John Wunder. Columbus: Ohio Historical Society.

Richardson, Laurel Walum
1981 *The dynamics of sex and gender: A sociological perspective.* 2d ed., rev. Boston: Houghton Mifflin Co.

Riley, Glenda
1981 *Frontierswomen: The Iowa experience.* Ames: Iowa State University Press.

Ritchie, Jean
1955 *Singing family of the Cumberlands.* New York: Oak Publications.

Roberts, Elizabeth M.
1930 *The great meadow.* New York: Literary Guild.

Roberts, Warren E.
1972 Folk crafts. In *Folklore and folklife*, pp. 233–52, ed. Richard M. Dorson. Chicago: University of Chicago Press.

Robinson, Archie
1982 *George Meany and his times.* New York: Simon & Schuster.

List of Works Consulted

Rohrbaugh, Joanna Bunker
   1979   *Women: Psychology's puzzle.* New York: Basic Books.

Romalis, Shelly, ed.
   1982   *Alternatives to medical control.* Austin: University of Texas Press.

Rosaldo, Michelle Zimbalist, and Louise Lamphere, eds.
   1974   *Woman, culture, and society.* Stanford, Calif.: Stanford University Press.

Roseboom, Eugene
   1944   *The Civil War era, 1850–1873.* Vol. 4 of *The history of the state of Ohio,* ed. Carl Wittke. Columbus: Ohio State Archaeological and Historical Society.

Roseboom, Eugene, and Francis P. Weisenburger
   1976   *A history of Ohio.* Columbus: Ohio Historical Society.

Rosenberg, Marie Barovic, and Len Bergstrom, eds.
   1975   *Woman and society: A critical review of the literature with a selected annotated bibliography.* Beverly Hills, Calif.: Sage Publications.

Rosenberg, Neil
   1978   *Folklore and oral history.* St. John's: Memorial University of Newfoundland.

Rossi, Alice
   1964   Equality between the sexes: An immodest proposal. *Daedalus* 93 (Spring): 607–52.

Rowe, Karen
   1979   Feminism and fairy tales. *Women's Studies* 6:237–57.

Roy, Marie, ed.
   1982   *The abusive partner: An analysis of domestic battering.* New York: Van Nostrand Reinhold.

Rupp, Leila
   1978   Nineteenth century American women: A selected bibliography. Unpublished.

Rusek, Sheryl Burt
   1978   *The women's health movement: Feminist alternatives to medical control.* New York: Praeger.

Russell, Anne, and Patricia Fitzgibbons
   1982   *Career and conflict: A woman's guide to making life choices.* Englewood Cliffs, N.J.: Prentice-Hall.

Safilios-Rothschild, Constantina
   1972   *Toward a sociology of women.* Lexington, Mass.: Xerox College Publishing.

Santmyer, Helen
   1962   *Ohio town.* Columbus: Ohio State University Press.

Scarborough, Dorothy
   1925   *The wind.* New York: Harper Bros.

Schaffer, Kay F.
   1981   *Sex roles and human behavior.* Cambridge, Mass.: Winthrop Publishers.

List of Works Consulted

Schaie, K. W., and K. Griffin
   1975 Adult development and aging. *Annual Review of Psychology* 26: 65–96.

Scharf, Lois
   1976 Employment of married women in Ohio, 1920–1940. In *Women in Ohio history*, pp. 19–26, ed. Marta Whitlock. Columbus: Ohio Historical Society.

Schatzman, Leonard, and Anselm L. Strauss
   1973 *Field research: Strategies for a natural sociology.* Englewood Cliffs, N.J.: Prentice-Hall.

Scheiber, Harry
   1969 *Ohio canal era: A case study of government and the economy, 1820–1861.* Athens: Ohio University Press.

Schlafly, Phyllis
   1978 *The power of the positive woman.* New York: Jove Publications.

Schlesinger, Arthur, Jr.
   1975 Main Street's revenge. *Wall Street Journal*, 29 October, p. 16.

Schulte, Renée K.
   1978 *The young Nixon: An oral inquiry.* Van Nuys, Calif.: Delta Lithograph Co.

Seeger, Pete
   1961 *American favorite ballads.* New York: Oak Publications.

Seward, Georgene H., and Robert C. Williamson, eds.
   1945 Cultural conflict and the feminine role. *Journal of Social Psychology* 22 (November): 177–94.
   1970 *Sex roles in changing society.* New York: Random House.

Shackelford, Laurel, and Bill Weinberg, eds.
   1977 *Our Appalachia—An oral history.* New York: Hill & Wang.

Sheehy, Gail
   1974 *Passages: Predictable crises of adult life.* New York: E. P. Dutton & Co.
   1981 *Pathfinders.* New York: William Morrow & Co.

Shostak, Marjorie
   1981 *Nisa: The life and words of a !Kung woman.* Cambridge: Harvard University Press.

Sicherman, Barbara, and Carol Hurd Green, eds.
   1980 *Notable American women: The modern period—a biographical dictionary.* Cambridge: Harvard University Press.

Simmons, Leo, ed., and Don C. Talayesva
   1942 *Sun Chief.* Published for Institute of Human Relations. New Haven, Conn.: Yale University Press.

Simpson, Jeannie
   1977 Personal interview, near Laramie, Wyo., 10 October.

Smith, Ralph, ed.
   1979 *The subtle revolution: Women at work.* Washington, D.C.: Urban Institute.

List of Works Consulted

Smith, Thomas H.
  1977 *The mapping of Ohio*. Kent, Ohio: Kent State University Press.
Snyder, Eloise, ed.
  1979 *The study of women: Enlarging the perspectives of social reality*. New York: Harper & Row.
Sousa, M.
  1976 *Childbirth at home*. Englewood Cliffs, N.J.: Prentice-Hall.
Spindler, George, ed.
  1970 *Being an anthropologist: Fieldwork in eleven cultures*. New York: Holt, Rinehart & Winston.
Stahl, Sandra
  1977a Introduction. *Journal of the Folklore Institute* 14:5–8.
  1977b The personal narrative as folklore. *Journal of the Folklore Institute* 14:9–30.
Steel, Ronald
  1980 *Walter Lippmann and the American century*. Boston: Little. Brown and Co., Atlantic Monthly Press.
Stevenson, Joanne Sabol
  1977 *Issues and crises during middlescence*. New York: Appleton-Century-Crofts, 1977.
Still, James
  1940 *River of earth*. New York: Viking Press. Rpt., Lexington: University of Kentucky Press, 1978.
Stoeltje, Beverly
  1975 A helpmate for man indeed: The image of the frontier woman. *Journal of American Folklore* 88 (January–March): 25–41.
Stone, Kay
  1975 Things Walt Disney never told us. *Journal of American Folklore* 88 (January–March): 42–50.
Strasser, Susan
  1982 *Never done: A history of American housework*. New York: Pantheon Books.
Stratton, Joanna L.
  1981 *Pioneer women: Forces from the Kansas frontier*. New York: Simon & Schuster.
Strobel, Margaret
  1977 Doing Oral History as an Outsider. *Frontiers* 2 (Summer): 68–72.
Studer, Jacob H.
  1873 *Columbus, Ohio: Its history, resources, and progress*. N.P.
Sundberg, Norman D.
  1977 *Assessment of persons*. Englewood Cliffs, N.J.: Prentice-Hall.
Swain, Donald C.
  1965 Problems for practitioners of oral history. *American Archivist* 28 (January): 63–69.

List of Works Consulted

Talland, G. A.
    1968   Age and span of immediate recall. In *Human aging and behavior,* pp. 93–129, ed. G. A. Talland. New York: Academic Press.

Tallman, Richard
    1978   Review of *People in the tobacco belt: Four lives,* by Linda Dégh. *Journal of American Folklore* 91 (January–March): 590–592.

Tallman, Richard S., and A. Laurna Tallman
    1978   *Country folks: A handbook for student folklore collectors.* Batesville, Ark.: Riverside Graphics.

Tax, Meredith
    1981   *The rising of the women: Feminist solidarity and class conflict, 1880–1917.* New York: Monthly Review Press.

Thomas, Sherry
    1981   *We didn't have much, but we sure had plenty.* Garden City, N.Y.: Doubleday/Anchor Press.

Thompson, Paul R.
    1978   *The voice of the past.* New York: Oxford University Press.

Treiman, Donald J., and Heidi Hartmann, eds.
    1981   *Women, work, and wages: Equal pay for jobs of equal value.* Washington, D.C.: National Academy Press.

Tuchman, Gaye, Arlene Kaplan Daniels, and James Benet
    1978   *Hearth and home: Images of women in the mass media.* New York: Oxford University Press.

Underhill, Ruth
    1936   *Papago woman.* Memoir 46, American Anthropological Association. Rpt. New York: Holt, Rinehart & Winston, 1979.

United States, Department of Commerce, Bureau of the Census.
    1972   *Census of the population, 1970: General social and economic characteristics,* Vol. PC (1)-C37, Final Report. Washington, D.C.: Government Printing Office.
    1976   *Current population reports: Series P-23; No. 58.* Washington, D.C.: Government Printing Office.
    1978   *County and city data book, 1977.* Washington, D.C.: Government Printing Office.
    1978   *Statistical abstract of the U.S.: 1978,* 99th Edition. Washington, D.C.: Government Printing Office.
    1980   *Current population reports: Series P-20, No. 349.* Washington, D.C.: Government Printing Office.
    1981a   *Statistical abstract of the United States,* 102d Edition. Washington, D.C.: Government Printing Office.
    1981b   *Current population reports: Series P-20, No. 365.* Washington, D.C.: Government Printing Office.
    1982   *Current population reports: Series P-20, No. 371.* Washington, D.C.: Government Printing Office.

List of Works Consulted

United States, Department of Labor, Bureau of Labor Statistics
    1977   *Bulletin 1977: U.S. working women: A databook.* Washington, D.C.: Government Printing Office.
    1982   *Employment and earnings* 29 (September):7–9.

Vansina, Jan
    1965   *Oral tradition: A study in historical methodology.* London: Routledge and Kegan Paul. Translated by H. M. Wright, from "De la tradition orale." In *Annales du Musée Royal de l'Afrique Centrale, Sciences Humaines*, No. 36, 1961.

Walker, Charles M.
    1869   *History of Athens County, Ohio.* Cincinnati, Ohio: Robert Clarke & Co.

Walshok, Mary Lindestein
    1981   *Blue collar women.* New York: Doubleday/Anchor Press.

Walum, Laurel Richardson
    1974   The changing door ceremony: some notes on the operation of sex-roles in everyday life. *Urban Life and Culture* 2:506–15.
    1977   *The dynamics of sex and gender: A sociological perspective.* Chicago: Rand McNally College Publishing Co.

Ware, Susan
    1981   *Beyond suffrage: Women in the New Deal.* Cambridge: Harvard University Press.

Waserman, Manfred
    1975   *Bibliography on oral history.* New York: Oral History Association.

Weed, John M.
    1942   Business—as usual. In *Ohio in the twentieth century*, pp. 159–97, comp. Harlow Lindley. Vol. 6 of *The history of the state of Ohio*, ed. Carl Wittke. Columbus: Ohio State Archaeological and Historical Society.

Weibel, Kathryn
    1977   *Mirror mirror: Images of women reflected in popular culture.* Garden City, N.Y.: Doubleday & Co., Anchor Press.

Weiner, Annette
    1976   *Women of value, men of renown.* Austin: University of Texas Press.

Weisstein, Naomi
    1968   *Kinder, Küche, Kirche, as scientific law: Psychology constructs the female.* Boston: New England Free Press.

Wekerle, Gerda R., Rebecca Peterson, and David Morley, eds.
    1980   *New space for women.* Boulder, Colo.: Westview Press.

Welter, Barbara
    1966   The cult of true womanhood: 1820–1860. *American Quarterly* 18 (Summer): 151–74.

Wertheimer, Barbara Mayer
    1977   *We were there: The story of working women in America.* New York: Pantheon Books.

Wertz, Richard, and Dorothy Wertz
    1977   *Lying in: A history of childbirth in America.* New York: Free Press.

List of Works Consulted

White, Linda
    1975 A development of woman's role on the farmstead. Paper presented at the Annual Meeting of the American Folklore Society, New Orleans, La. 24 October.

White, Theodore H.
    1961 *The making of the president, 1960*. Patterson, N.J.: Atheneum Publishers.
    1965 *The making of the president, 1964*. Patterson, N.J.: Atheneum Publishers.
    1969 *The making of the president, 1968*. Patterson, N.J.: Atheneum Publishers.

Williams, Thomas Rhys
    1967 *Field methods in the study of culture*. New York: Holt, Rinehart & Winston

Winkler, Karen J.
    1982 Transferring spoken words to print: The problems of the oral-history book. *Chronicle of Higher Education*, 24 February, pp. 19–20.

Woolf, Virginia
    1929 *A room of one's own*. New York: Harcourt, Brace & Co.
    1955 *To the lighthouse*. New York: Harcourt, Brace & Co.

Wrye, Harriet, and Jacqueline Churilla
    1977 Looking inward, looking backward: Reminiscence and the life review. *Frontiers* 2 (Summer): 98–105.

Yoder, Don
    1972 Folk medicine. In *Folklore and folklife*, pp. 191–216, ed. Richard M. Dorson. Chicago: University of Chicago Press.

Index

Adaptations, 212, 238 n. 26. *See also* Adaptive strategies; Conflict
Adaptive strategies, 236 n. 13, 237 nn. 16, 20, 21; "as if" behaviors as, 222, 237 n. 22; changing perceptions as, 223, 237 n. 24; changing a situation as, 222–23, 237 n. 23; compartmentalizing as, 223–24; Sarah's, 221–25
Ambivalence. *See* Conflict
Analysis: framework for, 211–12, 236 n. 3; of Sarah's life history, 212–25. *See also* Dimensions; Turnings; Adaptations
Anne (Sarah's daughter), 11, 13, 19, 75, 176, 178–79; grade-school memories of, 163–64; and interviews, 14, 19, 25, 121, 160, 169, 176; as official family adviser, 22; quotations of, 28, 129–39, 145–47, 151–53 n. 10; relationship of, to family, 165, 168, 175; sense of humor of, 162; as valedictorian, 159; views of, on local changes, 188–89
Appalachian Ohio: determinants of, 41, 42, 49 n. 2; lower income in, 158
Appalachian Regional Council, 41
Audio and visual research tools. *See* Research tools, audio and visual
Author. *See* Researcher as author

Barn raising, 99, 100, 139
Belief items, 254–61
Bellings. *See* Marriage patterns
Biblical interpretation (Sarah's): on families in conflict, 204; on nations in conflict, 205; on patriarchal role, 165–66; on woman's role, 3–4, 193, 199, 200, 216, 225
Biography: of "common person," 227; different terms for, 5–6; use of, in various disciplines, 6–7. *See also* Life history; Oral history
Birth control, 154 n.12
Block quotations, use of, 10
Boas, Franz, 23
Burial customs, 144–45, 184, 255
Butchering, 77, 99, 100, 133, 137–38, 144, 248–49

CCC (Civilian Conservation Corps), 120, 123–25, 151
Chautauquas (religious meetings), 97–98, 110
Children's generation: Adolf, 166; Barbara, 178; Denny, 141, 143, 151, 161, 164–65, 166, 174, 178; George, 62, 160, 176; Helen, 151, 161, 165, 166, 168, 175–76, 177, 178, 179, 181; James, 13, 19, 43, 44, 127, 132, 143, 161–62, 166, 167, 168, 174–75, 182, 185; Paula, 62, 127, 151, 160, 161 165, 168, 175, 177, 178, 179; Robert (Bud), 179, 181; Robert, 132, 160–61, 166, 177; Sally, 112, 121–22, 123, 127, 128, 159–60, 164, 178, 179–80, 182, 254, 258; Susan, 143, 175; Will, 159, 214. *See also* Anne
Chillicothe, 51, 74, 105
Church. *See* Religion
Cincinnati, 51, 53, 157
City-country: differences between 74, 119, 225–26; rivalry between, 29–30. *See also* Rural society; Urban Society
Cleveland, 53, 73, 124, 157
Coles, Robert and Jane Hallowell, 10
Compartmentalizing. *See* Adaptive strategies
Conflict, 5, 205, 209, 217–20, 221–24, 228–36, 238 n. 39. *See also* Adaptive strategies; Real/ideal rationale
Conflict management. *See* Adaptive strategies
Consultant, 3, 10–13, 32 n. 1, 218. *See also* Anne; Ellen; Martha; Sarah
Courtship. *See* Marriage patterns
Customs. *See* Burial customs; Food ways; Holiday customs; Marriage patterns

Deer Creek School, 56, 59–60, 63, 66, 87
Dégh, Linda, 18
Depression, the. *See* Great Depression, the
Dimensions of Sarah's life: biological, 212–13; cultural, 213–14; general discussion of, 212–20; psychosocial, 217–20; social, 214–17
Disease. *See* Health; Medicine
Donaldson, Mrs. (earlier consultant), 200–201

Education: and Bing Act (1921), 74; effect of, on traditional attitudes, 233–34; in Ohio, 52, 71, 157, 187–88, 237 n. 18; of rural teachers, 96, 107–8; of Sarah and siblings, 87–88, 220; in Sarah's vicinity, 48, 59–60, 61, 87, 94, 163–64, 173, 213–14 (*see also* Deer Creek School); as socializing agent, 93–96, 115, 142, 173, 231, 233–34; in southeastern Ohio, 48, 52, 54, 67, 74,

289

Index

Education (*continued*)
173, 214; and Teacher's Institutes, 54; as valued by farmers, 72; as valued by Sarah, 88, 106–7, 220; as valued by Sarah's mother, 87–88, 107, 115–16, 220

Ellen (Sarah's sister): on contemporary America, 185–88; on grandparents, 61, 64; on the Great Depression, 125–26; land purchase by, 45; marriage of, 112; miscarriage of, 126; nurses' training of, 107; as real estate trader, 221; on social change, 89; on World War I, 102–6

ERA (Equal Rights Amendment): controversy surrounding, 229–30; wording of, 238 n. 37

Family: as base of work and social groups, 148, 213–14; as cooperative unit, 213; size of Sarah's, 48; as social force, 52, 67; statistics on changing, 234, 235. *See also* Family economy; Farm income; Farming, subsistence

Family economy, 57–58, 60–61, 84–86, 154 nn. 15, 17, 213; children's contribution to, 131–32, 162; Sarah's contribution to, 129–31. *See also* Farm income; Farming, subsistence

Farm buildings, 171 n. 5. *See also* Farm layout

Farm income: in Appalachian Ohio, 158; from crops, 77–79, 99, 100, 117 n. 16, 121, 128, 129, 137, 144; from gas well drilling, 75, 79–80; during Great Depression, 119, 125–26; from livestock, 79, 80–81, 84; outside employment and, 79–80, 81, 128–29; for taxes, 80–81, 117 n. 18, 125; from women's work, 154 n. 16, 213. *See also* Butchering; Family economy; Farming, subsistence; Husking bees; Threshing

Farm layout: Penfield, 122; Sarah's, 42–43; Sarah's parents', 76; in southeastern Ohio, 42

Farmer's Institutes, 140, 146

Farming, subsistence: change in, 157, 173; in Sarah's vicinity, 42, 48, 77, 213; in southeastern Ohio, 42, 48, 115, 116 n. 15, 120, 158, 173. *See also* Farm income; Food ways; Ohio, state of: agriculture in; Ohio, southeastern: agriculture in

Flynn, Claire Rheinberg (Sarah's mother): and farm work, 81–83; as hard worker, 81, 84, 86–87; in later life, 150–51; as midwife, 126; as Sarah's model, 216–17, 219; sheltering daughters, 88–90; as valuing education, 87, 107, 115–16, 220. *See also* Parents' generation; Parents, Sarah's

Folkloristics: and use of life history, 6–7, 18, 23, 30–31, 36 n. 29, 250–61; and life history as new oral genre, 226. *See also* Belief items; Customs; Material culture; Personal narrative; Proverbs; Traditional songs; Verbal genres

Food ways, 43–44, 45, 77–79, 81–82, 98, 99, 100, 111, 129, 133–34, 135, 166–67, 173, 174, 175–76, 179, 213, 250; apple butter, 78–79; baking, 179; cider 78; freezing, 166, 179; gardening, 43, 81, 133, 179. *See also* Butchering; Threshing

Ford, Tennessee Ernie, 132, 217
4 H Club, 142, 149
Frank, Gelya, 8
Freud, Sigmund, 217, 219

Gallagher, Dorothy, 22
General stores, 83, 135–36, 144
Grandchildren's generation: Billy, 160, 175; Debbie, 13, 176–77, 178; Frank, 178; Heidi, 179; Nancy, 178; Penny, 175, 179; Polly, 252; Robbie, 178; Sarah, 178; Shelley, 143, 175
Grandparents' generation: Sarah's maternal, 56, 60, 63, 64–66, 100, 101; Sarah's paternal, 51, 54–61, 67; Robert's paternal, 56, 61, 62–63, 114
Grange, the, 98, 140–41, 155 n. 30. 173
Great Depression, the: impact of, on Ohio, 119–20, 123–26, 153, 192, 195
Grey, Zane, 101–2

Health: care of, 65–66, 68 n. 11, 101, 110, 126–28, 182–84, 259–61; Martha's, 48, 170, 182–84; threats to, 57, 74, 102–3; Robbie's (Sarah's son), 160–61. *See also* Medicine; Sarah: health of
Hocking Valley strike of 1884, 73
Holiday customs, 151–53
House(s): description of Sarah's, 43–45; design of Penfield, 122; design of Sarah's parents', 76; hotel as residence, 55, 57–59, 91; layout of Sarah's, 44; layout of Sarah's parents', 93–94; log, 42, 61, 68 n. 15, 75, 92, 114
Husking bees, 66, 99

290

Index

Ideology. *See* Women: influence of ideology on
Informant. *See* Consultant
Ireland, County Cork, 51, 55
Irving, Washington, 102

Kelley, Jane Holden, 12
Kluckhohn, Clyde, 18, 20

Ladies Aid (Society), 144, 147
Lancaster, 51, 73
Lange, Dorothea, 211
Langness, L. L., and Gelya Frank, 23, 26, 236 n. 3
Last of the Mohicans, 101–2
Lewis, Oscar, 10
Life history: contributions of, to scholarly research, 225–28; as document, 10, 18, 225; ethical problems with, 21–23; interdisciplinary approach to, 23, 30–32, 38 n. 50; as interdisciplinary document, 225–26; as new oral genre, 226; omissions in Sarah's, 21, 236 n. 13; representing larger truths, 228, 238 nn. 29, 35; research criticisms of, 212; Sarah's, as paradigm, 211, 228–36; in scholarly literature, 6–9, 27, 34 nn. 8, 10, 12, 13, 15. *See also* Biography; Oral history
Linguistic patterns, 27, 226
Log buildings, 53–54. *See also* House(s)
Lurie, Nancy, 14–15, 16–17, 131

McPherson, Amy Semple, 98
Malinowski, Bronislaw, 23
Mandelbaum, David: and model for life history analysis, 212, 236 n. 3
Martha (Sarah's sister): on contemporary American society, 127, 183–200, 205, 251–53; on the Great Depression, 125; on her family, 55–58, 63–65, 78, 80–90, 92–105; on her home life, 109–10, 112, 132, 151; life stages of, 106, 108–9, 112, 207, 219; personal profile of, 47–48, 100–101, 150, 169–70, 170–79, 181, 184, 219, 221, 223; as secondary consultant, 14, 19, 54, 75, 121, 154 n. 12, 250–61; on traditional songs and games, 251–53
Marietta, 73
Marriage patterns, 112–13, 214–15, 216, 220; bellings, 111; courtship, 66, 108–10; divorce, 219; weddings, 110–12
Material culture. *See* Barn raising; Butchering; Farming, subsistence; Food ways; Husking bees; Quilting; Threshing
Mead, Margaret, 27
Medicine, 45, 63–64, 103, 134, 256–59. *See also* Health
Men: emphasis on superiority of, 230–31; predominance of, as consultants, 27; role of, in Sarah's society, 213–14; as rural teachers, 96; and voting privilege, 117 n. 18. *See also* Sex roles
Mencken, H. L., 226
Merchant of Venice, 102
Methodology, research: anthropological, 23, 30, 34 nn. 12, 13, 15, 236–37 n. 13; and consultant, 3, 32 n. 1, 10–13, 218; and the editing process, 18–19, 36 n. 31; ethical problems in, 21–23, 36 n. 34; interviewing process in, 13–17, 35 n. 23, 218, 241–43 (*see also* Research tools, audio and visual); and linguistic patterns, 27; and participant observation, 26, 27; and reliability and validity checks, 26–27, 37 n. 43; and sampling, 27; and use of fictitious names, 23–24, 32 n. 3. *See also* Researcher as author
Midwifery. *See* Women's roles
Migration: effect of, on cultural mix, 226–27; in response to economics, 71, 121–23, 157–60, 214
Models: of "ideal" woman in nineteenth-century literature, 215–16, 229; Mandelbaum's, for analysis of life history, 212, 236 n. 3; of "nice" girl, 239 n. 43; Sarah as, 178–79, 226; Sarah's parents and grandparents as, 216–17, 219
Morgan, Marabel, 228
Mountain Wolf Woman, 15, 131

Odd Fellows Lodge, 140–41, 146
Ohio Canal, Hocking branch of, 52, 67
Ohio, southeastern: aggregate figures for fictitious place names in, 23–24; agriculture in, 42, 53, 67, 71, 73–74, 157, 158, 170, 173; agriculture societies in, 52, 53; geology of, 41–42; history of, 32, 52, 53–54, 67, 115, 120, 158, 170, 226; industrialization in, 67, 73, 158; lack of urban centers in, 73, 120, 158; literature on, 6, 25; mining in, 52–53, 73, 120, 158, 170; population of, 52, 53, 73, 120, 153, 158, 170, 173; recreation in, 74; as recreation area, 58, 158, 170; Sarah's family as historical prototype of, 48, 67; transportation in, 52,

291

Index

Ohio, southeastern (*continued*)
53, 67, 73, 120, 158. *See also* Appalachian Ohio; Education; Religion
Ohio, state of: agriculture in, 51, 52–53, 71, 73, 119–20, 157; geology of, 41; history of, 51–52, 52–53, 67, 71–73, 115, 119–20, 153, 157, 170; industrialization in, 51, 52–53, 71, 119–20, 157, 170; labor history of, 51, 53, 71–73, 119–20, 123–24, 151, 157; literature on, 6–7; politics in, 71–72, 120; population in, 38 n. 48, 51, 52, 53, 71, 157; townships, layout of, 56; transportation in, 53, 157; urban centralization in, 53, 71, 119; and World War I, 72, 120. *See also* Appalachian Ohio; Education; Religion; Ohio, southeastern
Ohio University (Athens), 52, 54, 107, 220
Oral history: focus of, in the literature, 7, 23, 30; as historian's term for biography, 6; problems in, 219. *See also* Biography; Life history

Panic of 1873, 53
Parent-Teachers Organization, 144
Parents' generation: Robert's father (George Penfield), 56, 114, 122, 123; Sarah's father (Joseph Flynn), 56, 66, 75, 79, 87, 97, 98, 100, 101, 115; Sarah's mother (Claire Rheinberg Flynn), 56, 66, 75, 81; Sarah's uncle (Harold Flynn), 75, 83, 100. *See also* Flynn, Claire Rheinberg; Parents, Sarah's
Parents, Sarah's: as hard workers, 84, 86; as models of behavior, 75, 98, 153, 175, 199, 208, 215, 216–17; preference of, for private sphere, 98; primitive mode of living of, 75–76, 115
Patriarchy, 224: biblical justification for, 165–66; in rural society, 213–14; traditional concepts as support of, 223
Pearl, Minnie, 182, 217
Peddlers, itinerant, 83–84
Penfield, Robert (Sarah's husband): Anne's memories of, 165; as a child, 56, 114–15, 121; in patriarchal role, 165–66; personal profile of, 101, 121, 123, 128–29, 137, 141, 152–53; and Sarah, 113–14, 121, 150, 107–8, 214–15; as shadowy figure, 165, 166, 219
Penfield, Sarah Flynn. *See* Sarah

Personal narrative, importance of, 48–49, 49 n. 10, 226
Place names (fictitious) for Sarah's vicinity: Blufton, 77, 98, 109, 112, 167, 168, 180, 193; Cloverdale, 58, 80, 107, 168; Deer Creek Hollow, 45, 59, 61, 66, 100; Greenfield 77, 83, 106–7, 127, 135; Harrington, 55, 56, 61, 135–36; Hillview, 127, 135–36, 167; Hillview School, 56, 87, 110; Madison, 125, 150, 176, 180; Northfield, 106–7, 112, 135, 183
Politics: in Ohio, 71–72, 120; in Sarah's vicinity, 106, 129, 144 167
Protracted meeting (church), 148–49, 155 n. 38
Proverbs, 253–54

Qualitative research materials, 225, 226
Quilting, 46, 137, 168, 176, 180–81, 190, 250

Reader's Digest, 181, 202
Real/ideal rationale, 5, 22, 205, 218, 219, 221, 244–45
Recreation: in Sarah's vicinity, 58, 66, 90–92, 94–98, 99, 109–10, 213
Red Man's Lodge, 141, 146
Religion: as socializing agent, 72, 93–94, 96–98, 109, 115, 141, 144, 173, 215; in Ohio, 52, 72, 157; in southeastern Ohio, 52, 54, 67, 74, 173, 214; in Sarah's vicinity, 59, 61, 96, 214. *See also* Chautauquas; Protracted meeting (church)
Research tools, audio and visual: genealogy, 12–13, 24, 54, 61–62, 246–47; map overlays, 24; photographs, use of, 12, 24–25, 33 n. 7; tape recorders, 16–17, 218
Researcher as author, 4–5, 9–20; and development of analytic framework, 211–12, 217, 218–20; personal conflicts of, 8–9, 21–23; professional conflicts of, 6–11, 20–31, 37 nn. 35–36, 38 n. 47, 218, 236 n. 13
Robinson Crusoe, 102
Roosevelt, Franklin, 119–20, 123–26, 138–39
Rural society, 157–58: aspects of, 45; in contrast to urban society, 119–20; cultural patterns of, 227; expanded perceptions of, 226–27; literature on,

Index

6–7; marriage in, 112–13; recreation in, 74; roles of men and women in, 213–15; as subculture, 27; and telephones, 145–46; values of Sarah's, 215–17, 221, 224. *See also* City-country: rivalry between; Urban society

St. Albans, 101
Sarah: adaptations by, 221–25; as consultant, 9–17, 20–23, 24–29, 48–49; and education, 87–88, 106–8, 115–16, 178, 214, 220; health of, 46, 176–77, 206–7, 212–13; influence of biological dimension on, 212–13; influence of church on, 215–17, 223; influence of secular literature on, 215–16, 217; and kinship relations, 169–70, 222–23; life stages of, 24–25, 106–8, 110–12, 121–23, 166, 170–71, 191, 220–21; life history of, as pattern for other women, 228; and neighbors, 145–48, 181, 190–91; profile of, 10, 12, 17, 19–20, 46–48, 101-2, 149–50, 167–68, 180–81, 213–17, 220, 223; in public roles, 46, 48, 107, 108, 121, 123, 129, 130, 133–35, 167, 170, 173–76, 207–8, 220, 221; reminiscences (historical) of, 105, 123–26, 192, 195; as role model, 178–79, 226; in traditional familial roles (grandmother, mother, wife), 9–10, 42, 47, 160, 166, 168, 170, 174–78, 179–80, 212–20; turning points for, 220–21; verbal art of, 250–61. *See also* Adaptive strategies; Conflict; Real/ideal rationale; Sarah's family; Sarah's generation; Sarah's husband; Sarah's mother; Sarah's views
Sarah's family. *See* Children's generation; Flynn, Claire Rheinberg (Sarah's mother); Grandchildren's generation; Grandparents' generation; Parents' generation, Sarah's; Penfield, Robert (Sarah's husband); Sarah's generation
Sarah's generation: Frank's brother-in-law (Percy), 138, 248–49; Robert's brother (Frank), 138, 149, 159, 165, 248–49; Robert's sister-in-law (Evvie), 138, 148–49, 166; Sarah's brothers, 55, 89, 93, 113, 184; Sarah's sisters, 54, 106, 107, 112. *See also* Ellen (Sarah's sister); Martha (Sarah's sister)
Sarah's husband. *See* Penfield, Robert

Sarah's mother. *See* Flynn, Claire Rheinberg
Sarah's views: on her family, 47, 148, 160, 165–66, 174, 178–79; on life, 47, 174, 196, 206–7, 223; on nature, 28, 45; on contemporary society, 29–30, 131, 167, 181–84, 184–209; on remarriage, 169, 171; on travel, 180–81; on woman's place "in the home", 179, 201–4, 223; on woman's roles, 3–4, 26, 179, 196–203, 204, 208–9, 216, 217, 219–23, 254; on women's work, 86, 160, 167–68, 191–203, 212–13; on work, 137, 212–13, 217
Schlafly, Phyllis, 229
Sex roles: contemporary, 192–195, 234; and cultural norm, 239 n. 49; delineated for women, 28–29, 142–45, 191–92, 213–14; and education, 87–88, 115–16, 173, 178; effect of World War I on, 103–4; and farm work, 85–86, 99–101, 131–32, 155 n. 30, 197–99; and socialization practices, 88–90, 237 n. 16. *See also* Men; Rural society; Sarah's views; Women
Simpson, Jeannie, 201
Socializing, agents of. *See* Education; Religion; Sex Roles; Work
Songs, traditional: "Down the Old Mississippi," 91; "Down the Old Ohio," 91; "Little Brown Jug," 251; "Old Dan Tucker," 91, 252; "Skip to M' Lou," 251
Subsistence farming. *See* Farming, subsistence
Sunday, Billy, 98

Taft, William Howard, 72
Threshing, 99–100, 128, 137, 144
Time (magazine), 205
Toledo, 124
Tradition: family nucleus of work and social groups as, 148–49; as generator of conflict, 230, 237 n. 20; in marriage patterns, 112–14; as role determinant, 8, 9, 10, 28–29, 213–15, 221; strength of, for women, 9–10; value of work as, 137, 155 n. 24; of women segregated, 144
Transportation in Sarah's vicinity, 58: lack of, 75, 80, 81, 99
Travel, 142, 149–50, 168, 179–81, 213–14
True Womanhood, concept of, 215, 236 n. 8

293

Index

Turnings (turning points), 212: in Sarah's life, 221–25, 237 n. 17

Urban society, 157–58: in contrast to rural society, 119–20; as subculture, 27; views on ecology of, 27–29, 37 n. 45. *See also* City-county: rivalry between; Rural society

Utilities: company as employer, 80, 81; electric, 75, 119, 132–33; gas, 75, 79–80, 81, 185

Verbal genres, 226; Sarah's 250–61

Wages: discrimination in, 198–99; for housework, 125, 192; of industrial workers, 120; of men, 72, 109, 192; of women, 72, 192

Wakes, 255

Weddings. *See* Marriage patterns

Western Reserve, 51, 52

Wilson, Woodrow, 72

Women: ambivalence of, 228–36; and biocultural dimension, 213, 236 nn. 4–5; conflict in, 228–36, 239 n. 49; and egalitarian marriage, 239 n. 48; as farm administrators, 213; influence of ideology on, 235; in labor force, 72, 173; as "noble pioneers," 211; role of, in Sarah's society, 173, 213–14; scholarly literature on, 6–7, 227–28; and segregation, 142–45; and self-image problems, 230–36, 239 n. 46, 239 n. 49; and social control, 239 n. 43; statistics on, 234, 235, 237 n. 18, 240 n. 54; and traditional role concepts, 228–30; working-class views on marriage, 237 n. 16. *See also* Conflict; Models; Real/ideal rationale; Sex roles

Women's roles: analysis of, 9–10, 26; as avenue to personal power, 222, biblical interpretation of, 3–4, as breadwinner, 64; change in, 191–96, 234; in midwifery, 53, 65–66, 101, 126; as teachers, 191–92, 220; traditional concepts of, 191–92, 213, 228–30; in work, 154 nn. 16–17, 191–94, 232–33. *See also* Researcher as author, Sarah: as consultant

Work: as form of socializing, 66, 99–100, 137–39, 213. *See also* Family economy; Men; Sex roles; Women

World War I: establishment of Camp Sherman during, 74, 102; Spanish influenza epidemic during, 74, 102–3; Ohio's participation in, 72, 120; Sarah's memories of, 85, 102–5

World War II, 120, 170, 214

Women of Crisis I and II, 10

WPA (Works Progress Administration) 120

Zanesville, 73

294